THE SOUTHWEST

Hippocrene U.S.A. Guide to
THE SOUTHWEST
A Family Adventure

Tish Minear and Janet Limon

HIPPOCRENE BOOKS
New York

For information, address:
Hippocrene Books, Inc.
171 Madison Avenue
New York, NY 10016

Library of Congress Cataloging-in-Publication Data

Minear, Tish.
    The Southwest : Hippocrene U.S.A. guide to the Southwest : a
family adventure / Tish Minear and Janet Limon.
      p. cm.
    Includes bibliographical references.
    ISBN 0-87052-640-5
    1. Automobile travel—Southwestern States—Guide-books.   2. Family
recreation—Southwestern States.   2. Southwestern States—
Description and travel—Guide-books.   I. Limon, Janet.   II. Title.
III. Title: Hippocrene USA guide to the Southwest.   IV. Title:
Southwest, a family adventure.   V. Title: Hippocrene U.S.A. guide to
the Southwest.
GV1024.M68   1990
917.904'033—dc20   89-77994
                                                                CIP

Printed in the United States.

Contents

Acknowledgments

We would like to thank the many people who helped us with this endeavor. Bruce Minear provided maps, as well as indispensable mental and moral support. This project could not have been completed without him. Diane Perkins willingly gave of her artistic talents to create most of the fine illustrations. We hope this is the first of many projects for her. Jim Ingwerson provided several photographs, computer expertise, and critical review of parts of the text. Sara White shared her knowledge of young children, and of Colorado and New Mexico. Kathy Parker and Chris Owens gave suggestions for traveling with children. Santa Clara Pueblo graciously gave their permission to use photographs of Puye Cliff Dwellings. Peggy Medina Giltrow and Marjory Poole of the New Mexico public library system provided some of the information for the bibliography. Chris Limon provided illustrations, pp. 220,237.

We are also grateful to the many people—friends, relatives, dedicated park rangers, local residents—who took the time to answer our numerous questions and to share their expertise, hospitality and encouragement. Most particularly, our mother, Lucille Lebsock, provided enjoyable travel companionship and unwavering support.

We would also like to thank all those writers mentioned in the Reading List who have inspired us with their own vision of the Southwest.

Finally, and most importantly, this project would never have been conceived without our children, Chris, Brian, Noah and Nita, who through the years have provided us with ideas, a fresh perspective on travel and many wonderful family vacations.

Introduction

People either love or hate the Southwest. It's too big to do anything else. Some see its starkness as beauty, sensing the basic truths laid bare here. Others just wish it weren't so hot, or dry, or barren, or so far to the next place to eat. It's hard to imagine the scale of time and size which operates in the Southwest. You can touch a million years ago in the rocks of Canyonlands, or see the future through the telescope in Flagstaff, Arizona. Vast sky, far horizon, air that shimmers clear—nothing seems to block the imagination and the possibilities. It takes stretching to adjust and to imagine the natural forces at work, powerful enough to buckle the earth and fold layers of rock.

The ruggedness of the land is mirrored in the faces of the old people who live there. Both are wrinkled by sun and wind and time, and the forces within. Hispanic, Anglo and Native American have all made their compromises with the land.

The Southwest is a place to explore, whether you are four or forty. Traveling here with your children will be an adventure, and like all great explorations, the trip may be wildly successful or dismally disastrous. We have written this book with the hope of reducing the disasters and increasing the successes.

You may think it will be easier to leave the kids at home or to postpone your vacation for several years until they are older. You're right! Traveling with children, especially young ones, requires advance planning and compromise. But the extra effort is well worth it. Broadening horizons, building family memories, discovering our great country together—these are just a few of the potential rewards of family travel.

To help keep young minds busy and stretching, Chapter XIII, "Discoveries for Children," includes numerous activities for each area. We have also included travel games, etc., at the end of Chapter III, "Getting There."

Although some of the activities in Chapter XIII are geared to specific places, most can be used throughout the Southwest.

9

For those that are place-specific, keep in mind that items in a museum, etc. are sometimes rearranged. If the item isn't relatively easy to find, assume it is no longer there. The "Discoveries for Children" are written to the kids. However, we strongly urge you to review them with your children before giving the go-ahead. Some are messy; others demand a certain amount of maturity on the child's part for safety.

When visiting national parks and monuments, keep in mind that many of them offer Junior Ranger programs. These involve activities children can complete to earn the designation of "Junior Ranger." Requirements vary with each place, and they may range from completing a mimeographed sheet of questions to attending ranger-conducted programs. Ask at the visitor center for details.

For each travel chapter in the book, we have included background information that covers the basic concepts that define the Southwest—the geology, culture, biology, history, etc. We have also included maps for each of these chapters and numbered areas to correspond with parts of the text. These maps are for your general information and are not meant to be comprehensive. We strongly recommend you purchase a more detailed road map.

In choosing places to visit, we have tried to pick those that will interest children, but if you find something we left out that your kids absolutely love—or something we've included that they absolutely hate—let us know, and we will consider it for future revisions of this book.

When listing attractions, we have made every effort to include current admission prices, hours, addresses, telephone numbers, etc. However, this information changes often. The Grand Canyon will still be there, but the visitor center may close earlier or later, depending on the current federal budget. The restaurant or motel may have a new owner, along with new prices. When in doubt, call ahead.

Most tourist attractions are not open on holidays, so we chose not to note that. When planning, be aware that Christmas, New Year's and Thanksgiving are common times to close, and that state facilities will probably be closed on state holidays.

In addition, we have not included extensive listings of places to stay and eat, although we do include a few in each chapter, either for their child-appeal or because of limited availability in the area. We also include toll free numbers for hotel/motel chains in the Southwest in Appendix C. Numerous other guidebooks focus on lodging and restaurants, and will give you more complete information. The local chambers of commerce are another source for lodging and restaurant information, as well as for attractions, tour operators, special events, etc.

Finally, we did not cover the entire area many consider the Southwest. To keep the size of this travel guide manageable, we included only the area which is roughly the Colorado Plateau. You may well find fascinating areas nearby that go beyond the scope of this book. By all means, explore them.

Consider the Southwest as part of your backyard. You already own much of it in the form of national parks, monuments and forests. But don't be afraid to desert the well-traveled route and see beyond the obvious. The heart and soul of this country is not found on the Interstate.

Visiting here will be a chance for you and your family to leave behind worn-out habits and attitudes. Sample a Navajo Taco or attend a Hopi ceremonial. Take a back road to a ghost town or camp out under the stars. Relax, explore a canyon, tour a Spanish colonial hacienda, visit a cliff dwelling, splash in the lake, and experience the satisfaction of adventure fulfilled.

Take a week—a month—a lifetime. There will always be more to discover. The Southwest reveals herself to those who take the time to listen. The spell she weaves is irresistible.

We have been held willing captives. Our hope is that you and your children will be captivated and changed by that same charm, so that a small bit of magic will follow you home to the everyday.

1

PREPARATION AND PACKING

Traveling can be a wonderful learning experience for you and your children, a unique opportunity to expand horizons. As Mark Twain said, "Travel is lethal to prejudice."

The more the children know about the area you're visiting, the more interesting it will be, and the more they will be able to see beyond the superficial. Take the time to try some of the activities for "Preparation and Packing" in Chapter XIII before you go. They will not only introduce the kids to the Southwest, they will give you, the parent, an idea of the kinds of things that interest your children.

Each child is different. Does she like learning about plants? Animals? How about the Anasazi Indians or the modern Navajo? Is he completely bored by any mention of rocks? Let your child's curiosity be your guide.

Preparation

Planning ahead is an important skill, and preparing for a trip is a great way to practice it. To impress this upon your child, give an example of the consequences of poor planning. If it happened to you, all the better. However remember to leave room for some flexibility in your plan. Nothing kills fun more quickly than rigidity.

Also, remember that for children, especially the very young, security is vital for happiness. The more they are involved in the preparation for a trip, the more confident they will feel. Give everyone an assignment, whether it's putting the apples in the car or arranging for pet care while you're gone, and let them know the whole family is depending on them. Speaking of pets, think carefully before bringing them along. Not only do national parks and many attractions have pet restrictions, being locked in a hot car in summer can be fatal.

The time of year you are traveling will do much to determine how you prepare. If you can, visit the Southwest anytime except July and August, when temperatures of 95 to 100 degrees, and hotter, are common. Not only will the crowds be smaller and temperatures cooler, you may save money on lodging and admissions during off-season. In addition, the desert Southwest has a period of monsoon rains from mid-July through August, and flash flooding is an ever present danger.

Most places are open all year, and although in some places temperatures at night may fall below freezing in winter, daytime temperatures are often quite pleasant. The exception to this is the high mountains, where snowstorms in September and May are not unusual. Of course, if you're looking for winter sports such as skiing or snowshoeing, winter is the only time to go. Just remember, the higher the altitude, the cooler the temperatures will be, and although daytime may be mild, the night will be chilly in the mountains, even in July.

You might want to plan around a festival or special event. Of course, there will be larger crowds during these times, but it may be worth it. Be sure to make lodging reservations early, and since some of the dates for special events vary a bit each year, make sure your sources are up-to-date. The local chamber of commerce is a good place to start. A list of addresses is in Appendix B.

Most people with school-aged children travel during school vacations, but if you choose a time during the school year, let your child's teachers know your plans. Not only can they indicate any make-up work, but they may have suggestions for projects your child can do to share with the class.

Before you gather information, get out the map. Show your child where you are going and ask her what she already knows about the Southwest, what her expectations are, and what she would like to know more about. She may already have some very definite ideas, especially on subjects such as cowboys, Indians, miners, deserts and mountains. Talk about some of the things you hope to see yourself.

Mark the date you plan to leave on a calendar so that every day your child can cross off another one.

READIN'

Reading books, fiction and nonfiction, is a great way to find out about the Southwest. Many parents set aside a special time to read together. Take an outing to a library or bookstore for titles on the Southwest. See the Reading List for a few suggestions.

Don't pass up picture books, even for older children. A picture is worth a thousand words (as the familiar saying goes) for understanding where you will be visiting. If your child is old enough to read, let her pick a book to read to someone else—a friend, a favorite doll, the dog, you.

Also, check the newspaper travel section for information about the Southwest and general travel tips. This is an especially good place for up-to-date information on new attractions, lodging, restaurants, etc.

WRITIN'

A good way to find out about the area is to write to local chambers of commerce and state travel bureaus. A list of addresses is in Appendix B. If you send a self-addressed stamped envelope, they will return free information on things to see and do, places to stay and eat, and a list of special events and festivals in the area. Many also provide maps. Be sure to specify if you want particular information about fishing, state parks, camping, etc., and the dates you plan to visit.

Another letter might go to an auto club, if you are a member, asking for help in planning routes and booking accommodations.

Put your child's name on the return envelope. Kids love to get mail. Ask your child if she wants to write the letter, and help her make it look official. If she is too young to write, let her dictate it to you and sign it herself. Make as many copies as you need, show her how to address the envelopes, and talk about why it is important to be able to read the addresses.

As information comes back, look it over with your child. Younger children might enjoy decorating a large envelope or file folder as a special place to keep it all.

Does your child like photography or archaeology? Ask around or look in the telephone book for special interest organizations that appeal to her and inquire if they have branches in any of the places you will be visiting. If so, contact the branches for suggestions of things to do when you get there.

'RITHMETIC

The financial aspects of a trip can provide practice in math skills.

Children enjoy having spending money of their own, and learning how to budget a fixed amount is a valuable lesson. Once she sees how you do it, help her come up with her own plan.

The amount of money provided, how often (daily, weekly, etc.), what expenses it will cover (souvenirs, snacks, gifts for others, etc.), and what portion of money the child contributes will depend on her age and the places you plan to visit. If she is contributing a portion, encourage her to start saving allowances, or suggest odd jobs she can do around the house or neighborhood to earn money. Let her follow your example of saving spare change to be used for the trip in a special place—a jar on the refrigerator works great.

Younger children might enjoy a graphic display to show how close they are to reaching their goal. A thermometer marked in increments and colored in as each amount is accumulated is a technique often used by charity fund drives. She can also make a special "piggy bank" from a can or box to watch the savings grow, or let her make regular deposits in a bank account. You can even act as "the bank."

Questions like "How much more do you need?", "What is the average you earned this week?", and "How much more did you make today than yesterday?", will give her practice with math concepts. Make the questions more difficult for older children. How about, "If you earn twice as much tomorrow as you did yesterday, and continue earning twice as much each tomorrow as you did each yesterday, how much money will you have in one week?" Of course, if the amount she's earned so far is zero, the answer will be relatively easy to figure out.

While traveling, have her help you keep a running list of expenses so you know how well you are adhering to your budget. Revise it if necessary—the sooner the better. Point out to her you would rather spend a previously unplanned night camping than run out of money for food the last two days.

Following is a list of sample budget categories to adapt. Once you have the categories, have her estimate a daily amount for each expense, then multiply by the number of days you expect to be traveling. As a guideline, AAA Auto Club has estimated a family of four spends an average of $192 a day for lodging, meals and 300 miles of auto travel.

Lodging—camping fees average $10 a night (less in national parks), hotels/motels average anywhere from $35 a night for two (economy) up to $125 (luxury hotel). Some hotels and motels offer discounts to auto club members.

Food—average is around $20 to $25 per day per person for

three meals a day. Some restaurants offer less expensive child portions, and fast food meals are usually under $5 per person. Picnicking will save money. You can even buy a picnic lunch from delis, bed and breakfasts, and some hotels to take along to that perfect picnic spot.

Car—pre-trip expenses include a tune-up, oil change, new tires, etc.; travel expenses include costs for gasoline (daily mileage divided by your car's fuel economy multiplied by the approximate price of a gallon of gas), oil, and parking. When figuring mileage, add 10% extra for sightseeing side trips, detours, backtracks, etc.

Entertainment—include admission to attractions, swimming pools, national and state parks and monuments, and cost of babysitting. A Golden Eagle Passport, which will admit you to all the national parks, can be purchased for $25 at any national park. Don't forget the cost of any guided tours you plan to take.

Gifts/souvenirs—you will pay a premium for anything you buy in a store that caters to tourists. Don't buy it on the road if you can purchase it at home.

Miscellaneous—laundry, magazines, film, local and long-distance telephone calls (a calling card from your telephone company can save time and money on this), boarding costs for the animals, film and developing. . . .

Emergency funds (car repair, medical, rained out of the campground, etc.)—at least $100 in cash and $100 in traveler's checks for those places that won't take plastic. Some credit card companies have emergency cash available from dispensers at airports, hotels, etc.

THE REST

If your child is young or hasn't traveled much, enlist her help in becoming a "veteran traveler." Start by observing the daily routine. A young child can make a list of regular morning and evening events, such as brushing her teeth, washing her face, and dressing.

You can play a game with the list, asking what would happen if she mixed things up and put her shoes on before her socks, or buttoned her shirt and then put it on. Encourage her to see what it would look like by asking her to draw a picture of the improbable results, then put the list back in order and talk about why things have to be done in certain steps.

Anticipate changes in the routine while traveling, and modify the list to include these changes. For instance, if you are camping, add "taking down the tent" to the morning routine; if staying in a motel, "packing the suitcase."

Visit a travel agent. Ask questions and gather brochures about accommodations and sights. They can be extremely helpful for making transportation and lodging reservations, as well as a good source of ideas.

Buy or rent a travel video, such as "Canyon Dreams" about the Grand Canyon or the award-winning "Desert Visions," and watch it with your children. Or how about "Butch Cassidy and the Sundance Kid" and "the Milagro Beanfield War."

Talk to people who have lived or traveled where you plan to visit. Your child can play "newspaper reporter" and interview them by preparing questions, writing down the answers, and reporting back to the family.

If you are camping, take a practice run in the backyard. Put up a tent, tell stories under the stars, and cook breakfast or supper on a camp stove.

Packing

Much of the Southwest is high, dry, and sunny, which means heat and cold are more bearable than in a humid climate. But the weather is also very changeable. Hot days are often followed by cold nights, especially in the mountains, yet sunny 50 degree days in winter are not unusual. Be prepared for wide temperature variations, no matter what the season. Bring rain gear, a warm jacket, sturdy walking or hiking shoes, a light long-sleeved shirt for a sun cover-up in summer, and a swimsuit. Don't forget the sunscreen, sunglasses, lip balm (with sunscreen), and plenty of lotion for dry skin. There's even a place for that old sun hat—on your head during the hottest part of the day.

The Southwest is fairly casual, and rugged, outdoor clothing that can be layered is the most efficient. Loose clothing of natural fibers such as cotton and wool "breath" and will be more comfortable in the heat **and** cold. Dark colors will absorb the sun and hold it close to your body, while light colors will reflect it away. (Let the kids prove it by putting water in both a dark colored bowl and a light colored bowl and placing the bowls in the sun for an hour.)

A packing system to help remember everything involves categorizing. To help a young child get the idea, start with ordinary items such as a coat, piece of fruit, and pan, and have her sort them into piles of similar patterns. Some possible categories include how the item is used (wearing, eating), how it looks (red, shiny), or how it feels (smooth, slippery).

Now develop the categories to use for packing. Some of the more obvious include food, camping gear, clothes for hot weather, and personal hygiene. Make a list of everything you want to include in each category.

Let your child make her own list of things to bring, and cover it with clear contact paper. Then, each day before you leave the motel, do a "pilot to navigator" check list. Anticipating her own needs not only gives your child practice in organization, but it also builds anticipation for the trip. (I'll need my swim suit because there will be a place to swim, and I love swimming. In the mountains I'll need warm clothes because there may be snow—Wow, snow in summer!)

When you begin packing, let your child sort things into piles using the categories you listed. Younger children especially will enjoy deciding which pile to put things in.

Consider giving your child her own suitcase. It will give her an added sense of responsibility and could save you countless frustrating moments searching for her toothbrush. (If it isn't in her suitcase, she obviously forgot it, so you might as well buy another one.)

One thing to remember when packing—keep it simple. Take only the essentials and do laundry on the way. An old pillowcase works great for dirty laundry. You might also consider packing a bag for one-night stops so you won't have to unload the whole trunk.

Organization in packing the car helps, too, at least for the first hour or so. Group things together by how you will use them. Put all the picnic supplies in one cardboard box (they hold up better than paper bags), all the overnight necessities in another.

DON'T FORGET THE SUNSCREEN—USEFUL THINGS TO BRING

Take a tape recorder with earphones if you have one, and don't forget extra batteries. Buy or check out from the library children's songs and stories, or make your own recordings of stories. You can also buy audio travel tapes for the whole family to listen to. Take along a blank tape for the kids to record animal sounds, interview people they meet, or to keep a daily log. If you have teenagers (*and* earphones), buy the newest tape by their favorite artist so they can blast themselves into senselessness.

Don't forget the recreation paraphernalia and other miscellaneous items—an inflatable ball, deck of cards, good book to read, jump rope, pad of paper, binoculars, magnifying glass, compass. Invest in a crossword puzzle book or travel activity book with games and puzzles to fill in, and magnetic games of chess, checkers or backgammon.

Fill a bag for the kids with inexpensive surprises from the discount store. A box of colored pencils or washable markers (crayons will melt in summer) and a pad of paper, play clay, a new miniature car, a new book, or paper dolls and blunt scissors are some of the things that can help children focus quietly on a long trip. Each day give your child something from the bag, or save it for when the going is tough.

Bring along useful information—maps, field guides, a star guide, telephone numbers (the neighbor watching your house, pediatrician, insurance agent, credit card companies and card numbers, lodgings), Rx for glasses and medicines, travel guide books (**The Southwest—A Family Adventure**), baby care book, and a duplicate list of travelers check numbers.

Other useful items include wash and dry packets (for hands, face, underarms, feet, toilet seats), litter bags, flashlights with extra batteries, first aid kit (be sure to include baby acetaminophen or aspirin for young children), bug repellant (and baking soda or calamine lotion for minor bites), Belinda's beloved blanket, Timmy's Teddy, spare set of keys for the car, canteens, electrical coil or hot pot for making hot chocolate and soup, wide-mouthed thermos, paper towels for wiping up the inevitable spills, travel sewing kit, plastic bags for soap and wet swimsuits, day pack for hiking, a small battery powered light for playing games and reading at night, pillows, blankets, and a folding stroller (even if you think your preschooler has outgrown it).

Let the kids pack a bag of their own—try a backpack—and fill it with their own things for entertainment that they will be responsible for (see Chapter XIII, Discoveries, the "possibles bag" under "Preparation and Packing" for ideas).

Staying There

HOTELS/MOTELS

Lodging may well be your largest single expense, but there are ways to economize. For a free directory from hotel/motel chains, call the numbers in Appendix C. For those not part of the large chains, invest in one of the numerous lodging guides for the Southwest that give complete listings and descriptions.

Be sure to ask questions before making reservations. Do prices vary according to the size of the room, furnishings, location? Are there special rates for kids? Would a longer stay or a slower time give a better rate? Are there activities for children? What about meal plans, babysitting, recreational facilities or special promotional rates? Are there cancellation penalties? How close are the major attractions?

Request written confirmation and take it with you. Include the rate you were promised and a cancellation number.

Don't overlook the availability of discounts from your auto club (if you aren't a member, consider joining), and if your vacation is during slow times, haggle. Hotel managers know a room rented at a discount is better than one not rented at all. If you are traveling during the off-season, you may be more successful getting a discount by writing or telephoning ahead (to the individual motel, not the toll-free central reservations). Ask for the "corporate" or "commercial" rate, or tell them you are planning to stay in the area if you can find a room for, say, no more than $30 a night. Once the lodging establishment realizes you are shopping around, they are likely to offer a better deal.

Don't wait to look for a room until the last minute during tourist season. Otherwise, you might be stuck with one you find totally inadequate at an outrageous price—or without one at all in places like southern Utah, northern Arizona, and on the Indian reservations, where motels can be few and far between.

If you can, stay a few nights in the same place. Why spend more time packing and unpacking than you need to? Besides, the kids will feel more secure (translate "happier") staying in one place. You can also take advantage of lower rates for multiple nights' lodging. Cities such as Moab, St. George, Flagstaff, Santa Fe, Taos, Albuquerque, and Durango make good base camps to leave your suitcases while exploring.

If you are willing to dispense with the frills, budget chains are conveniently located near highway exits. If you have time to search, small motels on the edge of town, far from the main tourist attractions, are often less expensive. Things you might not see in a budget place—bathtub (shower only—is this important to your 3-year-old?), color TV, sheets that fit, glasses (paper instead), a roomy room, a coordinated color scheme. Be sure to ask to see the room first. A quick look will tell you if the place is clean and will suit your taste.

For safety and convenience, ask for first floor rooms, those away from the stairs, near the soda or ice machine, and at the end of a hallway if the kids make a lot of noise (are there any who don't?). If necessary, toddler-proof the room by covering sharp corners, removing "bite-size" objects, locking windows within reach, and checking for frayed electrical cords. Consider suite hotels that provide extra space, kitchens, and sometimes play areas. For your sanity, if the budget allows, rent a separate room for the older children.

OTHER ACCOMMODATIONS

A bed and breakfast can be a good alternative to a motel, and a meal, usually breakfast, is included with the price of your room. Many are in someone's home and give you and the kids a chance to talk with a local resident in a homey atmosphere. Be sure to ask the proprietor if children are welcome. You might also want to know if the bathroom facilities are European style (down the hall) or in each room, and if there is a play area available either inside or outside.

You can rent an apartment or condominium even for a short stay. It is often cheaper than a hotel and sometimes comes with maid service. The *Hotel and Travel Guide* used by travel agencies and tourist offices lists short-term rentals. Ask for it at your library. You can also try a house exchange. See Appendix C for addresses, or contact local tourist offices or a travel agent.

A handful of college campuses in the Southwest offer inexpensive lodging, which sometimes includes use of campus facilities. *Travel and Accommodations Guide*, available from

Campus Travel Service, 1303 E. Balboa Boulevard, Newport Beach, CA 92661, has worldwide listings.

Youth hostels are inexpensive, as low as $4 to $10 per person per night. Most have separate male and female dormitories, but an increasing number are offering family accommodations. For a listing, send for the *American Youth Hostels Handbook* (see Appendix C).

The cheapest lodging will be your tent, even if you stay at the more expensive private campgrounds. National parks have well-equipped campgrounds for a reasonable price, although you can't make advance reservations at most of them (the Grand Canyon is one of the exceptions), so you do run the risk of finding them full. To be safe, get there before noon during tourist season.

You can find free campgrounds in rest areas, city parks, and national forests, but, again, spaces can't be reserved in advance. If showers aren't available, stop at the local swimming pool, gym, YMCA or large truck stop.

FOOD

Eating on the road is expensive. To cut costs, choose breakfast and/or lunch for a restaurant meal and a picnic in the park for supper. Consider staying in a motel room with a kitchenette, and keep the ice chest filled with healthful snacks.

If you are more concerned about the food than the atmosphere, try smaller restaurants. They are often less expensive. Look for local license plates, and ask the residents "Where do you eat?", not "What do you recommend?"

Keep a paper and pencil activity book for the kids to use in restaurants. With young children, play simple games such as "Simon Says" or "Twenty Questions," using something they can see. Look for buffets and salad bars that can offer quick fixes for stretched tempers and low blood sugars. In emergencies, grab the crackers.

The Foolproof Plan

If you have done your homework, you have a fairly good idea of the places you want to see and when you will be there. Be sure to leave room for serendipity. A trip too tightly scheduled makes it impossible to take that inviting trail, run in the park, or plunge into the swimming pool. Children, especially young ones, need time to just dawdle, and babies can be very unpredictable when away from home.

Plan alternatives. What if the museum is closed that day for renovation? Or Tommy doesn't want to see any more rocks? Or the hike is canceled because of rain? Take a deck of cards, a board game, or a good book for rainy afternoons in a tent or motel.

Balance your activities. Vary an amusement park with a quiet picnic, time apart with a family swim, a museum with a trip to the zoo. And be sure to include time for playing outdoors.

Young children won't last through a whole day of sightseeing, and three-year-olds won't be interested in scenery anyway, no matter how spectacular. They will be interested in the small and immediate—a new flower, splashing in the stream, a squirrel, or a funny looking stick. They may also be overwhelmed by large crowds. Consider visiting an attraction half an hour before closing, when the crowds are often less pressing.

Older teenagers might enjoy the freedom of a half-day excursion on their own. Make sure they know how to get where they are going—and back!

Don't forget that adults need entertainment and time alone. Give yourself permission to "get away" for a quiet walk or dinner. If there are two adults, one can watch the children while the other has free time. Or older children can take the younger ones to the park, the shopping mall or the movies.

Well-established hotels, city guidebooks, and the Yellow Pages have listings of babysitters. If you do use an agency, ask for references and specify your preference in a sitter—elderly, male or female, etc. Have them arrive early so they can get to know the kids before you leave.

You can also ask at local churches and senior citizen or day-care centers for sitters. Local colleges sometimes have babysitting as part of their student employment program, and before you leave home you can ask your friends if they know anyone with children where you are visiting who would be willing to babysit.

If all else fails, require your children to take a nap or quiet time to give you a breather. If an older child balks at "baby stuff," tell her the rest is for you. Play a game where everyone listens quietly for as many sounds as possible, or lie on your back and watch the clouds. Buy books your child can read, color, or fill in the blanks herself. If you are traveling in the summer, you'll want to avoid outdoor activity in the hottest part of the day anyway.

Other Tips

For healthy traveling, stop for the kids to stretch every few hours. Keep the food light and encourage them to drink plenty of fluids, preferably water or fruit juice.

Always carry one gallon of water per person per day when traveling in the Southwest. Buy bottled water to avoid the stomach upsets that can come from drinking different water. Remind the kids to drink frequently. They will perspire more in this climate. And never—repeat, never—hike in the Southwest without carrying water, even for short distances.

Changing time zones can be a problem for children. In general, try to maintain consistent eating and sleeping schedules. If you are only staying for a few days, stick to the kids' regular schedule. If you're going to be in the Southwest for an extended period, have them spend time outdoors in the sun to more quickly adjust their circadian rhythms to the new zone. And try to change schedules to the new time zone as soon as possible.

THE ALTITUDE

The air is thinner in the mountains of the Southwest. That means your lungs will find less oxygen than at lower altitudes. The result is a tendency to feel light-headed, headachy, and short of breath, and to tire more easily until your body has time to adjust. In more serious cases, usually not until above 11,000 feet, you may get altitude sickness—headache, nausea, anxiety, loss of appetite, shortness of breath that gets worse when one lies down. At the extreme (progressive difficulty in breathing, coughing, mental disturbances), altitude sickness can become life threatening. See a doctor and/or retreat to a lower altitude.

To help you and the kids adjust to the altitude, take it easy for a day or two and go to bed a little earlier. Drink plenty of water, and if the kids lose their appetites, concentrate on smaller, high-energy meals supplemented by snacks.

Because of the altitude, the kids will sunburn more easily. Use plenty of sunscreen, even in the lip balm, and don't forget the sunglasses, especially if there is snow or lake water that reflects the sun.

The altitude affects other things besides your body. Water takes longer to boil and food longer to cook. This is most noticeable camping, when impatient stomachs scream for supper. Plan accordingly.

THE BABY

Infants and toddlers present unique problems when traveling. Many will be fine with a little planning. Others won't, and postponing the trip until they are older may be the best alternative, especially if you have a colicky baby.

Keep in mind that a toddler's sense of time is immediate, and she won't be as interested in where you are going as in the trip getting there. Don't try to adjust her schedule to yours. Instead, gear yourself to toddler time.

Also, remember that babies require mountains of stuff. Allot about half of the car space for her necessities. Here are a few other tips.

—Make sure the clothes (easy-care) you bring have plenty of growing room—in case she does while on the trip.

—Maintain as much structure as possible in her daily routines.

—Stop frequently for expending toddler energy.

—Bring a plastic tablecloth for changing in unexpected places, or a portable potty for the newly trained. And don't be surprised if she reverts to old habits in the new surroundings.

—Expect the unexpected.

—Spend time talking and touching.

—Bring diversions, such as puppets, books, cuddly toys, snap-together blocks, sticker games.

—Whenever possible, drive at night while she sleeps.

—Keep snacks handy for waiting in lines or at restaurants.

—Consider investing in a harness. Many parents have mixed feelings about them, but they can prevent a disaster in the great outdoors, especially near cliff edges. Buy an identification tag or bracelet.

—Avoid overly crowded and noisy places.

—Bring a non-spillable cup or bottle, even if you think she no longer needs it.

—Cover the back seat of the car with a heavy towel to help protect from the mess.

—Bring a collapsible stroller, back or front carrier for hiking, car seat (required by law in many states) that can be used as an infant seat, and, if you have room, a portable crib (let your toddler sleep in it *before* you leave home to get used to it).

—If the car seat can be raised, do it so she can look out the window.

—Hang a soft mobile over the baby's car seat for visual stimulation.

—Make rhythm sticks out of paper towel tubes covered with
  contact paper. Have her copy rhythms that you tap out
  while in the car. Most kids love this!
—Include a baby food grinder, a shade for the car window to
  block the sun, and electrical outlet covers for the motel
  room.
—Be sure she drinks plenty of water in hot weather, even if it
  will increase the number of pit stops and wet diapers.
—When in doubt, feed her.

THE CAR

Preparing the car before you leave can save a lot of headaches. Give it a complete service and check-up, including
such things as a tune-up, oil change, replacing worn hoses and
frayed belts, and filling anything that sloshes. Don't forget to
have the air conditioner serviced and the muffler checked for
leaks, especially dangerous on a long trip.

If your car is inadequate in size or safety for the trip you're
planning, consider a rental. In particular, a mini-van can add
a lot of comfort and convenience for a large family, even
though it guzzles gas. You can defray some of the expense by
sleeping in it instead of a motel.

When driving in the mountains, use the engine gears rather
than the brakes to slow down on steep hills. And don't stop or
pass on curves. If you plan to stay at a high altitude for a
number of days, ask a mechanic to adjust the carburetor so the
car isn't sluggish.

Because of lack of oxygen at high altitudes, vehicles emit
more carbon monoxide than at sea level, and kids may develop
headaches or drowsiness after prolonged periods in the car.
The solution is simple—drive with a window or vent slightly
open. For hints on preventing motion sickness, see Chapter
III.

Snow can fall just about any time of the year in the high
country, so be prepared for possible winter driving conditions

in spring and fall, as well as winter.

Heat is the enemy when driving in the desert. Keep tires at normal pressure or slightly below and check them periodically for excessive pressure build-up. Keep an eye on the water gauge, and be sure you have extra for an emergency. If possible, avoid traveling between 1:00 pm and 4:00 p.m. during the summer, and keep your gas tank at least half full.

Local radio stations often broadcast unusual road conditions. Be alert for sudden rainstorms and flash floods, a serious danger.

Always inquire locally about unpaved roads; they deteriorate rapidly in the rain. Many cross dry washes that become raging torrents following a storm. If you come to a ford or muddy road, check the depth and firmness before trying to cross, and stay out of dry washes after a rain or downstream from storms.

Heed the areas closed to motorized vehicles. It can take the land years to recover from the damage done by vehicle tracks. And be aware that signs that say "Four-wheel drive vehicles only" usually mean it.

THE MUSEUM

Visiting museums with kids can be like cooking with hot chilies—a few add zest, too many make you cry. Here are some tips to help the kids appreciate them.

First, remember that you don't have to see the whole thing. Let the kids pick out what interests them and forget the rest. It's better to appreciate a few things than to be forced to take a quick glance at everything. Look for hands on exhibits and take frequent breaks at the snack bar or outdoor patio.

Try focusing on a particular item. Talk about it and ask the kids questions. What does this item tell you about another time or culture? What is the historical significance? What was it used for? Who could have used it?

Take along a tape recorder and have the kids make a narrative tape of the exhibits.

In art museums, encourage them to develop their own tastes by finding what they like. Have them look for a favorite painting and compare it with one of yours. Talk about the colors of the picture and how it makes them feel. Look for patterns, colors or lines that are repeated. Does the artist exaggerate anything? Why? What is the focus of the picture? Why did the artist choose this subject? Ask the children to tell a story about the picture. Where would be the perfect spot to display it in your home?

Play a game by having them study the picture, then close their eyes and try to describe it. For a different perspective, look at the painting through a camera viewfinder or use an empty paper towel tube as a telescope. If you are visiting several museums, see if they have a favorite southwestern artist whose works they can look for in other museums.

If the kids are artists, let them sit in front of a work of art and sketch it, or write a poem or story about it. Buy inexpensive art prints for their rooms, or let them start a postcard collection of favorite artists.

2

THE GREAT OUTDOORS

Camping Tips

Camping is a good way to save money—and a great way for children to learn about nature. It won't be quite as easy as staying in a motel, but with a little practice, you may find it more enjoyable. You can obtain good camping guides and maps from the National Forest Service and topographical maps for hiking from the U.S. Geological Survey. See Appendix A for addresses.

When packing, remember the high mountains are cold at night most of the year, and cool even in July and August. Throw in a warm hat and gloves.

Know how to put up your tent before you leave home, and be sure to arrive at the campground while it is still light. Setting up camp in the dark is difficult at best.

For shorter trips, grate cheese, peel vegetables, make meat patties, and do any other advance food preparation you can. You can also pre-cook dinners so all you have to do is heat them at camp. For long trips, carry freeze-dried dinners. If you start cooking as soon as you reach camp, by the time the tent is up, supper will be almost ready.

Use only well-established campsites and leave them as clean—or cleaner—than you found them. To escape the crowds, take along a 10-gallon jug of water, a shovel and a roll of toilet paper, and stay at a primitive campground without water.

When choosing a site, avoid those with potential dangers for the kids, such as nearby poisonous plants, sudden drop-offs, and heavily traveled roads. If possible, pick a spot with an open play area and removed from other campers so the kids won't disturb them.

Poison Ivy

Establish firm camp boundaries as soon as you arrive. Set up a play area, and for young kids, circle the camp with string or bright yarn to remind them of the boundaries. Include a discussion about the dangers of getting lost.

Give everyone a job in helping to set up camp. Older kids will enjoy a tent of their own (let them set it up by themselves if they are old enough), and ask them to make dinner. Little ones can help collect wood and wash dishes.

Nothing beats a campfire for roasting marshmallows, staying warm, telling stories, and just sitting around under the stars. If you are camping in an area that permits campfires, here are a few tips. If the kids are old enough, let them be in charge.

Use a fireplace that has been used before. If one is not available, make sure the spot you choose is away from any trees and fallen logs, and is on rocky or sandy ground, not near tree roots or soft humus that could catch fire easily.

Once you have chosen your spot, clear away everything that will burn in a circle between four and six feet wide. Make a small ring of rocks in the center of the circle for the fireplace.

Collect *all* the dry firewood you will need and stack it a few feet from the fireplace. You will need several sizes, ranging from match and thumb-size sticks to larger logs. If you have crumpled paper to help start the fire, fine. If not, collect dry pine needles, dry grass, tiny dead branches and bark for tinder.

There are many ways to build a fire, but one of the easiest is the tepee fire. Begin with tinder on the bottom, then arrange around it a circle of thin sticks in the form of a tepee. Gradually increase the size of the sticks as you build the tepee higher and thicker, making sure to leave room between the sticks for oxygen to feed the fire. To light the fire, hold a match to the base of the tinder.

Remind the kids of these safety rules:

—In campgrounds, build a fire only in approved areas.

—Never build a fire in high wind.

—Never leave a fire untended.

—Keep a bucket of water or sand near the fire in case of emergencies.

—Keep your fire small and manageable.

—Make sure your fire is out completely before you go to sleep or leave the area. Scatter the ashes and coals with a stick, then douse them with water until they are cold to the touch.

Hiking with the Tykes

For young children, practice before you leave home by taking frequent hikes to the park or store. To give them a sense of importance, let them carry the small backpack they will use when hiking on the trip and fill it with a few light items such as sunglasses and lip balm.

In the backcountry have them carry a signal whistle on a string around their neck. Tell them to stay put, hug a tree for comfort and blow the whistle loudly if lost.

Discuss basic safety rules—stay in sight at all times and

never throw rocks downhill. It can be hazardous to hikers below. Warn them about the Untouchables (see below) and the dangers of eating unknown plants and berries.

Remind them not to litter. You can even encourage them to pick up the trash others have left behind.

Keep your hikes short, around a mile or two, and remember that short people have short legs. Walk slower, stop for frequent rests and explorations, and if you never make it to your planned destination, well, who cares? Take along a magnifying glass, binoculars, and plenty of snacks. Tell stories, sing songs, count flower petals, play games, and if all else fails, bribe them to climb that last hill with a chocolate bar.

No matter what the age, gradual conditioning is important. Even your robust teenager is susceptible to the soreness and injuries that result from muscle overuse.

The Untouchables

Some things in the Southwest are downright awful—smelly, prickly, scary things. Some just look nasty; others really are. Caution the kids to walk carefully and not to put their hands, feet or faces into holes or hollow logs before looking, and let them get to know the dangerous desperadoes *before* they touch them.

The Southwest comes with plenty of bugs. Flies, gnats (especially the infamous no-see-ums), and mosquitoes are the most troublesome, and ants, bees and wasps can pack a powerful sting. Take along bug repellant and baking soda or calamine lotion for bites, especially during the rainy season.

One of the worst bugs is the wood tick, an arachnid related to spiders and mites. The danger comes from the diseases they transmit. Ticks are most active in spring and early summer, when temperatures are cool and humidity is high. They are most often found in brush on southern hillsides.

The best prevention is to find the tick before it burrows

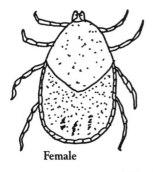 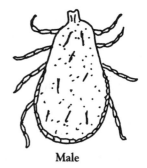

Female   **Male**

Wood tick

under your skin. They move slowly (always upward—they aren't too bright) and usually take an hour or more before they attach, so hold periodic tick checks. Also, when hiking in places ticks are likely to be, tell the kids to tuck in their trouser legs and shirttails and apply a commercial repellant with deet (diethyl-m-toluamide). Just be careful to spray it on your child's clothing and not directly on her sensitive young skin.

If you find a tick attached (the most likely places are the nape of the neck, the underarms, and the groin), but not yet firmly embedded, remove it by grasping the body firmly with tweezers, flipping it on its back and gently pulling until it releases. Be careful you don't pull off the head or the wound can become infected. Use an antiseptic on the bite and wash your hands. If you can't easily remove the tick yourself, see a doctor.

Tarantulas may look gruesome with their large, hairy

Scorpion

Tarantula

bodies, but they are actually slow moving and shy. Some people keep them as pets to rid the house of unwanted bugs, and in some places, they are symbols of patience and good luck. Their bite is usually no more poisonous than a bee sting.

The sting of the Arizona scorpion, on the other hand, can be fatal. These fearsome looking creatures have a gland filled with poison and a stinger under their tails. Stay clear and find a doctor if bitten!

Another poisonous animal is the Gila monster, although you won't find many until you travel farther south. This lizard has a large head with powerful jaws, and his pink skin is marked with yellow or orange and black patterns. Tell the kids to keep their distance.

The poisonous snake to watch out for is the Western Diamondback rattlesnake, whose bite can be fatal. You can tell him by the dark diamond patterns on his back and the series of horny sections at the end of his spinal column that sounds like buzzing when he shakes it. Other rattlesnakes with similar markings to the Western Diamondback are also found in the Southwest, and their bites have varying degrees of toxicity.

Rattlesnake

Since snakes are sensitive to ground vibrations, the best thing for the kids to do when they hear a warning rattle is to freeze until the snake slithers away. Any movement may cause him to strike. If the children are bitten, apply ice and get to a doctor as soon as possible.

Porcupines won't kill you, but that won't be any consolation if you get pelted with their brutal quills. They are slow-moving and slow-witted, so the kid's racket won't necessarily scare them off as readily as it will other animals, and since they love salt, you (and they) may be surprised when you find them gnawing on camp gear your sweaty hands have handled. They can't, however, throw their quills. Instead, these bundles of barbs forcefully flail their tails. It is effective enough. Tell the kids to stay as far away as possible!

Skunks won't be a problem unless they feel threatened. Then they raise their tails and stamp their feet, preparing to cloud you with stink. If the kids witness such an event, tell them to get out of the way—fast! These furry little guys have deadly accuracy up to ten feet.

Other critters, such as mountain lions, will probably try to stay as far away from you as you will from them. Don't, however, risk attracting large animals by leaving food or garbage out in the open, and never store food in your tent.

Animals aren't the only things to watch out for. The Southwest has some pretty mean plants, too. Cacti may be the most obvious. Warn the kids to watch where they step or put their hands.

Porcupine

You'll also find poison ivy everywhere in the Southwest except the desert, and unless you want miserable kids with itching, burning, stinging skin, tell them not to touch, even with the bottom of their shoes. The plant oil can easily be transferred from clothing to skin. Treat it by washing the exposed parts of the body with a strong soap and warm water, and applying calamine lotion to stop the itching.

Stinging nettles, irritating but nonpoisonous, are found among thick growth in canyons and along rivers. Ease the sting with vaseline or cold cream.

Also caution the children that many plants are poisonous if eaten.

Warnings and Rules

The Southwest has certain dangers for your children they won't find in the neighborhood park. Always keep an eye on them, especially near the edge of canyons. Also keep an eye on the weather. Flash floods and lightning storms can approach with alarming speed. Know your children's—and your—physical limits, and be sure to take into account the effects of the altitude, sun and heat.

It used to be the Southwest was big enough and uninhabited enough that people could do pretty much whatever they wanted. Not anymore. Man has left his mark, and it hasn't always been a good one. Litter, damaged ecosystems, polluted water, vandalism and crime—these are a few of the things he's brought. Only increased awareness by the multitude of visitors can prevent more damage in the future.

It is illegal to disturb or deface any natural feature or prehistoric object on public land. If the kids find pottery or other archaeological artifacts, caution them to leave them where they are. You can be fined up to $100,000 and imprisoned for five years for stealing or vandalizing antiquities on public land.

The plants and animals are also protected on public lands, so tell the kids not to pick the wildflowers. They wither & die within minutes anyway, even in water, and a picked flower leaves no seeds behind for future generations.

Don't let the kids feed the wild animals. Much of our food, high in salt, is deadly to animals, and if they become dependent on "people food," they will lose their ability to fend for themselves. Your children can also pick up fleas and ticks from them, as well as more serious injuries if the cute chipmunk bites.

Always stay on designated roads and trails. The ecosystems in the Southwest are fragile, even if they don't look it, and it may take years for the land to recover from your passing through.

The rangers have a motto—leave only footprints, take only photographs. Encourage your children to live up to it by making a game to see who can leave the least amount of evidence of having passed this way.

Also remember to lock your car and take your valuables with you, or hide them from view. Theft in the national parks and on the Indian reservations is an increasing problem.

The Camera

Vacations are great times for kids to learn about photography. Consider giving an older child a camera of her own. Here are a few tips to help her use it.

The Southwest is picturesque, but it's not always an easy place to take a picture. Wide vistas that dazzle in real life often disappoint on film. For broad panoramic shots and for shots of deep canyons, a wide-angle lens works the best.

The thin, clear air of high altitudes has an abundance of ultraviolet light that can be picked up as blue haze by color film. Using a filter will help to cut out the haze, as well as to protect the lens from dust and rain.

Underexpose when taking pictures that are largely of water or snow, or in the red-rock country where reflected light washes out colors if shot at a normal exposure. Try bracketing your pictures with one higher and one lower f-stop. The best time to take a picture to prevent that bleached look is early morning or late afternoon, with the sun at your back. On sunny days, lower speed films (25, 50, 64, and 100) usually work best.

Remember that, although a flash won't help light up a picture past 10 or 15 feet, it is useful in lighting up the faces of people standing against a bright sky.

For interesting pictures, be creative. Take a shot squatting below eye level or standing on a high rock shooting down. Position the subject off-center, or move in and take the subject as a close-up. Change to black and white film for a different effect.

Personalize pictures with family members posing in the foreground. Frame them with interesting foreground objects, such as rock overhangs or tree branches.

Do a study in some specific thing for the trip. For instance, look for colorful doors, humorous situations, red plants, neon signs, clouds, etc.

To take pictures of wildlife, pretend to be a predator. Pick a time when animals are active and hide near a water hole or feeding area. The early morning or late afternoon are best.

When approaching a small animal in the open, don't charge straight ahead or make direct eye contact. Instead, amble casually in a zigzag, always looking in another direction. This works especially well in national parks where animals are somewhat accustomed to people. And remember, these are wild animals. Don't approach an elk, bear or anything else that is likely to retaliate.

Take plenty of fresh film along and keep it in ziplock bags in the ice chest. It isn't always available in remote areas, and it will be cheaper at the local discount store. Buy mailers for exposed film and send in the roll as soon as the last shot is taken. That way, the pictures will be ready when you get home.

It is important to protect equipment from weather extremes. Dust, sand, sun and heat are all in abundant supply in the Southwest—and all are deadly to cameras and film.

Always load and unload film in the shade. Don't leave the camera in the sun or in a hot car. Try wrapping it in a light colored towel for extra insulation or store it in a waterproof bag in the cooler. Use a plastic bag for protection from wind and rain.

DID YOU KNOW?

—If you get lost in the desert, you can probably stay alive by eating the bugs. They are the most available source of nutrition. Some claim they taste better cooked (we've never tried them).

—You can collect water in the desert by tying a plastic bag over branches. Evaporation will collect inside the bag.

3

GETTING THERE: With You and the Children Still Sane

The bags are packed and you're on your way. It's too late to go back for anything you've forgotten. Adventure calls!

Is there someone with you who gets impatient when the old routines aren't there to rely on? Are you beginning to wonder if you should have stayed home instead of rolling down the road with your children in the back seat? "Mommy, she won't let me sit by the window!" "Daddy, tell Bobby to leave me alone!" "Are we there yet?"

Don't panic! Here are games and travel hints for keeping the young not so restless.

Travel Hints

We hope you brought along your flexibility and sense of humor. One of the greatest things about traveling is new experiences. Look for the slapstick in situations which might otherwise be unpleasant.

Remember this when you take that wrong turn. It might eventually lead to something wonderful. (Note: No matter how open you are to the unexpected, it's not advisable to tempt fate by starting across the desert with an almost empty gas tank, or to pass up the rest room because you're sure there *must* be a town closer than 80 miles—even though the map says otherwise.)

Remember that for the young child, his whole world has changed. He probably misses his friends, surroundings and routines. Hold him, reassure him, tell him how much you love him. An older child might enjoy a telephone call to his best friend back home.

Now's the time to set new guidelines. For instance, "You can only ask 'Are we there yet?' once an hour or we'll hang you from the antenna." "Put your apple cores in the litter bag (you did bring one, didn't you?), not in Mommy's lap." Decide what's important to you and set limits.

Make sure everyone is buckled up at all times, caution against playing with door handles and sticking hands and heads out of windows, and watch out for little fingers and toes in car doors.

Keep an ice chest of food handy. Chips and cookies may be easy in the short term, but the overload of sugar and fat can cause crankiness. Carrots, celery sticks, oranges, dry cereal, cheese, crackers, and apples are good alternatives. Sandwich fixings also come in handy for a spur of the moment picnic. Stock the ice chest with plenty of liquids. Fruit juice is better than pop, and water is a must in the dry Southwest.

Have diversions for your child when traveling loses its fascination. Put the teenager behind the wheel, switch seats on a frequent schedule, and let the older kids be in charge of entertaining the younger ones by reading stories and playing games.

And what if the kids get car sick? A few precautions will go a long way toward preventing motion sickness—and keeping the results off the floor of the car. Most young children will have no idea why they are getting sick until it is too late. Watching them will be up to you.

If the kids aren't used to riding in the car, take several shorter trips before vacation time. This will give them a chance to build up their resistance, just as a sailor needs a few days to get his sea legs.

Monitor the amount of time they spend in the car reading, coloring, or doing anything else that involves fixing their gaze to a page. Encourage them to look out the window and focus on objects in the distance, especially in the mountains.

Hunger pangs can also add to the nausea, as can gorging on heavy food. For some, a high-carbohydrate, low-fat diet for a few days before traveling helps with prevention.

It also helps to sit in the front seat rather than the back, to wear loose clothing, to crack a window for fresh air, to prop the head against the window with pillows, and to stop to walk around every hour or so.

If motion sickness has been a recurring problem, ask your doctor for medication before you leave—and have something handy for the kids to use if it doesn't work!

To enjoy traveling with the kids, avoid getting too tired. It may mean stopping earlier than planned, taking longer lunch breaks, or making it a point not to cram too much into one day.

Expect that traveling with the children will take longer than traveling alone. Plan on stopping every two to three hours. Let the kids out of the car into the fresh air, and encourage them to run around, throw a softball, and visit the rest room. Stop for the night while it is still daylight so younger kids can adjust to their new surroundings.

Keep the kids involved in the trip. When you stop for fuel, assign a job to each. One washes the windshield, one drains the cooler, one fills the water jug. At the motel, let them help unload the car. Assign everyone something to take in and back out. Even a toddler can usually find something to carry.

Once you are unpacked, explore with your young child or let more mature kids play "scout" looking for the swimming pool, fire exits, ice and soda machines, and game room. Send the older children to the pool or a nearby park with a watch and a time to return.

Take the younger kids for a swim or give them a bath to relax. Soap containers, paper cups, tea strainers, stick rafts, and anything that floats make good toys.

Play games in the room. Pitch paper wads or rolled socks into the wastebasket. Move the wastebasket around the room to change the angle or put it on the bed or a chair.

Make a hoop out of a bent coat hanger and hang it over the doorknob, then try to toss paper airplanes or socks through the target. Increase the difficulty by using your knees, elbows or head to get the object through the hoop.

Hide the thimble, or another small object, and have the kids look for it. "Colder," "warmer" and "sizzling" will give them clues. Or hide numbered squares of paper around the room.

Play "volcano erupting" by crossing the room without touching the floor of molten lava. Put paper on the floor as stepping stones if you don't want the children to use the furniture.

In addition to specific activities listed in each travel chapter, try the generic sanity savers listed below.

Entertainment for the Car

TODDLER ENTERTAINMENT

1. Play a guessing game: "What song am I humming?" "What makes this sound?", "What color is a ?", "What part of the body is this I'm pointing to?"

2. Chant nursery rhymes and jingles: "Pat-a-Cake" and "This Little Piggy Went to Market" are two favorites.

3. Chant the alphabet or the numbers. Let older tots add nonsense syllables (b bay bay, c cay cay, d day day).

4. Let babies pull off their socks (they'll do it as long as you

keep putting them back on) or play peek-a-boo.

5. Give them something to take apart (make sure it doesn't have any little pieces they can choke on).

6. Give them washable markers and paper to color a picture.

7. Play finger games: "Itsy Bitsy Spider," "Here's the Church," and "Where Is Thumbkin?".

8. Make a bracelet out of tape (sticky side out) for them to collect things.

9. Make a "touch bag" and let them guess what is in it by feeling inside.

10. Sing songs: "Ring Around the Rosie;" "Row, Row, Row Your Boat;" "I'm a Little Teapot;" "Twinkle Twinkle Little Star."

11. Have them compare the different sounds they hear at different times of day.

12. Make up your own rules for this game: "When we go through a tunnel, everyone makes a wish; when we cross a bridge, everyone stops talking; when we pass an exit, everyone holds their breath."

13. Give them a new toy or snack

POST-TODDLER ENTERTAINMENT

1. Collect sightings of these plants, animals, and signs of man. Check off each item when you see it. It may take the whole trip to find all of them, and a few you might not see, depending on where you're traveling. You can add your own if you want.

SIGNS OF MAN

__old fence	__power lines	__cut tree stump
__windbreak	__swimming pool	__hospital sign
__well	__roadside litter	__cigarette butts
__abandoned building		__abandoned car or truck
__mine shaft		__old railroad or roadbed
__S-shaped curve sign		__fire station

PLANTS AND ANIMALS

___rabbit brush
___pinyon pine
___aspen
___kangaroo rat
___greasewood
___horned toad
___prairie dog

___mormon tea
___bristlecone pine
___prickly pear cactus
___rainbow trout
___columbine
___mule deer
___coyote

___sagebrush
___yucca
___mule
___cholla cactus
___hawk
___chipmunk
___fairy shrimp

Chipmunk

2. Categorize license plates by state. See who can find the most from out-of-state. Or look for those with red on them, with two 6's, from eastern states, dealer plates, from your home state, with a state name ending in the letter S, with white letters, with two A's, or any other category you decide to include.

3. Have a contest to collect things you see along the highway: bicycle, car with hood open, station wagon, luggage carrier, jeep, convertible, foreign car, trailer, boat, dump truck, car same color as yours, semi without a trailer, white horses, cars the same make or model as yours. Whoever finds the most gets to make a wish.

4. Collect signs such as barber pole signs, stop signs, old burma shave signs, information signs, "No Vacancy" signs.

5. Use your lapboard to write postcards or letters to relatives and friends. Enclose a few pine needles or a special feather found along the way.

6. Compare fingerprints with your family by rubbing a pencil

on a piece of paper to make a coating of lead, rolling your thumb in the lead, then taking a piece of scotch tape and sticking it over the print to pick up the impression. Paste the tape to a piece of paper to examine it with a magnifying glass.

7. Write in your journal.

8. Pretend you are a pioneer. What would you eat and drink? Where would you camp? What are the dangers? How far would you travel in a day? What are the landmarks on the trail?

9. Play a game of Twenty Questions, making sure the answer is something you can find in the Southwest.

10. Play a game of Facts in Five. Choose a category, such as desert plants. Randomly choose five letters of the alphabet and write them on a sheet of paper, leaving space for six names under each letter. At the signal, each player tries to write as many examples as he can of items that begin with each of the five letters. Give each player bonus points for letters that have six examples.

You can also play this without paper. Each player takes turns adding to the list under a specific letter, then dropping out when he can no longer add a word.

11. Make pipe cleaner figures. Put them together in a scene.

12. Make up rhyming riddles. For example: I am thinking of something with four legs and brown eyes. It rhymes with "here" (deer). I am thinking of something thin and slithery that rhymes with "cake" (snake).

13. Play a memory game: I'm going on a trip and I'm taking an apple; I'm going on a trip and I'm taking an apple and bandanna; I'm going on a trip and taking an apple, bandanna, and cat. Add one item for each letter of the alphabet. Make it more challenging by naming only fruits, or using two words that start with the same letter, such as "awful aardvark" and "bashful boy."

14. Start a story and leave it in mid-sentence. The next person picks it up where you left off. See how long you can keep the story going.

You can do the same thing with drawing a picture. Have

someone draw a line, and let others add to it. Don't be surprised if what the next person adds isn't what you had in mind.

15. Have someone in the car draw a simple face with cartoon eyes, nose and mouth. You add a mustache, glasses, hat, eyebrows and whatever else you can think of to diguise it.

16. Write the name of something on a slip of paper and have each player draw a paper and describe the item for the others to guess. Animals can be described by imitating their sounds.

17. Put on a blindfold and draw something. If you're young, try shapes such as a square or egg; if you're older, try a map of the United States.

18. Draw a picture using letters of the alphabet or numerals, or draw a picture on graph paper, "squaring off" the rounded parts.

19. Sing songs together.

20. Make up a rebus message or story. See who can figure it out (I C U).

21. Ask your parents to tell you stories about when they were growing up, or talk to them about what is important to you.

22. Look at clouds and see what pictures they suggest.

23. Find all 26 letters of the alphabet on signs, license plates and billboards. Make it more difficult by finding them in order. Have your younger brothers and sisters look for shapes instead of letters, such as a yellow circle or a red square.

24. Each player picks a make of car and counts how many they see in a certain amount of time. The player who finds the most wins.

25. Play navigator for your family and follow the map. Duties can include keeping track of the mileage and/or expense records for the trip.

26. Write a poem with one word per line, using the consecutive letters of the alphabet to begin each word. Can you use all 26 letters?

27. Play car bingo: Make bingo across, down or diagonally by finding the following:

oil well	horse	pink house	purple car	cow
juniper tree	saguaro	motorcycle	airplane	hawk
red flower	windmill	FREE	bumper sticker	boat
tractor	red rock	prairie dog	elevation sign	river
KS license	NY license	CO license	mile marker	mountain

4

A SOUTHWEST PRIMER

Once upon a time, around 4½ billion years ago, Mother Earth was hot, reckless, and full of the energy of youth. Driven by a liquid fire that covered her with seething rivers of lava, her surface moved, constantly, unexpectedly, in massive thrusts that sent tons of rock flying for miles and left deep wounds oozing with molten rock. Electrical storms charged her thin air, and steam blanketed her barrenness.

After millions of years, Earth's great fire burned lower. She hid it, forcing her power underground to seethe in private, except for those times it pushed through volcano doorways, wrenched out earthquakes, and twisted upheavals into new shapes.

As Earth's fire cooled, so did her blanket of steam, and it condensed into rain. Onto the still-hot rock it rained—and it rained, and it rained—in a deluge that lasted countless years. When the rain stopped, Earth was covered with primordial seas.

On the 130,000 square miles where Arizona, New Mexico, Colorado and Utah now meet (the Colorado Plateau), a deep depression formed and eventually filled with warm saltwater. For 600 million years the waters here retreated and returned, again and again, leaving layer upon layer of compressed sand and mud in the 12,000-foot rock bed. But under this shallow sea, Earth was still restless.

Between 60 and 80 million years ago, She thrust up thousands of tons of earth, twisting and cracking her crust. Sand, gravel and clay were cemented together on the ocean floor, mixed with hard, brittle igneous rock, then jutted skyward, giving birth to the Rocky Mountains and the Colorado Plateau. Then, around 10 million years ago, the Plateau was lifted even higher, nearly a mile above the surrounding terrain.

Although Earth is still as restless as she was 60 million years go, the most noticeable forces of change on the Plateau since the uplift have been water and wind. Earth's past exuberance left behind exposed softness, the sedimentary rock that yields easily. Erosion now pounds against this weakness.

In the last ten million years, deposits a mile thick have eroded from the Plateau. Imagine the scenery here if everything was covered with 5000 feet of dirt!

The rain scrubs spires and mountainsides, washing away the soft rock, dripping holes in it and relentlessly pushing it to the ground. Wind carries the dust, depositing it hundreds of miles away. And the power of the Colorado River and its tributaries, magnified by the uplift, washes the debris to the sea.

Each year, the mighty Colorado relentlessly carries away millions of tons of earth, rock and sand. As the river cuts deeper into the skin of Mother Earth, it exposes her past. Each layer travels farther back in time, until at the bottom of the Grand Canyon, you can see some of the oldest uncovered rock in the world.

Today, most of the Colorado Plateau is hot and dry, a desert that parches with an average of under 10″ of precipitation a year and temperatures that can reach 110 degrees Fahrenheit in the summer shade. But it is also thousands of feet above sea level, so January can bring below-zero temperatures, frigid winds and roaring blizzards.

Life is not easy here. The plants are tenacious, sturdy, and sparse: scraggly pinyon and juniper trees cluster in pygmy forests; low-growing bushes flourish while looking half-dead; thorny cacti live on water stored in their plump flesh; hardy grasses scorch and freeze unconcerned.

Occasionally, the dry land surprises with small oases of flowers, hanging gardens tucked into shady, moist alcoves. They are a harbinger of the momentary lushness found in narrow bands along the Colorado and other rivers, and the occasional display of life in all its glory on mountain slopes.

The animals on the Colorado Plateau are as hardy and well-adapted as the plants, and although diversity is great, you will usually have to look for it. Most animals avoid the heat by staying in their burrows until the cool evening air creeps in.

Many have elaborate ways of coping with the lack of water, such as the fairy and tadpole shrimp who live in rain-filled potholes and lay eggs that can lie dormant for decades until the shallow depression again fills with water. Snakes and lizards are shielded with tough skins that allow for little evaporation of moisture. The kangaroo rat drinks no water, getting all it needs from the plants it eats.

When man came to the Colorado Plateau thousands of years ago, he also had to adapt to survive. Much of his story remains a mystery, but the current theory is that somewhere between 12,000 and 30,000 years ago, he crossed over from Asia on a land bridge in the far north.

As a hunter, he followed his prey, the paleolithic mammals, southward. He probably traveled no faster than an average of ten miles every year, but he eventually reached the tip of South America. This nomad left little evidence of his passing—a fluted spearpoint here, an occasional hand-chipped stone there.

Slowly, early man evolved distinct cultures. Many of today's Southwest Indian tribes are descended from three of these societies—the Hohokam who settled in the central desert of Arizona, the Anasazi in the area of the Four Corners, and the Mogollon in the southern mountains of present-day New

Mexico.

The Mogollon, hunters and gatherers, were the least advanced of the three, and lived between approximately 300 BC and AD 1300. They made their homes in partially underground pit houses covered with mud-plastered roofs. It was a perfectly adapted house for the extreme climate of the high mountain valleys, affording insulation from both the frigid winds of winter and the hot sun of summer. These pit houses were eventually abandoned as dwellings in favor of one-story adobe pueblos, but they did not disappear. Many believe they became places of ritual and worship called kivas.

The Mogollon clustered into small, isolated villages. Far from the major trade routes, they were never able to develop an agriculture or culture much beyond the primitive stage.

The second group, the Hohokam (Pima for "those who are gone"), was a sophisticated culture that took pride in creating finely decorated clothing, masterful stone sculptures, and etchings. Although vital archaeological evidence has been lost because they cremated their dead, much is still known about this vanished culture that flourished between 500 BC and AD 1500 around the Gila River in Arizona.

Like other farmers of the Southwest, corn was their primary sustenance, with supplementation from wild game—jackrabbit, mule deer, and an occasional bison. A sturdy people, the Hohokam labored in the fields, digging canals and building earthen dams.

Their canals were a marvel of early engineering, dug narrow and deep to reduce evaporation from the sun and lined with clay to prevent water infiltration. Water flow was directed with floodgates of woven mats, and an extensive maintenance system included frequent patching of the canal walls and hauling away silt accumulated on the bottom. Their ancient waterways eventually became the basis for the modern water system used by Phoenix, Arizona today.

In their leisure time, the Hohokam played games on large ball courts (the largest one found is 132 feet long by 33 yards wide) reminiscent of those used by the Mayans. Flanked by three-foot high earthen banks, these courts were probably the playing field for a game similar to one played by their Meso-American neighbors. Two teams tried to knock a rubber ball through the opponents' hoop at one side of the court. Only the knees, thighs and buttocks were used. Touching the ball with the hands or feet was prohibited.

Around the time of Christ, the third group, the Anasazi, began settling down in the Four Corners area. By AD 100 they had become successful farmers, dominating the area and prospering for over 1000 years.

The Anasazi are thought to have been an industrious and relatively peaceful people, resilient in the face of adversity. Through the centuries, they elevated their society to one of beauty and complexity, living amicably in close-quartered pueblos.

They were a deeply religious people who spent hours watching the heavens. Master artists and craftsmen, they learned to weave, fashion shell jewelry, and mold beautiful yet durable pottery. Master merchants, they developed an elaborate road and trade network that stretched from one of the centers at Chaco Canyon to outlier towns over a hundred miles away, and extended as far away as the Pacific Ocean. Master farmers, they coaxed life from the arid land with a sophisticated system of irrigation. And master builders, they erected grand apartment complexes of stone.

A satellite culture, the Sinagua, emerged at the melting pot of Wupatki, where farmers from the three main cultures peacefully mingled to take advantage of optimal conditions after the eruption of Sunset Crater. After exhausting the soil at Wupatki, the Sinagua moved south to Walnut Canyon and the Verde Valley.

The Anasazi, Hohokam and Mogollon cultures flourished. And then, sometime between the late 1100's and 1300, in what is one of the greatest mystery stories of all time, a dark age settled over the Southwest. The richly populated cities were abandoned, and the inhabitants disappeared.

Throughout the Southwest, their ancient houses stand

empty, but many think their descendants still live, faded into other times and places—along the shores of the Rio Grande River, on the Hopi Mesas, in the Zuni Pueblo and in southern Arizona.

The first major influx of foreigners into the area was the Navajo and Apache Indians. By 1500 they had arrived from the north, fierce nomadic hunters who brought raiding and wars.

They were followed in 1540 by the Spanish, who embarked some years before on a grand adventure searching for the fabled Seven Cities of Cibola. It began in 1492 when Spain sent Christopher Columbus to find a western water route to the Eastern Orient. At the same time, the country ended a struggle of over half a century to rid their land of the infidel Moors. Holy Spain was infused with a new destiny, that of saving the souls of the world from the heathen.

New dreams were born when the first galleon loaded with Aztec gold left Mexico for Spain. Young men, unhappy with bleak prospects of gaining financial comfort in Europe, heard the stories. Who could believe the wealth that had been found? And once it was proven, who was not willing to believe it could happen again?

No one was surprised when it did—in Peru, where an entire room was filled with gold to ransom the Inca emperor. Surely, the New World held more glory for those brave enough to risk it.

Spanish conquistadors set sail for the New World. Close behind were devoted friars and settlers. For years Spain claimed dominion over what is now the American Southwest, until in 1821 the country of Mexico declared its independence and took over the northern lands.

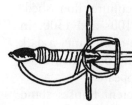

Conquistador sword

Then, in 1846, the United States gained possession at the end of the Mexican-American War. With the explosion of the California gold rush in 1848, the area received an onslaught of new residents—weary prospectors who decided this was as good a place as any to get rich. The settlers weren't far behind. This, in spite of what was described by a newsman of the time as "A barren, deserted, dreary waste, useful only as a dwelling place for the coyote, the owl, the rattlesnake and the prairie dog."

The next few years saw a series of bloody Indian wars that ended with the final defeat of Geronimo in 1886, but many of the southwestern Indian tribes were saved from extinction by the ruggedness of their land, the strength of their character, and the reservation system that eventually provided a sanctuary from further encroachment by the white man. Today, many maintain the customs, land and villages their ancestors did hundreds of years ago.

In the early part of this century, Americans began to put a different value on the Southwest. Parts of this incredible landscape were set aside to protect it from vandals, looters of the past, and the careless. The amazing variety of public lands found in New Mexico, Utah, Arizona and Colorado attests to that desire to preserve nature's uniqueness for posterity. These lands are like a huge billboard, shouting to the world—the Southwest, brought to you by Mother Earth!

Still, much of the land remains unprotected, and every year more is lost to development and twentieth-century treasure seekers in pursuit of mineral wealth. In a strange twist of fate, Native Americans (in particular, the Navajo) who fought so hard to preserve their land now find themselves the caretakers of vast tracts packed with rich deposits of coal, oil and uranium. Should the earth be laid bare to provide badly needed income for the tribe, or should it be preserved as it was in the time of their ancestors? It is an issue on which members of the tribe still do not agree.

In many other ways the reservations are changing as modernism seeps in around the edges of tradition. For some Native

Americans, such as many of the Hopi, the influence of white man's society is actively opposed. For others, such as the Navajo, it is a force the tribe is striving to adapt to its own beliefs. For all, it is a power that has brought turmoil and cannot be ignored.

The weather is another force to be reckoned with. It was just as hot and dry here during Anasazi times as it is now. During their Golden Age, prolonged drought was a major factor in the collapse of civilization. Could it happen again?

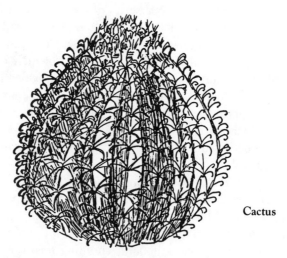

Cactus

Developers are betting against it, and to hedge their bets, they've built vast water reclamation projects such as Lake Powell. Others point to the stagnant lake that will eventually fill with silt and wonder if the short-term solution has been worth the environmental losses.

What will life in the Southwest be like a hundred years from now? It is just as unpredictable as the future was when the Spaniard Coronado strode into the Zuni pueblo of Hawikuh in 1540 and changed history. But for now, visiting is a chance to see the meeting of man and nature. Even in a time of moon walks and atom splitting, life here is molded, melded and shaped by the land, an adaptation to the dominating power of Mother Earth.

If you come to the Southwest, experience her grandeur. Perhaps no place else in the lower 48 states remains so much like it was before the handprint of humanity.

Man seems inconsequential here. He is a visitor who can observe and curse and love the country passionately, but who, ultimately, must leave the land to its own wisdom if he is to survive. May it always be so.

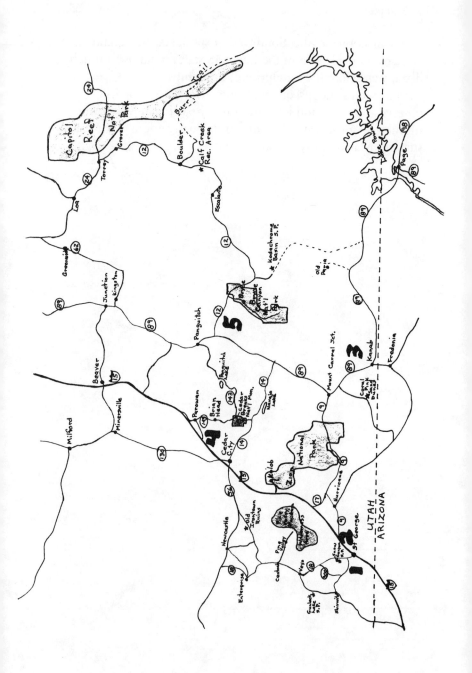

5

SOUTHWEST LIFE ZONES: From Bottom to Top in Southwestern Utah

You can find six different life zones in the arid Southwest. Each of these life systems has a unique combination of plants and animals that live together in a circle of cooperation, competition and dependence for survival, and each has its own climate: its own pattern of temperature and precipitation. precipitation.

The six life zones in southwestern Utah typify those found throughout the Southwest. In this jagged part of the country, altitude yo-yos temperature up and down with dizzying speed. For every thousand feet of elevation gain, the temperature rises an average of three degrees Fahrenheit, the equivalent of traveling 600 miles north. That explains why plants and animals which thrive on top of Thousand Lake Mountain (elev. 11,295 feet) are more similar to those in the Arctic than they are to those a few miles away in Capitol Reef (elev. 5,400 feet).

The lowest elevations in southwestern Utah are in the

Lower Sonoran life zone. This is the zone of the American deserts, and its inhabitants are those that can survive with little moisture. Plants such as the barrel cactus store their own water, and animals such as the kangaroo rat get all they need from the seeds they eat. Lizards and snakes hide in shady spots from the sun's blaze, and most of the animals are active in the cooler morning and evening hours.

Water in the Upper Sonoran zone may not be abundant, but if it's around, it is usually easy to find. Just look for bushes and trees and a wide assortment of birds. If you travel a short distance from the water, the land changes to a desert grassland dotted with prairie dog mounds and sagebrush, inhabited by lizards, pronghorn antelope and jackrabbits.

Prairie dog

The Transition zone is the pygmy pinyon-juniper forest that dominates vast areas of the Southwest, especially the mesa country around the Four Corners. Ground squirrels, chipmunks, and wild turkeys are abundant, as well as lizards and snakes.

The Canadian is the true forest, where ponderosa pine grows in open, park-like stands, often accompanied by Douglas fir and scattered with aspen and mountain meadows blooming with columbine and wild rose. Bear, mule deer, bighorn sheep, and mountain lion sometimes spend the winter here, ranging to higher zones in summer.

In the Hudsonian zone, the bristlecone pine and the majestic Engelmann spruce thrive. At treeline, these giants become naked and dwarfed, their gnarled, windblown bodies clinging to the rocky slopes.

The Arctic-Alpine is the treeless tundra above timberline. Lichens, sedges, and compact alpine meadow flowers rush from sprout to flower to seed to death in a few short weeks. Marmots survive the winter by hibernating; the pika by storing food. Although it seems hardy, this zone is one of the most fragile.

Some species are found in several different zones, and many adapt to the changing weather, such as the yarrow plant which starts out at a height of three feet in the lowlands and ends up only three inches tall above the timberline.

In nature, life systems exist in a delicate balance. What affects one member affects all—often disastrously. Take, for instance, the Grand Canyon in the early 1900's. Park authorities, spurred by a desire to protect the deer that so many visitors enjoy, waged their own war on natural predators. Thousands of coyotes, eagles, mountain lions and bobcats were destroyed.

This championing of the deer worked only too well. With no natural check, their population exploded, and by 1924 the herd was estimated to be 100,000. Unfortunately, nobody asked how the land was to support these huge numbers.

The deer quickly stripped every leaf from every bush and tree, turning next to the bark in their quest for survival. The countryside was left barren, the trees dying, but even that wasn't enough to stave off widespread starvation. Within a few years, the herd had fallen to 20,000, with many of the survivors sick and degenerate.

But when white men first came to Utah, the wilderness was still pristine. The first settlers were the hardy Mormons (The Church of Jesus Christ of Latter-day Saints), driven here by ridicule and persecution. They were followers of a man named Joseph Smith, who claimed to have received from God tablets of gold that outlined the tenets of a new religion restoring the true gospel of Jesus Christ. These tablets were then transcribed into the Book of Mormon, hence the name "Mormons."

Although Mormons adhere to the teachings of the Bible, the Book of Mormon added new beliefs. One of these involves the organization of the church. Rather than a paid ministry, the Mormon church is run by male members of the congregation who take turns conducting worship services and serving in leadership capacities.

Mormons also believe Christ visited the Western hemisphere after his resurrection and was known as the Great White God by the Aztecs, Mayans, and other native peoples. As he did in the Middle East, Christ healed the sick, performed miracles, and promised to return someday.

The church stresses the importance of family and teaches that marriages will last for eternity if they are sealed in a temple. A more controversial belief involves polygamy, a practice defended on the basis of statements in the Old Testament, although no longer officially sanctioned.

In the East, Joseph Smith and his followers were spurned because of their unorthodox beliefs. When Smith was killed by an angry mob, his followers bundled their belongings into covered wagons and migrated westward. Led by Brigham Young, many settled in Salt Lake Valley in 1847, establishing the state of Deseret. Valuing industry and competence, they prospered and spread throughout much of what is now Utah.

DID YOU KNOW?

—In addition to altitude, two things that affect average temperatures are latitude and north or south slope.

—Many of the early Mormons lived in cooperatives where the livestock herds, grain fields and industries were owned jointly by the community. In some cooperatives, at the end of the year, each worker received the same pay and all debts were cancelled.

From St. George to Capitol Reef in Southwest Utah

1. St. George to Cedar City
2. East from St. George to Zion National Park
3. South from Mt. Carmel Junction to Lake Powell
4. East of Cedar City through Mormon Country
5. Scenic Route 12 to Bryce and Capitol Reef National Park

1. ST. GEORGE TO CEDAR CITY

St. George
Zip Code 84770   Area Code 801

St. George, at the heart of Utah's Dixie, has plenty of sun. The town was settled in the 1860's by members of the "Cotton Mission," faithful Mormons sent from Salt Lake City to find a hot, dry climate to grow cotton. They found it here in the picturesque Virgin River Valley, surrounded by red rock cliffs and black lava ridges. In addition to cotton, they planted mulberry trees to feed silkworms imported from China. The trees thrived, the silkworms did not.

Today, about half of the people in Washington County live here. It's a good place to stay while touring Zion and other nearby attractions.

THINGS TO DO

The most visible landmark is the **Mormon Temple,** 401 South 300 East, begun in 1871 but not finished until 1877. Brigham Young selected the site for this first Mormon temple in Utah, but after digging only a few feet, the workmen hit a water table. Between draining the water and other problems, it took a year just to complete the foundation. For stabilization, drainage pipes were installed, and tons of volcanic rock were pounded into the earth, using an old cannon for a pile driver.

Although the Temple is open only to Mormons, the grounds and Visitor Center are open to non-Mormons. The Center has a slide presentation and guides to provide you and the children with more information about the Temple and the Mormon religion.

Brigham Young's Winter Home and Office, in the middle of town, was the religious leader's haven from the harsh Salt Lake City winters. Free tours are given of the refurbished house. You can see cotton growing in the garden, fig trees, and a large, 1870 mulberry tree split by lightning and tied together. While you're there, have the kids ask what potato peelings have to do with the naming of St. George.

Brigham Young Winter Home and Office, 89 West 2nd Street North, 673-2517. Tour hours: daily between 9:00 am– 8:00 pm in midsummer, 9:00 am–6:00 pm during the rest of the year, except for Sundays from late October to late March. Admission is free.

The **Chamber of Commerce** has brochures, maps, and a walking tour of the city that will fill you in on the local history. It also has information on tours and scenic flights over the national parks in the area and Lake Powell. The offices are at the corner of St. George Boulevard and 100 East in the old Washington County Courthouse.

McQuarrie Memorial Hall (Pioneer Museum) adjoins the Courthouse to the north and exhibits early-day relics of the region, including furniture, clothing, tools and an old clothes washer. Kids might enjoy seeing the Crystal Room with its collection of miniature tools and dolls. Hours are 10:00 am– 2:00 pm, Tuesday through Saturday. Admission is free.

DID YOU KNOW?

—The original cost of building the Mormon Temple was close to $1,000,000. It has almost as much rock below ground as above ground.

—Tabernacles are used by Mormons for large meetings; temples are used for special ordinances and ceremonies such as marriages and baptisms. Only the initiated and specially prepared may enter a temple.

CIRCLE WEST FROM ST. GEORGE TO CEDAR CITY

A trip west of St. George on State Highways 18 and 56 includes volcanoes, hot springs and history. Leave a full day for leisurely exploring.

A few miles west of St. George off State Highway 18 is Santa Clara, settled by Swiss immigrants. Stop to visit the restored **Jacob Hamblin House.** Hamblin was a Mormon trailblazer, missionary and peacemaker among the Indians. The sandstone house he built in 1862 has two bedrooms, one for each wife. Free tours are conducted daily, 9:00 am–8:00 pm.

Follow the signs from Santa Clara a few miles to **Snow Canyon State Park,** a 3 mile long trough of intricately sculptured red sandstone cliffs and canyon walls splashed with desert varnish. Cradled between are soft dunes of silky sand, Indian pictographs and pottery shards, and a valley floor blobbed with lava that came bubbling up through the ground.

It's a good place for exploring and picnicking. Take the kids to the **sand dunes** to play and to look for the tracks of chuckwallas, sidewinders, Gila monsters, bobcats, and cottontails.

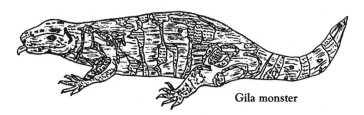

Gila monster

Hike the short trail to Johnson's Arch (a natural land bridge with pioneer names and dates carved in the sandstone) or the lava caves. Drive to **Panorama Point Overlook** to see the confluence of ancient (3 million years) and modern (1000 years) lava. And if all else fails, let the kids chase lizards.

The campground has trailer hook-ups, water, electricity and showers, and the picnic area has interpretive displays. A private concessionaire offers horseback and hayrack rides that can include a campfire breakfast.

For more information on this and other attractions in Southern Utah, contact **Washington County Tourist and Visitor Center,** *97 East St. George Boulevard, St. George 84770, 801/628-0505. The park is open daily year-round. Fee for day use is $3, for camping with hook-ups $10, without hook-ups $8.*

Take State 18 north past extinct volcanoes. In the town of Veyo is the **Veyo Pool Resort,** a small swimming pool fed by hot springs. The pool has a slide and is pleasantly situated beside a stream and shaded picnic ground. It is open mid-March to Labor Day. Admission is $.50 for ages 2–5, $1.75 for ages 6–11, and $2.50 for ages 12 and over.

Southwest from Veyo a road leads to **Gunlock Lake State Recreation Area.** The mild year-round temperatures make it popular for water sports, camping, and fishing.

From Veyo continue to the turnoff to **Pine Valley,** 25 miles from St. George. **Pine Valley Recreation Area** has campgrounds, picnic sites, and hiking trails in the mountains.

The village of Pine Valley, seven miles from the highway, was once a logging center. The small white chapel, built in 1865 by Ebenezer Bryce (the one who lost his cow in Bryce Canyon), is Utah's oldest church in continuous use. Bryce, a former shipbuilder who had never tried his hand at churches, first assembled the walls on the ground, then raised and joined them with rawhide and wooden pegs.

Continue north on State Highway 18 to a side road to the site of the **Mountain Meadows Massacre.** A monument was erected here in memory of the massacre of Missouri pioneers by Mormons. The incident occurred in 1857 during a time of hot tempers, when U.S. troops were sent to remove Brigham Young from office and enforce military authority.

Turn right at the junction with State Highway 56 to the ruins of **Old Irontown.** The town was established in 1868 by a

Mormon cooperative. It was part of the first iron manufacturing industry west of the Mississippi and one of the largest open pit mines of the time. You and the kids can still see the blast furnace walls and the beehive brick kiln, which operated night and day, producing 800 pounds of iron every eight hours.

Watch for signs to Old Irontown by the small lake around ten miles from Cedar City. The dirt road travels three miles.

Covered wagon

Cedar City
Zip Code 84720   Area Code 801

Cedar Fort was settled in 1851 by Mormon pioneers who volunteered to establish it as a base for iron mining and manufacturing. In addition to hostile Indians, the members of this "Iron Mission" battled floods, crop shortages, furnace failures, and the Utah War. By 1858, the foundry was defunct, and the Mission members were encouraged to go elsewhere.

Today, the town serves as a base for touring Zion, Bryce Canyon, Cedar Breaks, and the other sites in the area.

THINGS TO DO
To learn more about the iron industry, visit **Iron Mission State Historical Park**. In addition to a diorama of an 1850 iron foundry, the museum has an interesting collection of horse-drawn vehicles. Have the children look for the forerunner to the compact car (the Stanhope Phaeton) and the bullet-scarred stagecoach.

Other artifacts kids might enjoy include Indian games collected by William R. Palmer, pioneer barbed wire, and an iron jail. In the park outside is old farm machinery and the George L. Wood Cabin, built in 1851 and claimed to be the first log cabin in southwestern Utah.

The museum is less than a mile north of downtown on Main Street (Highway 91), near the cemetery.

Iron Mission State Park, PO Box 1079, 585 North Main Street, 586-9290. Hours: daily, 9:00 am–7:00 pm from June to mid-September, 9:00 am–5:00 pm the rest of the year. Admission is $1, children under 6 are free.

The **Chamber of Commerce** is downtown in a park with a playground. Ask for the historical tour brochure of the town and information on the numerous cultural and sporting events.

One of the most popular annual events in town is the **Utah Shakespeare Festival.** Hosted by Southern Utah State College for several weeks in July and August, this outdoor festival on campus features student actors from across the country. Children will enjoy the pre-performance entertainment held on the green called the Greenshow. Storytelling, dancing, music, juggling, and acrobatics abound. It's also a great time to sample Elizabethan food, or to learn more about the evening performance by attending the Play Orientation in the Indoor Theatre.

If you have children ages 6 and under, you can take advantage of the Festival childcare facilities (they will not be allowed at the play). Cost is $5.

For reservations/information, contact the Shakespeare Festival Box Office, Southern Utah State College, 586-7878.

To see a bit of Mormon pioneer history, visit the **Daughters of Utah Pioneer Museum,** 86 E. Center. The small museum is open Monday through Saturday from 9:00 am–5:00 pm, June through September, with guides available from 1:30–5:00 pm. Admission is free.

Across the street is the **Mormon First Ward Chapel (Old Rock Church),** built during the Depression using varicolored native stone, including iron, copper and gold ore, petrified wood, limestone, sandstone and quartz.

If the weather is hot, take cover under the shade trees in the park on the road to Cedar Canyon, or try the swimming pool and water slide at the middle school, open Monday through Saturday.

Guided tours to nearby national parks and scenic flights can also be arranged. For more information, write Utah Parks Company, 221 North 100 West Street, Cedar City 84720.

DID YOU KNOW?

—Old Main Building on the college campus, built 1898, was the first higher education building in Utah.

—One of the first passengers at the Union Pacific Depot was President Warren Harding.

I-15 Between Cedar City and St. George

Between Cedar City and St. George on I-15 is exit 23 and the road to Leeds and the **Silver Reef Mining area.** Silver Reef was a lusty silver mining town which prospered between 1887 and 1888. Part of the area looks like a western movie set, with old iron ore buckets and mining ruins, and part is exclusive homes and a still active mining area. The red sandstone Wells Fargo building has been restored as an art gallery operated by a well-known local sculptor.

At the Leeds turnoff there is also a road to **Red Cliffs Recreation Site,** which has camping, picnic sites, and a nature trail.

The entrance to the **Kolob Canyons section of Zion National Park** is 27 miles north of St. George off I-15. The Visitor Center has information on the Finger Canyons of the Kolob, which are narrow box canyons jutting out like deep red fingers.

For the adventurous, the trail to **Kolob Arch** will take you

over seven strenuous miles one-way to the largest freestanding
arch in the world. For the more sedate, **Kolob Canyons Road**
climbs across the Hurricane Cliffs to a splendid overlook 5½
miles from the freeway.

2. EAST FROM ST. GEORGE TO ZION NATIONAL PARK

At Harrisburg Junction on I-15 north of St. George take
State Highway 9, the Zion National Park/Hurricane exit.
You'll pass **Quail Creek State Park,** a popular fishing and water
recreation area.

The town of **Hurricane** has a small museum and visitor
center in city park, and you can see turn-of-the-century canals, including Hurricane Canal, which took 11 years to build
using wheelbarrows to haul away the dirt. Ask at the visitor
center about the hot springs in the area.

Rockville, begun in 1862, once produced crops of cotton,
cane sorghum, and silk. At the end of town, look on the right
for Bridge Road. Cross the bridge and turn right again to
backtrack four miles to the ghost town of **Grafton.** When the
road forks, keep to the right.

Grafton was a peaceful farming town which was settled in
the 1860's and survived until the 1920's. You can still see the
brick church and some of the old houses, and you may
recognize it as the locale for the filming of the movie "Butch
Cassidy and the Sundance Kid."

In the town of **Springdale** is the outdoor **Obert C. Tanner
Amphitheater,** where each night at dusk the film "Odyssey" is
shown on a 24-foot by 40-foot screen. This film chronicles the
history, prehistory and scenery of the Grand Circle, which
includes state and national parks, monuments, and historical
sites. Tickets are $3 per adult, $2 per student and ages under
12, and $8 per family. Telephone 673-4811 for more informa-
tion.

You can stay in town at the moderately priced Bumbleberry

Inn (named for its bumbleberry pies), 801/772-3224. Behind the motel is **Ghost Town,** a pioneer village of buildings moved here from other places in Utah. Kids will enjoy walking the old board sidewalks, sampling an old-fashioned sarsaparilla, riding in the stagecoach or watching a gunfight. In the bank is a safe that Butch Cassidy hijacked, but could never open. Behind the village is a large collection of farm and road equipment, a horse-drawn hearse, and an old school wagon.

Ghost Town is open April to October, 10:00 am until dark, during July and August, 5 pm until dark. Admission is $3.

East of town one mile on State 9 is Zion.

Zion National Park

Zion, "the heavenly city of God," is a fitting name for this timeless, massive place. Part of Zion is a lush valley carved by the Virgin River, which alternates between rage and placidity; part is perpendicular walls of sculpted Navajo sandstone decorated in shades of red, blue, yellow and white.

Here and there, the vertical walls are bubbled with alcoves and amphitheaters. Hidden within are pilasters, towers, delicate arches and waterfalls cascading into quiet pools. In winter, a shock of white snow on top contrasts the vivid colors of the lower walls. In autumn, the golden aspen foliage adds its own luster, and in spring, cascades of multicolored sand and water tumble down the escarpments.

Geologic change is still rampant in Zion. The river drags sand grains scouring across the valley floor, floods tumble boulders downstream, rains loosen the cement that holds the quartz together, and water seeps through rock, bringing with it pieces of sandstone.

The Basketmakers once called the eastern section home. Later the Virgin Anasazi built small houses in Zion Canyon and grew corn, squash and melons. The Paiute Indians came next, and in 1858, Nephi Johnson led Mormon pioneers to the flat land between the towers and thought he had reached heaven on earth.

The Mormons named many of the great monoliths in the canyon and called the place "Zion." Brigham Young visited the area and said, "This is not Zion," so for awhile that's how it was known—"Not Zion."

THINGS TO DO

Zion is on a grand scale. Bring it down to child-size by looking for the small among the huge. Smell the flowers and pine trees; watch a butterfly in the sun; touch a smooth rock and scratchy juniper tree; listen for falling grains of sand, a waterfall, the wind or footsteps; and look for the shadow of a soaring raven, a seashell fossil, or shifting sand dunes that have turned to stone. (If you have one, use a cardboard cylinder as a telescope to focus on the small. If not, roll your fingers.)

The **Visitor Center and Museum,** one mile from the south entrance to the park, sits in a canyon with towering walls. In the Center are a topographical map and relief model of the park, slide show, an extensive bookstore with trail guides and maps, and excellent exhibits on geology, wildlife and early Indian cultures. Inquire about the naturalist-led hikes and evening talks from late March through early November, as well as booklets for the self-guiding trails and backcountry permits. Also check for possible travel and parking restrictions for oversized vehicles in the tunnel and on the Zion Canyon road. More information is also listed in the park newspaper.

The Visitor Center and Museum is open 8:00 am–5:00 pm, October through April, until around 6:00 pm during May and September, and until 9:00 pm in the summer months.

Sign the kids up at the Nature Center for the nationally-known **Junior Ranger program,** which transforms Zion into a hands-on experience of hikes, games and other activities. Registration for this excellent program is from 8:15 to 9:00 am and 1:00 to 1:30 pm for full or half day sessions. The one-time fee is $1. The program is for ages 6 to 12 and operates Tuesday through Saturday, Memorial Day to Labor Day.

The **Nature Center,** located just north of the South Campground, also operates as a mini-visitor center with nature exhibits for children.

Take the **Zion Canyon Scenic Drive** to the heart of the park. A favorite for kids is the easy, paved **Emerald Pools Trail.** It is an approximately ½ mile hike to the Lower Pool, and includes walking behind a waterfall. To reach the larger Upper Pool, continue for another mile and a more strenuous climb.

The **Grotto Picnic Area** is a pleasant place for a picnic lunch. The self-guiding trail to **Weeping Rock** is an easy stroll (½ mile round trip) to an alcove where water drips from overhanging cliffs decorated with hanging gardens.

The road ends about 6½ miles from the Center at the **Temple of Sinawava,** a natural amphitheater almost completely surrounded by sheer cliffs. During spring rains, vivid hued waterfalls, colored yellow, red, chocolate, orange and black by the sand from the plateaus above, give a knock-your-socks-off display.

Take the **Gateway to the Narrows Trail,** with trailside exhibits on geology and natural history. This one mile paved trail follows the Virgin River through towering sandstone cliffs and past trailside exhibits, ending at hanging gardens.

During some times of the year, it is possible to continue on a more strenuous trail into the heart of the Narrows, where at one point, the walls tower 1000 feet high and the width at the bottom is only 20 feet. It is essential to ask first at the Visitor Center for safety conditions that can change daily. The trail can be extremely dangerous at certain times of the year because of flash flooding.

You can continue through the park on the **Zion–Mt. Carmel Highway** (State Highway 9). The road is an engineering marvel that took three years to build, cutting through rock for a mile at Zion–Mt. Carmel Tunnel, completed in 1930. Windows in the tunnel give a tantalizing glimpse of the intriguing landscape to come, but please don't create a hazard by stopping to look.

From the parking area at the east end of the tunnel is a ½ mile trail to **Canyon Overlook.** This easy self-guiding trail takes you to the top of Great Arch and ends at an impressive view.

Just before the eastern park boundary is Checkerboard Mesa, a mountain of sandstone crisscrossed with weathered beds and joints.

The northwestern section of Zion is **Kolob Canyons.** It can be reached from the Kolob Visitor Center off I-15 (see page 75).

The Kolob Terrace Road leaves State Highway 9 a few miles south of the park's south entrance. This narrow road is partially paved, and eventually ends up on State Highway 14 east of Cedar City, passing by Kolob Reservoir and a primitive campground.

Zion Lodge, near the visitor center, has lodging, a restaurant, gift shop, and snack bar. Plans are to be open year-round, beginning in 1990. For reservations, contact TW Recreational Services, Inc., PO Box 400, Cedar City, 84720, 801/586-7686. Moderate.

A tour by tram operates daily during summer months from the lodge. Cost is $4 for adults, $2 for children 4-12, under 4 free. You can also make arrangements at the lodge for horseback rides.

The National Park Service operates three campgrounds, one open year-round. The primitive campground at Lava Point has no water, but the other two in Zion Canyon have tent and trailer sites, fire grates, rest rooms and water.

Superintendent, Zion National Park, Springdale, Utah 84767, 801/772-3256. Zion Canyon is open year-round; Kolob Canyon is closed by snow during the winter. Admission is $5 per vehicle.

DID YOU KNOW?

—The Virgin River carries about 180 carloads of ground rock out of the park each day, which equals over 1,000,000 tons a year.

—One of the interesting rock formations in Zion is a hoodoo,

a footstool-shaped rock of sandstone capped with iron.
—The brownish-black Zion snail is about the size of a pinhead.
—At the bottom of the Narrows, sunrise is around noon, and sunset is about an hour later.

3. SOUTH FROM MT. CARMEL JUNCTION TO LAKE POWELL

Continue on State Highway 9 to Mount Carmel Junction, then turn south to Lake Powell or the North Rim of the Grand Canyon. A few miles south of Mt. Carmel Junction on US Highway 89 is the turnoff to Coral Pink Sand Dunes, 11 miles on a paved spur road.

Coral Pink Sand Dunes State Reserve is a basin of pink, fine sand. Kids think it's a huge playground! It was formed when the wind carried sand from Rosy Canyon (southeast of Pipe Springs) and over Moccasin Mountain, merging in this boiling pileup of dunes.

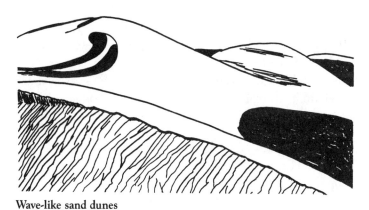

Wave-like sand dunes

Here you can see the struggle to survive. The plants stand far apart so as not to compete with each other for water and nutrients. The sunflower and the wild rhubarb, relished by the Indians, are two of the most common.

Have the kids look for the tracks of kangaroo rats, sidewinders, scorpions, jackrabbits, and the lacy patterns left by beetles. Watch the dune buggies on weekends (keep an eye on the kids when they're around), or rent your own at Mt. Carmel Junction. Write your name in the sand, draw a picture, leave a footprint, build a sand castle, or bury yourself. When you are through playing, the fine sand will pat off.

Coral Pink Sand Dunes State Reserve, Box 95, Kanab 84741, 801/874-2408. Cost is $3 for day use, $8 a night for camping. The campground has improved camp sites, hot showers and rest rooms open from Easter to the end of October. In winter, the main rest rooms are closed and only primitive toilets are available.

Continue on US 89 to Kanab. Several miles outside of town is the privately-owned **Moki Cave,** with extensive black-light mineral displays, Indian artifacts, original dinosaur tracks, and a replica of a Moqui Indian village.

Kanab
Zip Code 84741   Area Code 801

If the canyons around Kanab could talk, they would tell of Hollywood legends. Dozens of movies and television shows have been filmed here, including "Gunsmoke," "The Lone Ranger" and "Planet of the Apes." Many of the stars have left behind their autographed photos at **Parry's Lodge** on Main Street, still one of the nicest places to stay in town for a moderate price.

THINGS TO DO
Lopeman's Frontier Movie Town is the re-creation of a western town, with entertainment, gunfights, shopping, music and food. The town is open 10:00 am to 10:00 pm daily, and is located behind the large tepee outside of Gift City, where craftsmen cut and frame wonderstone.

City Park has fun playground equipment, including a merry-go-round swing and spiral slide. From the park take

Squaw Trail for an enjoyable, but strenuous, hike for children around ages 8 and older. Pick up a self-guiding booklet at the trailhead.

Denny's Wigwam, across the street from Parry's Lodge, is an ice cream parlor with homemade hot fudge. Behind is a small replica of a frontier town.

Heritage House Museum is located at 14 E. 1st South and is open by appointment, 644-2422. Admission is by donation.

Take time to explore the caves and canyons outside of town. Let the kids collect colored sand to make decorative filled bottles. Or reserve a scenic flight over the Grand Canyon from Kanab airport. Stop at the Visitor Center, 48 South 100 East, for more information.

DID YOU KNOW?

—Kanab is a Paiute word meaning "place of the willows."
—Zane Grey lived here in 1912 while writing *Riders of the Purple Sage.*
—Kanab is often called "Little Hollywood."

Kanab to Lake Powell

From Kanab you can travel south to Pipe Springs National Monument and the North Rim of the Grand Canyon (see Chapter XI); or east on US Highway 89 to Lake Powell and Page, Arizona.

At highway mile marker 55 on US Highway 89 turn left to **Johnson Canyon.** About 5½ miles from the highway is an old movie set on the right-hand side of the road. About 2½ miles farther is a panel of ancient petroglyphs. Look for the rock amphitheater and the red cliffs dotted with barn swallow nests. Unfortunately, the petroglyphs have been accessible to modern man, and you can see the resulting vandalism. The road continues through Johnson Canyon. Rock hunting and climbing are popular along this road.

Return to US 89 and continue east. At mile marker 31, a sign points to the town site of **Old Pahreah,** a ghost town and an old movie set, 4½ miles along the fair-weather dirt road.

The abandoned set was built for the filming of "Sergeants Three," starring Sammy Davis, Jr., Frank Sinatra, and Dean Martin. Stop there to pick up a map or to eat lunch in the picnic area.

The set is still sturdy and a great place for the children to use their imaginations. Have them pretend they are directors of a western movie. Which of the buildings will be the saloon? General store? Jail? Hotel?

Film the production if you have a movie camera. If you have a still camera, tell the kids to pose in a window, depicting different emotions—alarm because of a gunfight, sadness because of a lover's jilting, excitement because a wagon load of goods from the East is approaching. The second floor window is fun with a close-up lens. If you don't have a camera, be the audience for their production.

From the movie set, it is less than a mile past the old graveyard to the ruins of the original pioneer settlement. It's over the river and through the tamarisk. Pahreah (Paiute for "muddy water") was built in 1870 by settlers relocating from five miles upstream.

If you can make it to the town site across the river, ask the kids to compare it to the movie set. Is it bigger or smaller? Which is in better condition? Why?

Back on US Highway 89, the highway travels through rugged scenery. Side roads lead northeast into this frontier wilderness of labyrinthine canyons. Cliff dwellings, strange fossils, dinosaur tracks, and inaccessible tablelands on Smokey Mountain and the Kaiparowits Plateau all wait to be discovered in this land almost completely devoid of man. Continue on US 89 to Lake Powell and Wahweap Marina.

4. EAST OF CEDAR CITY THROUGH MORMON COUNTRY

Take State Highway 14 southeast of Cedar City to the turn-off to Cedar Breaks National Monument. Several miles past the turn-off on State 14 is **Navajo Lake,** one of the most picturesque mountain lakes in Utah. The crystal clear water is ideal for fishing and boating, and camping and cabins are also available. **Cascade Falls** is a natural tunnel in the mountain where lake water tumbles down to the canyon below. **Duck Creek Pond** has a playground and campground, and interpretive programs and hikes conducted by the National Forest Service.

Cedar Breaks National Monument

State Highway 148 leads north of State Highway 14 to Cedar Breaks, a vast amphitheater of eye-piercing white and orange cliffs topped by rose and coral. Almost half a mile deep and over three miles from rim to rim, it encloses several semi-circular basins jammed with intricate designs and time-worn ridges.

This "circle of painted cliffs," as the Indians called it, blazes with color, and the rollick of cliff tint is echoed by the alpine flowers. In spring and summer, you can drive through the spruce-fir forest on the Markagunt Plateau for a striking contrast to the naked rock.

THINGS TO DO

Keep the children's jackets handy. Temperatures in the high-country (elev. 10,300 ft.) can be surprisingly cool.

Stop at the **Visitor Center** for more information on the geology, wildlife and wildflowers of the park. A stuffed mountain lion at 4-year-old eye level, a touch table with animal tracks to match, and an exhibit to test rock samples make it particularly interesting to kids. Ask for information on ranger-led walks and programs available in summer.

The Visitor Center is open daily, Memorial Day to mid-October, depending on snow, 8:00 am–6:00 pm. The rest of the year, information is available at the Kolob Canyons Contact Station in Zion National Park.

The **Rim Drive** will take you five miles past the scenic attractions. In summer, the wildflower display is extraordinary. The road is open mid-May to late October, depending on weather. The most dramatic view of the park is from **Point Supreme;** the most splendid time is sunset.

If the kids want to hike, try the two-mile rim **Wasatch Ramparts Trail** past a stand of bristlecone pine at Spectra Point and ending at an overlook. Another easy trail is the self-guided one to **Alpine Pond.** It curves through lava outcroppings, wildflowers, and a beautiful forest glade to the pond.

The campground near Point Supreme is open mid-June to mid-September.

Superintendent, Cedar Breaks National Monument, Box 749, Cedar City, Utah 84720, 801/586-9451. Admission is $3 per vehicle.

DID YOU KNOW?

—Bristlecone pine trees like the ones on the Wasatch Ramparts Trail are some of the most ancient living things in the world. Some in California are over 4,600 years old.

—Cedar Breaks was named by the Mormons—"cedar" for the fragrant juniper or cedar trees and "breaks" for the eroded landscape.

—The Fremont Indians hunted and gathered fruit in Cedar Breaks during the summer.

—There are over 150 species of flowering plants in the park. You can't find such a variety anywhere else in southern Utah.

State Highway 143 Northwest to Parowan

State Highway 148 continues through Cedar Breaks to a Tintersection with State 143. Look for the 11,315-foot high **Brian Head,** a lava mountain named because it resembles the profile of William Jennings Bryan. A three mile gravel road open in summer will take you to the summit view.

Left on State 143 is **Brian Head Ski and Summer Resort,** with horseback riding, camp-outs and backcountry trips in the summer, and downhill skiing and other winter sports in the winter. The road then descends through Parowan Canyon on steep switchbacks. It is not recommended for trailers.

The town of **Parowan** was settled by Mormon pioneers in 1851. It is now southern Utah's oldest permanent settlement, and several historic buildings still stand.

Rock Church in Townsquare Park on Center and Main Street offers tours. Call 801/477-8901 or 477-3549 to make arrangements. The park also has a playground and the town library.

Across the street is the restored **Jessi Smith Home.** Built of adobe and lumber in 1856, the original house had joints held together only by wooden pegs. For hours and tours, call 801/477-8143 or 477-8728.

The park in the south part of town has a picnic area and swimming pool.

Windmill

To see a good example of petroglyphs, including the Fremont Indian "spacemen," take Main Street north then turn west on 400 North to **Parowan Gap,** a deep gorge cut through the Red Hills. The road becomes gravel in about four miles, then continues another four miles to the gap in the mountains. As the Indians passed through here, they pecked images of snakes, lizards, mountain sheep and other messages on the rock. You can continue to Cedar City on the gravel road that connects with State 130 or return to Parowan.

DID YOU KNOW?

—The name Parowan, meaning "evil water", came from a Paiute legend which claims that hundreds of years ago, while the Indians camped beside the nearby Little Salt Lake, a monster rose from the lake and dragged one of the maidens into his watery lair.

—John C. Fremont, the Pathfinder, came through Parowan in 1854. By the time he and his party got here from the Green River, the snow was deep, and they had no shoes and not much food.

State Highway 143 Northeast to Panguitch

About fifteen miles northeast of Cedar Breaks on State Highway 143 is **Panguitch Lake,** one of the best fishing lakes in the country. Lodging, camping, a general store, restaurant, trailer parks, marinas, and rental boats are all available June through October. The campgrounds close in the winter, but the resorts stay open for winter sports.

In the town of **Panguitch,** look for the prevalent red brick architecture provided by the communal brick factory. Building in town flourished as workmen at the kiln were paid in bricks rather than money. North of town on US Highway 89 is the **Visitor Information Center** in a park with a picnic area and playground.

The town's **historical museum** is on Center and First Street, open 4:00–8:00 pm during the summer.

On the east side of Main Street is the old Blue Pine Hotel, where Butch Cassidy is said to have met his mother for the last time. Butch's real name was Robert LeRoy Parker, and he grew up in the area. Some of his relatives still insist he was not killed in South America, as commonly believed, but that he returned to visit his hometown and later died an old man somewhere in the Northwest after changing his name and going straight. The old Parker homestead Butch visited in later years still stands beside US 89 near Circleville north of Panguitch.

DID YOU KNOW?

—Panguitch is Indian for "big fish."
—In 1894 Butch Cassidy, who grew up near Panguitch, was convicted of rustling. He asked for one more night of freedom, and the lawmen agreed. Cassidy returned the next day to serve a two year jail sentence.

5. SCENIC ROUTE 12 TO BRYCE AND CAPITOL REEF

Seven miles south of Panguitch on US 89 is the turnoff for Scenic Route 12. The road travels through **Red Canyon,** a small Bryce, with many of the same erosional forms and colors found in its bigger brother. Continue to Bryce Junction, then turn south to Bryce Canyon.

Bryce Canyon National Park

Bryce is dramatic, its carved pink pinnacles abundant with scenery. Wildlife also abounds, with mule deer, bobcats, porcupines, and chipmunks roaming freely in this surreal fairyland of color. Maybe that's what prompted Ebenezer Bryce to make it his home.

He homesteaded here in the 1870's. Five years later he gave up, saying "It's a hell of a place to lose a cow." Looking down at this enormous amphitheater with its labyrinth of side canyons, you might echo his sentiments.

Unlike Zion and the Grand Canyon, Bryce Canyon has no river. Rather, it has been washed out of the side of a plateau by thousands of rain-filled cascades, patient, intricate carvers exposing 60 layers of stone. Some of the most bizarre, intensely colored rock formations in the world have been left behind. Even kids are amazed!

THINGS TO DO

Although jammed with tourists in summer, Bryce is still worth a visit.

The **Visitor Center,** just past the entrance, has exhibits, maps, audiovisual programs, and a schedule of the numerous ranger-led programs and hikes. The Center is open daily, June through August, 8:00 am–8:00 pm; September through May, 8:00 am–5:00 pm.

Several times a week the **Sunrise Nature Center** conducts programs for children ages 5–10. The park also has a Junior Ranger Program. Ask at the Visitor Center for more information.

Rim Road, claimed to be the most colorful 20 miles in the world, will take you past numerous lookout points from where you can see the main geological formations. The most spectacular are the five closest to the center—Fairyland, Sunrise, Sunset, Inspiration, Bryce and Paria Points.

Hiking is another good way to see Bryce Amphitheater. The **Rim Trail,** easy to moderate, follows the canyon rim 5½ miles. You can walk the entire trail or just a section between two lookout points, depending on your children's ambition. Between Sunset Point and North Campground the trail is relatively level.

Another easy to moderate trail is the **Bristlecone Loop Trail.**

This one mile loop leaves from Rainbow Point. **Navajo Trail,** a moderate 2 mile round trip, leaves from Sunset Point.

Queen's Garden Trail, a 1½ mile round trip from Sunrise Point, is the easiest trail that descends the cliffs. A self-guiding leaflet is available at the Visitor Center. This moderate trail descends 320 feet. Young children may find hiking back out of the canyon is difficult. Consider renting a horse for the trip.

Bryce Canyon Lodge, open between early May and mid-October, offers lodging, a gift shop, service station and the historic General Store. Also, a slide show is shown nightly in the Lodge, and you can make arrangements here for horseback ·rides and van tours. Make your reservations early. TW Recreational Services, PO Box 400, Cedar City, Utah 84720, 801/586-7686. Moderate.

The Park operates two campgrounds, North Campground (open all year) and Sunset Campground (open June–October).

Another good place to stay in the area for a moderate price is **Ruby's Inn Resort,** at the north entrance to the park. Open year-round, it includes a motel, campground, swimming pool, restaurant, Old Bryce Town, a general store, wild west shows, chuck wagon suppers, trail rides, and helicopter rides, as well as snowmobiling and cross country skiing in the winter. Telephone 801/834-5341 for reservations.

Bryce is open year-round, but the road south of Inspiration Point is usually closed by snow November through April. At that time, you can see the rest of the park on the free snow-shoes available at the Visitor Center.

Superintendent, Bryce Canyon National Park, Bryce Canyon, Utah 84717, 801/834-5322. Admission is $5 per vehicle.

DID YOU KNOW?

—The Paiute Indians called Bryce "Unka-timpe-wa-wince-pack-ich," which means "red rocks standing like men in a bowl-shaped canyon."

—Erosion eats away another foot from the canyon rim every 50 or 60 years.

—The Paiute Indians have a legend that tells of sinful ancestors whom the gods turned to stone, forming the strange formations in Bryce.

—Bryce is really made up of twelve amphitheaters eroded out of the limestone cliffs.

Between Bryce and Capitol Reef

From Bryce, take State Highway 12 southeast to Cannonville. From here, a gravel road travels about eight miles south to the turnoff to **Kodachrome Basin State Park,** named by the National Geographic Society because it was so impressed with the scenery. Be aware that the road can be impassable after a rain. However, there are currently plans to pave it.

Kodachrome is a delightful place filled with unique geological formations and brilliant colors that shift with the sun like a chameleon. The self-guided nature trail is short and easy, and there are a few other good trails for kids in the park. The campground has picnic tables, grills, water and firewood. The Trail Head Station, a private concession in the middle of the Park, has picnic items and gifts, as well as rentals for horseback and horse-drawn coach rides through the park.

About 10 miles southeast of Kodachrome is another side trip to **Grosvenor Arch,** a superb example of a double sandstone arch. This 152-foot high, cream-colored expanse was formed by ancient freshwater springs. The road is fair-weather and deeply rutted under the best of circumstances. It connects to the dirt road through **Cottonwood Canyon,** which leads to US Highway 89 and Lake Powell, about an hour away. This is one of the most scenic areas in southern Utah.

Kodachrome Basin State Park, PO Box 238, Cannonville, UT 84718-0238, 801/679-8562. The park is closed in the winter. Admission is $3 per vehicle for day-use, $8 for camping.

Continue on State Highway 12 to the town of Escalante. About two miles east of town, turn off to **Escalante Petrified Forest State Park.** The park includes Wide Hollow Reservoir and a tent campground with picnic sites.

You and the kids can fish, swim and water ski in the reservoir, or take the nature trail that leaves from the campground. This one-mile loop winds past balanced rocks and petrified logs. Cost for camping is $8, day use is $3.

The town of **Escalante** exudes frontier isolation and rugged rusticity. The Mormons settled here in 1876, calling it Potato Valley. Early history and relics are in the Daughters of Utah Museum, in the old tithing office beside Griffin's grocery store. Call 801/826-4242 or 826-4288 for the museum to be opened.

Fifteen miles east of Escalante is **Calf Creek Recreation Area.** This BLM campground is a super place for kids. The shallow Escalante River is easily accessible for warm water wading and tubing, and the campground has picnic tables with firepits, firewood, showers and a playground. Arrive early to assure yourself of a campsite. The area is a U.S. fee area, but the Golden Eagle Pass does not apply.

Take the 5½ mile round-trip hike to **Lower Calf Creek Falls** on a self-guided nature trail that leads past small Indian ruins, rock art, a pioneer fence, and a miniature natural arch. The trail ends in a blue-green oasis of hanging gardens and a 126-foot high waterfall where you can swim. The hike crosses and recrosses the shallow river, so have the kids wear canvas shoes or boots. Part of the trail is through thick sand, so plan to take your time.

After Calf Creek, the highway climbs on steep curves. At one point, the road becomes a twisting, narrow neck over the hog backs, called Hell's Backbone. How long do you think the road will be here before it washes away?

Boulder is an isolated farming community claiming to be one of the last United States communities to become accessible by automobile. The village, like the nearby mountains, was named for the volcanic rocks littering the ground.

Visit the **Anasazi Indian Village State Historical Monument,** where 11th-century Indians once lived. The visitor center–museum has historical and cultural displays, including a diorama of the original village, a storage granary, and replicas of rock art. You can also buy packages of Anasazi beans or blue popcorn.

Outside are the partially excavated small village, a replica of an Anasazi dwelling, and a forest service weather station where daily precipitation measurements are taken. Have the kids look for the grinding and mealing bins against the outside wall, and for the clues archaeologists used to predict where to find the ruins. Call ahead to make special arrangements for atl-atl throwing and flint knapping demonstrations.

Superintendent, Anasazi Indian Village State Historical Monument, PO Box 393, Boulder, UT 84716, 801/335-7346. Hours: daily 8:00 am–7:00 pm from mid-May to mid-September, 9:00 am–5:00 pm the rest of the year. Cost is $.50 for adults, children under 6 are free.

If you have time, drive the ruggedly beautiful **Burr Trail.** This graded dirt road winds east through the Waterpocket Fold of Capitol Reef National Park, eventually ending at Bullfrog Marina on Lake Powell. This is 66 miles of unparalleled scenery.

The Burr Trail is not a highway, although some are currently lobbying to make it such. Weather can adversely affect conditions, so check with the rangers at the Anasazi Indian Village for up-to-date information from the local road department.

North of Boulder, State Route 12 passes through **Dixie National Forest,** stately evergreens, mountain meadows and rushing streams. Boulder Mountain is a lava mountain with a remarkably flat summit, 50 square miles of rolling tableland called Boulder Top. It has three easily accessible campgrounds for cool summer camping and numerous small lakes and streams where the kids can try their fishing luck.

Descend from the mountains past the Neapolitan-striped boulders of black, white and brown, and turn east on State Highway 24 to the entrance to Capitol Reef.

DID YOU KNOW?

—The Escalante River was the last major river to be mapped in the United States.

—Anasazi Indian Village is believed to have been the largest Anasazi community west of the Colorado River.

—Bull Valley Gorge near Cannonville is so narrow it is said stars can be seen in broad daylight from the bottom.

—A legend claims Montezuma's Treasure is hidden on White Mountain in Johnson Canyon. An actual treasure map from Mexico pinpoints petroglyphs and hand-cut steps leading to a maze of tunnels. Locals followed the map and found many of the tunnels, which led to booby-trapped rooms, but they never found the treasure.

—The petrified geyser holes (white sediment plugs standing upright) found in Kodachrome Basin have been seen nowhere else on earth.

—The bones of what may be the longest dinosaur ever found (between 100 and 120 feet) were discovered recently in Escalante Canyon.

—Until 1938-39 Boulder's mail delivery was via pack mule and packhorse.

Capitol Reef National Park

Some think Capitol Reef is grander than Zion and more fantastic than Bryce. It is 378 square miles jammed with carved spires, goblin rocks, arches, grand buttes, cliffs and gorges, and spattered with a dose of history and archaeology.

Colors here are vivid blues and greens, purples and orchids, whites and reds. Look for the white domes of Navajo sandstone that cap the red Wingate sandstone cliffs. One of the park's high points, Capitol Dome, is every bit the replica of the Capitol Building in Washington, D.C., hence the name "Capitol." Like an ocean reef rising from the valley floor, cliffs have been a barrier to travel, hence the name "Reef."

Millions of years ago, inland seas covered this area, depositing sediments. Later, giant sand dunes were deposited when the seas receded. In time, the sand was cemented together by minerals in the groundwater, turning to stone. In layers that were once tidal flats, you can still see the ripple marks and prehistoric tracks.

Then, 60 million years ago, the earth's crust buckled in a great uplift that created the Colorado Plateau and the Waterpocket Fold, a 100-mile long crinkle in the earth extending from Lake Powell to Thousand Lake Mountain. After that, erosion took over, exposing deeper and deeper layers of the earth.

The Fremont Indians once lived in Capitol Reef, using the river water to irrigate their fields of corn, squash and beans, and storing the surplus in sheltered bins called moki huts. Later, the Paiutes passed through Capitol Reef on hunting expeditions. They were followed by Mormon pioneers who homesteaded in the area and eventually planted orchards and settled the town of Fruita.

THINGS TO DO

There are easy hikes, interpretive programs, evidence of Mormon pioneers, wildlife and orchards—kids like it here!

The Park is divided into north, south and central districts. The central district contains the area's most renowned canyons, its only paved highway (State Highway 24), and the visitor center. Fair-weather and four-wheel drive dirt roads take you into the other two sections.

As you enter the park from the west, stop at **Panorama Point** for an overview of the park.

Continue on State 24 to the **Visitor Center,** which has information, exhibits, slide shows, a three-dimensional map of the area, and touch tables of rocks, dinosaur bones and other fossils. It's also the place to obtain backcountry camping permits and to find a schedule for the natural history programs and naturalist walks conducted May through September.

The center is open daily during the summer, 8:00 am–6:30

pm. Memorial Day to Labor Day, 8:00 am to 4:30 pm the rest of the year.

Near the Visitor Center is a pleasant year-round, cotton-wood-shaded campground with an old barn; orchards planted by the Mormon pioneers; and a **blacksmith and implement shop** with a recorded message detailing early farm life. Stop for the kids to pick their own cherries, apples, peaches, pears and apricots in the **orchards.** During harvest times, there is a small fee. Other times, it is free, as long as the fruit is eaten on the spot. Ask at the Visitor Center.

A gravel **Scenic Drive** travels south from the center past the campground (25 miles round trip). Allow a minimum of 1½ hours. You can purchase a self-guiding brochure from the center, or pick up a less elaborate one at the first stop. As the road travels through the numerous dry washes, imagine what it would look like after a cloudburst, and you will know why one of the most important things to do on this trip is watch for rain and the resulting flash floods, especially July through September.

A spur road from Scenic Drive takes you one mile past the Oyler uranium mine into **Grand Wash,** a steep-walled canyon that is a beautiful place to explore. The level, two mile trail travels along the wash bottom edged by steep sandstone walls, then branches to several points of interest.

At the end of Scenic Drive is **Capitol Gorge,** with narrows of Wingate sandstone. A short stroll down the canyon (one mile) will take you past Basketmaker petroglyphs, the record early travelers left at the Pioneer Register, and to The Tanks, where erosion has carved pockets in the rock. The first part of the trail is enjoyable for even the youngest, with wonderful holes to crawl in to. A more strenuous trail leaves from the parking area to the Golden Throne, a gold dome of sandstone sitting 3000 feet high on the crest of Capitol Reef.

Return to the Visitor Center, and drive one mile east on State Highway 24 to the old **Fruita** community and **Historic Fruita Schoolhouse,** built in 1896. During the week, eight school grades were taught in its one room. On weekends it was used for Sunday school and social gatherings. The kids can listen to a recorded message from one of the early teachers, and the schoolhouse is sometimes staffed by graduates telling stories about attending school here. Ask at the Visitor Center for schedules and an informative handout.

The self-guided trail to **Hickman Natural Bridge** is a moderate one-mile hike that children particularly enjoy, with alcoves and potholes to explore, a massive sandstone bridge, and abundant wildlife. Take your lunch and your time for exploring.

Other good trails that are a bit more strenuous include **Fremont River, Cohab Canyon and Chimney Rock.**

Farther east on State Highway 24 is the **Behunin Cabin,** the one-room home of a family of ten. Built in 1882, this small house offered just enough sleeping room for the father, mother, and the two youngest children. The older girls slept outside in the old wagon box and the older boys slept in "dugouts" in the cliff behind the cabin. Ask the kids which one they would choose for sleeping.

The **North District** of Capitol Reef is reached by a four-wheel drive road. The **South District** is part of the wilderness of the Waterpocket Fold, red and white rock jutting up as high as 2000 feet. A fair-weather graded dirt road parallels the eastern edge of the Fold and eventually intersects the Burr Trail. Ask the rangers about hikes and road conditions for the North and South districts.

Other than the park campgrounds, the nearest places to stay in the area are in the towns of Torrey, Bicknell and Loa. The **Rim Rock Motel,** seven miles west of the visitor center, also offers guided tours of the area. Call 801/425-3843 for reservations. Inexpensive.

Superintendent, Capitol Reef National Park, Torrey, UT 84775, 801/425-3791. Although Capitol Reef is open all year, trails and unpaved side roads may be closed during rains or midwinter. Admission is $3 per vehicle.

DID YOU KNOW?

—Old Fruita's population averaged 10 families.

—Waterpockets are shallow depressions eroded in the rock that collect rainwater. They are also called potholes and tanks.

—The Navajo called Capitol Reef the "Land of the Sleeping Rainbow."

—In the 1920's uranium from the Oyler Mine was ground up and used as medicine, either by mixing with drinking water or by placing it on the joints as a cure for rheumatism.

—Cassidy Arch was named after Butch Cassidy, who hid out from the law nearby. He and his Wild Bunch occasionally used the Waterpocket Fold as a route to escape southeast into New Mexico.

—The last student graduated from Fruita School in 1941.

—The name of Cohab Canyon refers to the polygamous Mormons who are said to have hidden in the canyon to avoid federal officers.

From Capitol Reef to Hanksville

From Capitol Reef continue about 40 miles on State Highway 24 to the town of Hanksville. The river valley between Caineville and Hanksville is called the Blue Valley. This scenic drive takes you through badlands with barren slopes of hardened sand, eroding columns, and porous igneous rock.

Stop so the kids can see if the ground here is as soft as it looks. Have them make up a story about how this land was formed. Why are the rocks red? Who sprinkled in the black?

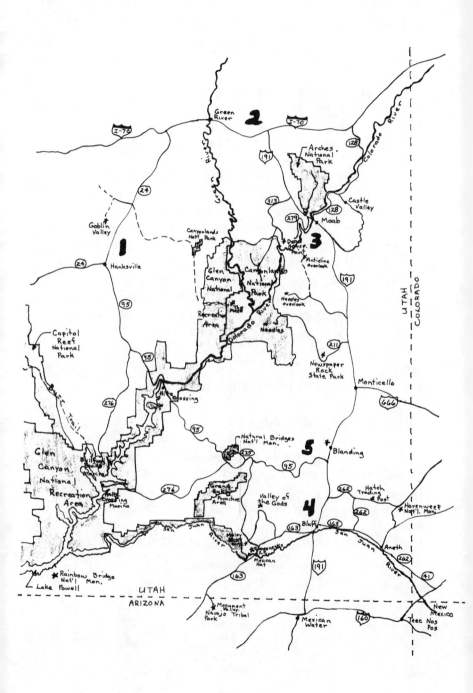

6

CANYON COUNTRY: The Fractured Earth in Southeastern Utah

Southeastern Utah is at the heart of the Colorado Plateau. Mother Earth is fractured and naked here, stacked in wedding-cake layers of stone from primordial bottom to newborn top. It's a jagged land, a place where mesas and spires, pinnacles and needles, natural bridges and arches are shuffled into an astonishing jumble. "A wilderness of rocks," John Wesley Powell called it.

If you're a geologist, canyon country is a living university. In most of the rest of the world, the yardsticks of earth's past are invisible, hidden beneath the sediment of today. Here, they stand exposed, and there's probably no place else on earth you can see such a wide variety of stone sculpture.

The earth is made of three types of rock—igneous, sedimentary and metamorphic. Sedimentary is formed when sediments such as sand, soil and shells are bonded together by pressure, usually beneath a lake or sea. Metamorphic rock is generally sedimentary in origin, and has been changed by intense heat or pressure. Igneous is formed from rock that was once so hot it was liquid. When it cooled, it hardened.

Much of canyon country is sandstone, a sedimentary rock deposited as sand dunes during the Paleozoic era or under ancient oceans. It is held together, often tenuously, by a relatively soluble cement. Although rain here is rare, only 10″ or less a year, it usually comes in torrents that carve the landscape with a fluid knife. The stone yields, in some places more, some less, as the water rushes headlong towards the sea, dragging along with it millions of tons of debris.

During flood times, you can stand on the banks of the San Juan River and hear boulders crashing against each other as they are flushed downstream. The rivers, heavily loaded with sediment, look like liquid dirt then. The Mormons called them too thin to plow and too thick to drink. As the water hastens seaward, it leaves behind towering ruins—and a parched land.

It wasn't always so. If you look, you can find fossils from another time: the shellfish and snails and worms that lived here a few hundred million years ago when earth's thirst was quenched and life was lush and abundant. But today this massive place emanates starkness, not the green of life, and its colors are the tonings of dirt, the reds and yellows and oranges of minerals.

Much of the rock is coated with "desert varnish," shiny ribbons of dark gold and black. The varnish is formed when minerals (clay, manganese oxide and iron oxide) leached from the rock by water seepage are mixed by bacteria with a coating of airborne dust.

In the few places where moisture gathers, life makes a grandstand effort at display. Luxuriant hanging gardens drink the water seeping through the porous rock to cliff-face springs and add an occasional splash of color. Where canyon walls widen out from river's edge, plant roots tap into the water table a few feet below the surface, and cheat grass, tamarisk and pennycress bloom. In some places, quicksand forms, jealously

Eagle

sucking any potential for life into a soggy grave.

The history books in southeastern Utah aren't as full as in other parts of the country, but a few names have become synonymous with the ruggedness of the land. Major John Wesley Powell captained an expedition down the unexplored Colorado River, a trip he called riding on "the back of the Dragon." In what is an amazing tale of bravery, resourcefulness and foresight, he contributed to the understanding of the geology and ecology of the area. Butch Cassidy, the American West's version of Robin Hood, hid out from the law in the unexplored maze of canyons.

Although the coming of the railroad in the 1880's opened some of the area to settlement, much of this battlefield of nature is not easily accessible even today. Few paved roads exist, so one of the best ways to explore is on foot. For the wilderness enthusiast, canyon country is a giant playground.

If you do take the time to explore, don't be surprised if in some remote place, you discover an unexpected Anasazi ruin, a mute reminder that ancient man was once so in tune with the land he could survive here without air conditioning and indoor plumbing. Whatever else you do, enjoy your visit to this skeletal earth. The solitude may renew you, the rugged beauty inspire you, the awesome power of nature humble you. If nothing else, you may leave hoping to someday return to this tough and lonely, alluring and magnificent land.

DID YOU KNOW?

—The temperature range in San Juan County, Utah is one of the widest recorded anywhere in the world. It varies from 115 degrees to −29 degrees Fahrenheit (a 144-degree change). Daily variations of 50 degrees are common.

—Bands of sedimentary rock related by location and composition are sometimes grouped as a formation. In the Southwest, examples of these formations are Chinle, Moenkopi, Navajo, and Cutler.

—In southeast Utah, only the Colorado, San Juan and Green rivers flow year-round. The rest vanish almost as quickly as they appear after a rain.

—During a flash flood, a stream may rise ten feet in an hour and recede to a trickle in the next hour.

—During one extraordinary flood day, October 14, 1941, the San Juan River carried an estimated 12 million tons of sediment past the town of Mexican Hat.

—Each year, the San Juan and Colorado rivers together deposit enough sediment in Lake Powell to cover 80,000 acres a foot deep.

—Although introduced from western Asia for its attractiveness and for erosion control, the tamarisk has become a pest in the Southwest, invading most river drainages and displacing the native plants such as willows and cottonwoods.

From Hanksville Through Moab to Natural Bridges

1. Hanksville to Green River—A Maze of Rocks
2. From Green River to Moab—Gateway to Canyon Country
3. Moab to Bluff—Past the Trail of the Ancients
4. Bluff to Grand Gulch Primitive Area—Towers of Stone
5. Blanding to Natural Bridges National Monument

1. HANKSVILLE TO GREEN RIVER—A MAZE OF ROCKS

Hanksville
Zip Code 84734   Area Code 801

Hanksville was used by Butch Cassidy and his Wild Bunch as a rendezvous point in the 1880's and 1890's. Because he and his gang were big spenders, and because the large cattle companies were their chief victims, many of the locals welcomed them to their small community.

Mining has been important to the development of Hanksville. You can visit the **Wolverton Mill,** a gold-processing mill. It was built in the early 1900's in the nearby Henry Mountains at the same place three prospectors claimed to have found a lost mine.

According to legend, the old Spanish mine they found had been worked by Indian slaves. When they were rescued by their kinsmen, the Spanish masters were killed, the mine filled in, and the place cursed by the medicine man. The lives of the three original prospectors seemed to bear out the curse. Two died shortly after they found the mine, and the other claimed bad luck and sickness followed him for 40 years until his death.

The mill is made of hand-hewn logs, and it took E. T. Wolverton ten years to complete it. The water wheel, which weighs 3200 pounds, is so perfectly balanced it can be turned with one hand. After Wolverton's death, the mill was moved by helicopter to its present location and rebuilt.

To visit, turn south from the main road in the center of town at the sign for the Henry Mountains and drive a few blocks to the BLM office. Ask at the office for a free brochure on the history of the mill. Admission is free.

For a home-cooked, inexpensive meal, eat at **Tropical Jeems Cafe,** one mile north of town on State Highway 24. Remember that home cooking takes time. This is not a fast food joint.

Young children might enjoy a quick stop at **Hollow Mountain,** a grocery store built into the side of a hill. It's easy to see from the front door, but once inside, you won't know you are in a big rock unless you look through the back door.

Southeast from Hanksville, State Highway 95 winds through beautiful red rock country to Lake Powell (see Chapter XI).

North from Hanksville, State 24 travels to I-70 and Green River, Utah. The road is a good place to pull off and look for animal tracks among the Mormon tea and sagebrush. If you find any tracks, let the kids practice their detective skills. What animals were here? How long ago? How many? What were they doing? Where are they now?

At Temple Mountain Junction, around 21 miles north of Hanksville, turn southwest approximately 14 miles to Goblin Valley State Park. The surfaced road changes to improved gravel.

Goblin Valley State Park

Ghoulish forms greet you from this valley of weirdly eroded sandstone. Most kids love running through the small, accessible valley.

Water created this unique sculptured rock garden. Intense cloudbursts and flash floods washed away the softer rock, exposing the harder rock underneath. But it only takes a smattering of imagination to picture ancient goblin carvers working their magic in the stone of this enchanting land. Maybe on some moonlit night, you will see them at work.

THINGS TO DO

Drive to **Observation Point,** which has a covered picnic pavilion and an overlook of the valley. Have the kids pretend the stones were once alive and are frozen in time. What were they? Imagine what this place looked like when rock layers filled in the open areas. What will it look like in 100 years? What will be gone first?

Short trails descend to the valley floor, where you and the kids can walk among the squat, stubby forms and feel like Alice through the Looking Glass.

Carmel Canyon Trail begins along the edge of the valley. Look at the effects of erosion on both sides of the trail and see if you can figure out why each side is so different. Find a rivulet bed and follow it to the bottom. You can continue on the trail, 1½ miles, or descend directly to the valley floor.

On the floor, have the children look for E. T. and Howard the Duck. Hint: The easiest way to find them is to enter the valley from the Carmel Canyon Trail. Play "Swing the Statue" or "Freeze" to see what shapes you can become. Or try a game of hide and seek among the "goblins." Let the kids explore on their own and take a picture.

The campground has water, RV hookups, picnic tables and grills. Showers and rest rooms are also available. Telephone 800/284-CAMP for reservations.

Goblin Valley State Park, PO Box 93, Green River, UT 84525-0093. Admission is $3 per vehicle.

Canyonlands National Park—The Maze District

If you and the kids are adventurous, visit the Maze District of Canyonlands (for more information on Canyonlands, see page 110). The Maze is a wild and rugged place. Only about 8000 people a year challenge its remoteness. But for the serious hiker or four-wheel drive enthusiast, it is an unparalleled opportunity to be immersed in the wilderness.

Primary access is via a dirt road passable to regular vehicles except during stormy periods. The road takes you 46 miles off State Highway 24 to the **Hans Flat Ranger Station,** telephone 801/259-6513 (between 8:00 am and 9:00 am daily). Be sure to bring your own water.

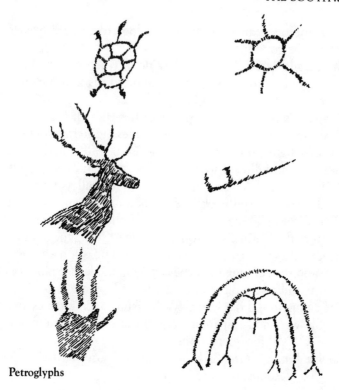

Petroglyphs

Stop at the ranger station for backcountry and natural history information, topographical maps, and emergency aid. From here, a two-wheel drive road leads to the top of the Flint Trail. All other roads in the Maze are four-wheel drive. If you plan to do any hiking, realize that trails may be marked only by rock cairns. Exploring them will sharpen your map reading skills, but be sure you have some before you start. Getting lost can be hazardous to your health!

One of the star attractions in the Maze is **Horseshoe Canyon,** with some of the best examples of rock art in the Southwest. It can be reached from the ranger station via a four-wheel drive road, but most people use the two-wheel drive dirt road that travels 32 miles from State 24 to the west rim of the canyon, or the 45 mile dirt road from Green River. A hiking trail (around 6 miles round trip from the west rim) leads to the ghostly life-size figures staring out from a rock panel called the "Great Gallery." Primitive camping with a permit is available.

Another four-wheel drive road leads to the **Maze Overlook.** Look for the Chocolate Drops. Older children can take the trail to the **Harvest Scene pictographs,** deep in the canyon complex. You'll have to scramble down the steepest parts of the trail using footholds and handholds carved in the rock.

To really see the Maze, plan at least three days by four-wheel drive, more if hiking. Admission is $3 per vehicle for a seven day pass good for all three sections of Canyonlands.

From The Maze to Green River

North of the Maze, State Highway 24 passes through the eastern edge of the **San Rafael Swell and Reef,** 1000 square miles of wilderness reminiscent of a miniature Colorado Plateau. Access to the area is by dirt road and hiking trails, most of them near Price, Utah. For more information, write Castle Country Travel Council, Box 1037, Price, Utah 84501.

At I-70, turn east to the town of **Green River.** Once part of the Old Spanish Trail, the major trade route between New Mexico and California, it is still the easiest place to cross the river. The town is also a popular departure point for expeditions down the Green River.

Green River State Recreation Area is on the west bank of the river. This 50-acre site is open April to October. You can camp and shower, or take a swim in the river. The park also has picnic tables, a large grassy area and pleasant shade trees. During the summer, rangers conduct nightly slide programs, many of interest to children.

For more information on the area, as well as guides for river raft, canoe, horseback and jeep tours, contact the Green River Visitor Center, 240 East Main, Green River, Utah 84525, 801/564-3526. The center is open April through October.

2. FROM GREEN RIVER TO MOAB—GATEWAY TO CANYON COUNTRY

From Green River, continue to Crescent Junction, then turn right on US 191 to the turnoff to Dead Horse Point State Park and Canyonlands National Park.

Canyonlands National Park

Canyonlands National Park is 527 square miles of wilderness, most of it inaccessible by passenger car. The noise and hurry of humanity haven't invaded its vastness yet, and a pervading peace coats the landscape, just as the desert varnish lacquers the rock.

Canyonlands has three districts, divided by the "Y" confluence of the Green and Colorado rivers. The northern district, an elevated plateau between the Green and Colorado rivers, is called **Island in the Sky**. From this island of rock, the land falls away to the river gorges below in a series of terraces resembling huge stair steps.

The southeastern district, to the east and south of the river confluence, is **The Needles,** named for its hundreds of colorful rock spires. This is a complex series of unusual canyons, meadows and spectacular arches (see page 123 for more information on The Needles).

The Maze is the wild western district, a complicated labyrinth of gorges cut into the layered sandstone below the Orange Cliffs (see page 107).

Superintendent, Canyonlands National Park, 125 West 200 South, Moab, UT 84532, 801/259-7164.

Island in the Sky District and Dead Horse Point State Park

Hiking and four-wheeling are two great ways to explore the

interior of Canyonlands. Another way to the heartland is via the Colorado and Green rivers. The rigors of John Wesley Powell's 1869 expedition are in the past, and today, numerous commercial tours make these trips relatively safe, yet exciting, for older kids. The Moab Visitor Center and Canyonlands National Park headquarters in town have a list of commercial operators.

For those limited by time and/or money, some of the most breathtaking overlooks are in Dead Horse Point State Park and Island in the Sky. To reach these, take US 191 south of Green River to the paved State 313. This road travels approximately 23 miles to the Park, part of it through Sevenmile Canyon, filled with giant cottonwoods and interesting rock configurations. At 18 miles, the road forks, with the left fork continuing to Dead Horse Point and the right fork leading to Island in the Sky.

Dead Horse Point is an isolated mesa. Here, on the rim of the Orange Cliffs escarpment, the view is magnificent. Some 5000 square miles of vivid colors and rugged Colorado Plateau stretch before you. Two thousand feet below is a loop of the Colorado River, eating its way through layer after layer of sandstone, mudstone, conglomerate, and limestone as old as 200-300 million years.

The place was named for a band of wild ponies. Corralled here by the cowboys who had rounded them up, confused by the topography, they wandered in circles for days, finally dying of thirst.

The **Visitor Center** has a museum with geological displays. Ask about ranger-led activities in the summer, canyon rim hikes, and backcountry maps and permits. Take the kids on the informative ¼ mile, easy **nature trail** that will teach them much about Utah deserts.

The park has the most highly developed **public campground** in the area, with water, electrical hookups and sewage dump stations. Near the end of the Point is a picnic site, a large shade-pavilion and walkways to the cliff rim. Be sure to closely supervise your children. It's a long way down!

Dead Horse Point State Park, PO Box 609, Moab, 84532, 801/259-6511. The Visitor Center is open daily, 9:00 am to 5:00 pm in winter, 8:00 am to 6:00 pm in summer, but the park is open from 6:00 am until 10:00 pm daily. Admission is $3 per vehicle, camping is $3.

Island in the Sky is the northern border of Canyonlands. It is an irregular mesa of rock connected to the "mainland" by The Neck, a 40-foot wide sliver of land that drops off in sheer cliffs on either side.

Be sure to bring your own water when visiting. There is none available in the park.

Stop at the **ranger station** near the entrance for maps, guides, books, and information on the four-wheel drive trails. As you explore the park, keep children away from the cliff rims. People have been killed falling over the edge.

About 6½ miles from the station is **Mesa Arch Trail.** This trail travels through the pinyon forest to Mesa Arch and affords excellent views. You can pick up an interesting self-guiding booklet at the trailhead. This ½ mile, easy loop is one of the best short hikes in Canyonlands.

The road travels past overlooks to **Grandview Point.** Be sure to stop for the impressive view into the heart of Inner Canyonlands, the Needles, and Monument Basin below. A level, 1½ mile walk will take you to the southernmost tip of Island in the Sky and back.

Have the children look for the three worlds of Canyonlands—the high plateaus, the benchlands of lower buttes and mesas halfway to the bottom, and channels of the Green and Colorado rivers at the deepest level. Imagine all the rock that has eroded away to make this.

Return to the main road and the junction with the road to **Green River Overlook and Upheaval Dome.**

The view from Green River Overlook includes a panorama of the 60,000 acres in the rugged Maze District. The rimside **Willow Flat Campground** has primitive camping with no water available (the closest water is at Dead Horse Point State Park). Campfire programs are conducted here several nights a week in summer.

Upheaval Dome, three miles wide, is a geologic oddity thought to have been created by salt. This 1500-foot deep hole has grayish green rock spires jutting from the center.

At the parking lot is a viewpoint and a half-mile trail that leads to another overlook. Pick up a self-guiding brochure at the trailhead which explains the geology of the area. There is also a tree-shaded picnic area by the parking lot.

The primitive **Whale Rock Trail** will take you and the kids to the outer dome. It is a ¾ mile, easy self-guided trail, but does include a moderate climb.

Various trails and 4-wheel drive roads lead into the park. One is the **White Rim Trail** that takes you 100 miles over slickrock along a ridge 1000 feet below the mesa top. Primitive campgrounds are situated along this popular trail, and are available by reservation only. Check at the Visitor Center for more information.

Guided tours of the interior of the park are also available. These usually require advance reservations, especially May through September. Contact the Moab Visitor Center for tour operators.

The ranger station, telephone 801/259-6577, is open daily during the summer, 8:00 am to 4:30 pm, with reduced hours and days in the winter, but the park is open daylight hours. Admission is $3 per vehicle for a seven day pass for all three districts. An annual pass for both Arches and Canyonlands is $10.

DID YOU KNOW?

—Sandstone covers about 20% of the earth.

—In summer, the sun heats the desert ground to over 150 degrees Fahrenheit.

—Butch Cassidy's famous hideout, Robber's Roost, is 30 miles west of the park. It can be reached by a four-wheel drive road.

—The first vehicles entered the Maze in 1957.

—Cataract Canyon, below the confluence of the Colorado and Green rivers, has some of the most exciting white water rafting in the world. In the canyon the riverbed drops 30 feet in about a mile.

Arches National Park

Arches National Park is about five miles north of Moab on US 191.

Windows, pinnacles, arches and balanced rocks cluster in this area of geological wonders sculpted by water and time. Much of the geology here was influenced by a unique element—salt.

Arches is part of the Paradox Basin, 10,000 square miles that was once the arm of an ancient sea. When the water evaporated, it left behind a mile-thick layer of salt deposits mixed with shale and limestone eroded from the surrounding hills.

Arches National Park

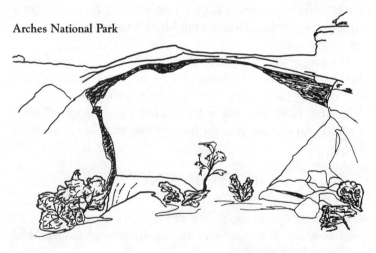

Eventually, hardened sediment covered the deposits. At the northeastern edge of the Paradox, thousands of tons of rock washed down from the mountains, burying the basin floor.

But salt in the earth flows just like salt in your saltshaker.

The weight of rock on the northeastern edge squeezed the salt toward the southwest, where the covering rock layers were lighter. As it bulged, it lifted and fractured the earth above, and pushed itself into vertical walls within the rock, forming upfolds (anticlines) filled with salt.

Sedimentary deposits continued to accumulate until the dramatic uplift of the Colorado Plateau, 10 million to 60 million years ago. Then water and frost took over, wearing away layers of the anticlines and their foundation of salt. When the salt dissolved, the anticlines collapsed, forming cliff-walled valleys.

Arches were formed later. Beginning first as small holes in the cliffs, they were enlarged by weathering to freestanding rock bows. Today, the same forces of erosion are at work in the park as old arches collapse and new ones are born. Most of the changes are visible only after thousands of years, but some are more dramatic, such as the 1940 collapse of a large block of stone from Skyline Arch which suddenly doubled its size.

Have the children look for arches in different stages of formation. And know that the time between the life and death of some of the oldest arches (probably tens of thousands of years) is but a brief chapter in the history of the planet.

THINGS TO DO

Numerous short hikes in Arches make this a fun place for children to explore. If it is summer, however, plan your hiking for the early morning or evening. Temperatures can easily exceed 100 degrees.

The **Visitor Center** has natural history and archaeological displays, as well as information on the summertime campfire talks and naturalist-led hikes that children will enjoy. Ask for the mimeographed information sheets and about purchasing the auto tour guidebook of the park.

Before you leave, take the excellent, self-guided **Desert Nature Trail.** This short walk is a great place for you and your children to get to know the desert plants. Ask at the desk for the free trail brochure.

The 18-mile **scenic drive** goes through the park past unusual rock formations. Have the kids make up their own
names for them. Also look for the different plant communities, especially the blackish cryptogamic earth that forms a
thin crust over the sandy soil. It is composed of spore-re-
producing plants similar to fungi. Be sure the kids stay on the
trails to protect this fragile earth.

The road passes viewpoints and short hikes to the base of
many of the arches, and ends in a one-way loop at **Devil's
Garden,** a natural amphitheater surrounded by domes and
fins. The majority of the Park's arches and windows are in this
section. There are also picnic sites and the park campground.
If you plan to camp, arrive early, especially during the busy
spring and summer months.

On your way to Devil's Garden, stop at **Wolfe Ranch,** where
John Wesley Wolfe and his son homesteaded in 1888. They
lived in this isolated place for 20 years.

The foot trail from the ranch continues 1½ miles to the
free-standing **Delicate Arch,** one of the best known and most
photographed arches in the park. This is a strenuous hike,
climbing 500 feet from the cabin, but the view is worth the
struggle, and the hike includes walking across a swinging footbridge that spans Salt Wash. Don't miss it with the older kids!

A less spectacular view of the arch can be seen from a short
trail that leaves from Delicate Arch Viewpoint, 1.3 miles
further up the dirt road.

Take the ¼ mile hike near the campground through a
narrow crevice in the slickrock to **Sand Dune Arch.** Hidden
from the sun most of the day in the cool recesses of a small
canyon, it is a popular resting place for those passing through,
animals as well as people. Children will enjoy playing in the
small sand dune under the arch.

Another good hike for children is the self-guiding trail to
Landscape Arch, beginning at the Devil's Garden parking lot.
A bit more strenuous trail, with several possible side trips,
continues from Landscape Arch to Double-O Arch.

Other short hikes the children will enjoy are the trail around

Balanced Rock, a boulder balancing on an eroded projection of sandstone, and the trails to several arches in the **Windows Section.** More difficult trails lead to Park Avenue and to Tower Arch in Klondike Bluffs.

Superintendent, Arches National Park, Box 907, Moab 84532, 801/259-8161. Hours: daily, 8:00 am–6:00 pm April to October, and 8:00 am–4:30 pm the rest of the year. Admission is $3 per vehicle or $10 for an annual pass for Arches and Canyonlands.

DID YOU KNOW?

—Landscape Arch is the second-longest natural arch in the world (306 feel long). Kolob Arch in Zion is the longest.

—One of the arches of Double Arch is large enough to span a 15-story building.

—When water freezes, it can exert as much as 1000 pounds of pressure per square inch, which is one reason it is such an effective force of erosion.

—Arches National Park contains more natural stone arches than anywhere else in the world, over 900.

—The black cryptogamic earth found in Arches is rare now, but was common before livestock overgrazed the Southwest. It reduces erosion, retards moisture evaporation, and collects patches of soil where other plants can take root.

—An arch is eroded away by weathering; a natural bridge is carved by a river or stream.

—Anasazi and Fremont Indians quarried the chert and jasper rocks here for spearpoints and arrowheads.

—Ribbon Arch, one foot thick and 1½ feet wide at its narrowest point, is one of the slenderest arches in the park.

—One of the most recent arches to be discovered is named Anniversary Arch because it was discovered by a couple on their wedding anniversary.

Moab
Zip Code 84532   Area Code 801

The small town of Moab was founded by Mormons. Their first settlement, in 1855, was established to convert the Ute Indians. The Utes, however, weren't interested, and after killing three of the Mormons, they drove the foreigners away. Over 20 years later the Mormons tried again. This time they stayed, and they named their new town after a remote kingdom on the edge of Zion in the Old Testament.

Moab still has an aura of isolation about it, despite a brief heyday of mining activity. Around a hundred years ago, prospectors began searching for gold in the nearby La Sal Mountains and river gravels. In the early 1900's, copper was mined, as well as small amounts of uranium ore. None of these endeavors amounted to much until after World War II, when the demand for uranium skyrocketed, along with the number of prospectors.

In 1952, uranium king Charles A. Steen discovered a $60,000,000 lode in his "Mi Vida" mine. The resulting "uranium rush" turned Moab into a modern boom town. You can still see Steen's mansion high on a red hill beside US 191 north of town. Farther north, a giant uranium mill and tailings pond dominate this end of the valley.

Moab saw its share of cowboys and outlaws in the early days, and Butch Cassidy used the Moab Ferry on his escape route after robbing his first bank in Telluride, Colorado. Today, the town is the largest in the area (pop. 6000), and it makes a good place to stay for a few nights while touring canyon country.

THINGS TO DO
The **Hollywood Stuntmen's Hall of Fame** will give you and the kids a glimpse into the life of a stuntman. There are trick saddles and other props, and the auditorium shows movies in the evenings and on Saturday afternoons.

Hollywood Stuntmen's Hall of Fame, one block north of Main Street at 111 E. 100 North. Hours: 10:00 am–9:00 pm *weekdays, 2:00–6:00 pm weekends. Cost is $2 adults, $1 ages 12 through 18, $.50 ages 4 though 11.*

Moab Museum has a black light display of minerals, as well as Indian artifacts and exhibits on the history, archaeology, geology and uranium mining of the area.

Moab Museum, 118 E. Center, 259-7430. Hours: 1:00– 5:00 pm and 7:00–9:00 pm in the summer, and 3:00–5:00 pm and 7:00–9:00 pm in the winter. Admission is free.

If the kids are rock-hounds, let them browse through the quality selections in the rock shops. You might try **Moab Rock Shop,** 137 North Main, telephone 259-7312, which also has a free nightly slide show on the geology of the area, as well as 4-wheel drive tours.

The kids can cool off at the municipal **swimming pool** in City Park, several blocks west of the highway at W. 400 North. The south side of the park also has picnic tables under pleasant shade trees.

If you want to work up an appetite, take a horseback ride followed by a chuck wagon dinner and western entertainment. If it's excitement you want, catch a river boat down the mighty Colorado, a horse or four-wheel drive vehicle through the surrounding countryside, or an airplane over Canyonlands and Arches. You can also rent a mountain bike for exploring some of the four-wheel drive trails. **Moab Information Center** on US 191 at the north edge of town has a list of area tour operators and rentals.

If you have the time, take one of the scenic drives from town. **Scenic Route 128** takes you 42 miles northeast to the junction with I-70. The road parallels the Colorado River most of the way and offers a beautiful panorama of the La Sal Mountains.

The turnoff is just north of town at a pleasant riverside park, complete with shade trees, picnic tables, rest rooms, and a roadside display of the early history of Moab. Across the river is a boat launch for river runners down Cataract Canyon.

Around 16 miles on Scenic Route 128, a partially paved road leads southeast to Castle Valley. This outstandingly scenic road

(**La Sal Mountain Scenic Route**) ascends through the La Sal Mountains to the upper Spanish Valley, and eventually joins US 191 nine miles south of Moab. You and the kids may recognize the lofty finger of red sandstone called Castle Rock from old General Motors commercials or western movies. Parts of Castleton, an early mining boom town, still remain.

The La Sal (Spanish for "salt") Mountains, once the hunting grounds for the Ute Indians, offer a welcome relief from desert heat and crowds. They were so named by the Dominguez-Escalante expedition because the snow on the peaks was mistaken for salt. Excellent public campgrounds in the Manti-La Sal National Forest are usually uncrowded and offer good hiking trails, and abundant fish are in lakes nearby. Stop at the Moab Ranger District office, 446 South Main in Moab, for a trail guide.

State 128 continues to a sign for Fisher Valley, around five miles east of Castle Valley junction. This fair-weather dirt road follows **Onion Creek,** a small stream flowing through a complex series of grotto-like canyons. In the maze are fins, balanced rocks, and weird formations in a rainbow of colors. The road up Onion Creek to Fisher Valley is about 60 miles round trip from Moab.

Less than a mile past the turnoff to Onion Creek is a graded dirt road that leads two miles to **Fisher Towers,** slender spires also known as the Colorado River Organs. There is a picnic site and rest rooms (but no water) at the base of the towers, as well as a hiking trail 2.2 miles through the rocks to a panoramic view. Tell the kids to look for cairns (piles of rocks that mark the trail) and to test for echoes. Be sure to take along water.

Another road north of Moab is **Potash Road** (Scenic Route 279), on the left past the Colorado River Bridge and Court House Wash Bridge. The eighteen paved miles of this road that parallel the Colorado River won an award as one of the most scenic roads in the country.

The road travels past the uranium mill's huge settling pond, dinosaur tracks in a slab of rock, Fremont petroglyphs that look like broad-shouldered spacemen, and arches. Points of interest are marked, as well as hiking trails to some of the arches.

The paved part of the road ends at the potash plant. In good weather, you can continue to the evaporation ponds, filled with a salt solution that has been pumped from deep in the mines. The round trip from Moab will take an hour or so, and is especially pleasant on summer evenings.

Evergreens

3. MOAB TO BLUFF—PAST THE TRAIL OF THE ANCIENTS

Take US 191 about 25 miles south of Moab to the two mile, graded dirt road that travels west to **Looking Glass Rock,** a large, unusual window in a dome of sandstone. Water seepage and wind formed an immense cave here, and when it collapsed on one side, the window was created. In some seasons during the late afternoon, sunlight on the cave wall resembles shafts of light reflecting from a mirror.

Continue on US 191 another mile or so to **Wilson Arch,** a large arch that can be seen from a parking area beside the highway.

Thirty-three miles from Moab is a paved road that leads northwest to **Canyon Rims Recreation Area** (BLM). This highly scenic drive takes you on the rim of a plateau to the Needles and Anticline overlooks. **Needles Overlook** has interpretive exhibits, picnic tables, trails and safety fencing, and some say the **Anticline Overlook** is the most spectacular view of Canyonlands you can find.

The two campgrounds have water, grills, and picnic tables in picturesque settings, and usually have space available. Canyon Rims is open year-round, although occasionally closed by snow.

DID YOU KNOW?

—The town of La Sal was once a remote outlaw hideout for rustlers driving horses to Telluride, Colorado.

—The La Sal, Henry and Abajo mountains are laccolithic mountains, which means they were formed from a dome of molten lava that squeezed into the surface layers of sedimentary rock. After the lava cooled, the sandstone and shale eroded away, exposing part of the igneous core.

—The onion odor of Onion Creek comes from minerals in the water.

Canyonlands National Park—The Needles District

To reach the Needles District of Canyonlands, turn west at the junction of US 191 and paved State Highway 211.

The Needles is jammed with so many pointed spires and pinnacles, Powell called it "Land of Standing Rock." Much of it is primitive and accessible only on foot or by four-wheel drive, but State 211 will take you farther into the area than any other passenger-car road.

The highway leads through over 30 miles of scenery to the national park boundary. It first descends through Indian Creek Canyon.

Stop at **Newspaper Rock State Historical Monument,** where the kids can see at least 350 distinct petroglyphs and pictographs. For a thousand years, Anasazis and Utes, Navajos and whites have chipped and painted their messages on this rock face blackened with desert varnish. The ¼ mile interpretive trail explains the natural areas on both sides of the road. There is also a primitive campground (no fee) with pit toilet, grills and picnic tables, but no water.

Past Newspaper Rock the road enters open country. Have the kids look for North and South Sixshooter Peaks and the sandstone formation that looks like a giant wooden shoe.

Just inside Canyonlands National Park to the right is a graveled road to **Needles Outpost,** which has a snack bar, fuel and supplies. You can also rent four-wheel drive vehicles and camp.

A short distance inside the park on the main road is the Needles ranger station, telephone 801/259-6568. Stop for information, maps and backcountry permits.

Just beyond the ranger station is an enjoyable nature trail to **Roadside Ruin.** This easy ¼ mile loop leads to a prehistoric Indian granary. A self-guiding brochure points out many of the native plants in the area and their Indian usage.

Farther on, a side road on the left takes you to **Cave Spring,** a great hike for kids. The short (.6 miles) nature trail includes walking through a huge alcove and climbing old wooden ladders. Cave Spring, tucked in a rock recess, was used as a camp by cowboys during the cattle era. The self-guiding brochure gives more details on the history.

The main road forks, with the left branch continuing to **Squaw Flat Campground** and to Elephant Hill, where the road becomes one of the most difficult four-wheel drive trails in the country. The campground, $5 per night, has piped in water April through September, a picnic area and evening campfire programs in summer. Children will be delighted with the cornucopia of shapes, colors and sizes of the surrounding rock formations and can spend hours exploring.

Older elementary schoolchildren can take the six-mile round trip hiking trail to the grassy meadow of **Chesler Park.** It begins at Elephant Hill with a steep climb, then levels out, traversing slickrock, narrow crevices, and ending in a natural meadow surrounded by stone spires.

The right branch of the road takes you to **Big Spring Canyon Overlook.** Along the way stop for the **Pothole Point** nature trail, about a half mile round trip. During a rain, depressions in the rock here fill with water and teem with life. Not only do larger animals stop to drink, but tiny aquatic life thrives, having hatched from eggs which lay dormant in the dried mud at the bottom of the pothole.

Ask at the ranger station for jeep and more difficult hiking trails in the area.

Monticello to Blanding

The mountain community of **Monticello** sits at the base of Horsehead Peak, where vegetation grows on the slope in the shape of a bald-faced horse. Summer temperatures that rarely exceed 90 degrees are a welcome relief from the nearby blazing canyons.

The Visitor Center in the library-museum building on Main Street has information on the several public campgrounds in the nearby Manti-La Sal National Forest and at

Lake Monticello. They also have a list of local tour operators for river trips, trail rides and jeep tours.

Continue on US 191/163 to the town of **Blanding.** If the children are thirsty, stop at the **Elk Head** for what one frequent visitor says is the best milkshake in Utah. Four miles north of town on US 191/666 is **Recapture Lake,** a popular spot for fishing and swimming.

Follow the directional signs to the main attraction in Blanding, **Edge of the Cedars State Historical Monument.** The ruins of a small Anasazi village are being excavated here. A short, self-guided trail leads through the ruins and includes a climb into a kiva.

The Visitor Center has an interesting museum with exhibits depicting the history of man in the Four Corners area. There are also living history films, Indian crafts demonstrations, a gift shop, a garden of native plants and a Navajo vegetable garden.

The park is also the departure point for the **Trail of the Ancients,** a 180-mile scenic loop past unique geological features and other points of interest. The trail includes the site of the last armed encounter between Indians and whites on the frontier (1923), prehistoric ruins, Natural Bridges National Monument, Valley of the Gods, the towns of Mexican Hat and Bluff, Hovenweep, and other attractions. A map and orientation film are available at the museum.

Edge of the Cedars State Park, 660 West 400 North, PO Box 788, Blanding, UT, 84511, 801/678-2238. Hours: daily, mid-May to mid-September from 8:00 am to 7:00 pm, mid-September to mid-May from 9:00 am to 5:00 pm. Admission is $3 per vehicle.

South of Blanding, State 95 branches west past Valley of the Gods and Natural Bridges National Monument to Lake Powell (see Chapter XI). Fifteen miles south of town, State 262 forks east to Hovenweep and the Four Corners (see Chapter VII). US 191/163 continues to the town of Bluff.

DID YOU KNOW?

—Some of the trails in the Needles pass by pack rat nests dating back 10,000 years.

—This area had its share of colorful cowboys. A sampling of their names includes Yarn Gallus, Latigo Gordon and Doc Few Clothes.

—The country around Horsehead Peak has been the setting for novels by Zane Grey and Louis L'Amour.

—Rock art that depicts horses was etched after the mid-1500's, when the Spanish explorers brought horses to America.

Pack rat

Bluff
Zip Code 84512   Area Code 801

The sleepy town of Bluff was named for the red sandstone hills edging the town. It was the first white settlement in southeast Utah, and its original inhabitants were the intrepid members of the Hole-in-the-Rock wagon train that crossed the Colorado River during the winter of 1879-80.

The Mormons weren't the only ones who called this rustic place home. The first Clovis Man hunting site to be found on the Colorado Plateau is nearby. Later, the Anasazi lived in cliff alcoves along Comb Ridge. The Navajo followed, and today the town borders the Navajo Reservation.

THINGS TO DO

Take State Highway 216 east towards Aneth. One mile east of St. Christopher's Episcopal Mission (just past mile post 4) turn right to a picturesque cable-support **footbridge across the San Juan River.** Most kids will love practicing the rhythmic art of walking on a suspension bridge. This was once the only access from the Navajo Reservation to Bluff. The trail on the other side leads to Anasazi ruins in the cliffs.

In town, follow the signs to **Cemetery Hill,** where many of the original settlers are buried.

The **Sunbonnet Cafe** on the Historic Route is a good place for Navajo tacos, and the **Cow Trading Post** on the highway has Indian rugs and baskets for sale, as well as a restaurant open for lunch and dinner, Wednesday through Sunday.

Bluff is a pleasant place to spend the night. Try the inexpensive, historic **Recapture Lodge,** which has nightly slide shows, a swimming pool, and geologist-guided tours, telephone 801/672-2281, the **Bluff Bed and Breakfast,** 672-2220, or the **Scorup House,** 672-2272 (to open in the spring, 1990). Bluff is also a good place to arrange for boat or vehicle tours of the area. Ask at the Recapture Lodge for tour operators.

4. BLUFF TO GRAND GULCH PRIMITIVE AREA—TOWERS OF STONE

Three miles west of Bluff on US 163 is **Sand Island,** a public campground on the banks of the San Juan River. The boat launch is a principal departure point for San Juan River trips. The dirt road to the right of the campground leads to a large petroglyph panel on a low bluff.

US 163 continues to the town of **Mexican Hat,** named for the stone formation that resembles a sombrero. The town is a popular put-in place for San Juan River trips through the Goosenecks. If you or the kids have wanted to take a raft trip but are daunted by churning white water, try one of these. You won't find the same hair-raising rapids you find in places on the Green and Colorado, but the scenery is still magnificent.

From here, US 163 continues to the Navajo Reservation and Monument Valley (see Chapter XII).

Before the town of Mexican Hat, State 261 forks north from US 163, and travels past Goosenecks State Reserve and over Cedar Mesa, eventually joining State 95 near Natural Bridges National Monument.

Goosenecks State Reserve is an overlook on the rim of the San Juan River Canyon. From here, you can look down 1000 feet to the goosenecked switchbacks eroded by the river—a geologic feature called an entrenched meander. This primitive reserve has picnic sites, but no water.

The nearby Honaker Trail, built by gold miners, descends 1,235 feet in switchbacks to the river below. This strenuous hike is only for the adventurous and the older child. Rangers at Edge of the Cedars State Park or Natural Bridges will give you more information on where to find the trail.

A few miles farther on State Highway 261 is a fair-weather dirt road that loops about 17 miles through **Valley of the Gods,** a dreamscape of weirdly eroded buttes and spires. Use your imagination to see the valley inhabitants in the sculptured sandstone—an organ grinder's monkey with pillbox hat on a sleigh behind a Trojan horse, an Old Fashioned Girl, Stately Gods, and Five Sailors. Have fun making up your own names.

The valley has relatively few visitors, partly because the dirt road is crossed with dry washes that can flood when wet. If you don't want to drive, local guides in Bluff or Mexican Hat will take you there.

State 261 continues to the crest of Cedar Mesa on **Moki Dugway,** a three mile gravel road ascending 1000 feet in tight switchbacks. At the summit, a dirt side road leads another four miles to **Muley Point,** a finger of land with a stupendous view of Glen Canyon, Monument Valley, and Navajo Mountain.

There is also an interpretive display on the geology of the area.

State Highway 261 continues past the entrance to **Grand Gulch Primitive Area,** a great place for camping, hiking, and exploring for Anasazi ruins. Because it has been set aside by the BLM for non-vehicle use, to see this natural/archaeological preserve, you and the kids will have to go on foot or horseback, but if the kids are archaeology buffs, it may be worth it. The box canyon has several hundred cliff dwellings, few of them fully explored, and an uncounted number of petroglyphs.

Access to the area is via a five hour round trip hike, and to visit, you must apply for one of the limited permits granted by the BLM. Stop at the Kane Gulch Ranger Station beside State Highway 261 a few miles south of State Highway 95, or register with the BLM offices in Monticello.

5. BLANDING TO NATURAL BRIDGES NATIONAL MONUMENT

State 95 west from Blanding cuts through Comb Ridge, a rock barrier that once daunted pioneers. Several miles farther is **Mule Canyon Rest Area,** a partially restored prehistoric settlement with tower and kiva.

Thirty-five miles from Blanding is a dirt road to Valley of the Gods and access to Grand Gulch. About three miles farther on is the junction with State Highway 275, which travels five miles to Natural Bridges National Monument, three giant natural bridges.

Natural Bridges National Monument.

A natural bridge is unique. Unlike an arch, which is created by wind and rain, a natural bridge is carved by a stream. There aren't many natural bridges anywhere in the world, but at Natural Bridges, you can see three of the most spectacular.

The **Visitor Center–Museum** has exhibits, a slide show,

and information on the bridges, trails and Indian sites in the area. The park also has a primitive campground (no water) comfortably situated in the juniper forest. Ask at the center for a schedule of evening campfire programs.

A **scenic eight-mile loop road** travels from the center to overlooks of the three bridges, but the best way to see these magnificent structures is by hiking. A seven mile round trip foot trail connects the three, but shorter trails leave from roadside viewpoints. In summer, 100-degree temperatures make these hikes more pleasant in the morning or evening rather than midday.

The ½ mile round trip trail to **Owachomo Bridge** is the easiest for kids. The pale salmon pink Owachomo is the oldest, smallest (106 feet high with a span of 180 feet), and most fragile of the bridges. Beneath it is a pothole known as Zeke's Bathtub, once a source of drinking water for people of the desert. Armstrong Canyon, on the other side of the bridge, is a place where the kids can explore for wildlife. Encourage them to take a nature walk, or to just sit and listen.

The trail to **Sipapu Bridge** is not long (1½ miles round trip), but it does include a steep descent on wooden ladders and steel stairs. Sipapu is the largest of the bridges and is big enough for the Washington, D.C. Capitol to sit underneath, with 50 feet to spare!

The 1½ mile round trip trail to **Kachina Bridge** is also more demanding. This deep red arch is the youngest of the three and is still growing. It is also the most massive and is decorated with the most prehistoric artwork.

Modern man has added his own attraction to the monument. A **solar energy system,** one of the largest in the world, uses 250,000 silicon solar cells and provides 90% of the electricity for the visitor center and ranger residences. A special display in the center lets the kids flip a switch to power the lights.

Natural Bridges National Monument, Box 1, Lake Powell, UT 84533, 801/259-5174. Hours: daily, 8:00 am–4:30 pm. Admission is $3 per vehicle.

DID YOU KNOW?

—Sipapu Bridge is the second-largest natural bridge in the world (Rainbow Bridge is the largest).

—Shallow depressions in the rock (potholes) teem with life when they are filled briefly by summer rains. Tadpole and fairy shrimp are some of the inhabitants. They can complete their entire life cycles in two weeks, leaving behind eggs that may lie dormant for decades until conditions are again right for hatching.

—The first white man to see the three bridges was Cass Hite in 1883. This prospector also established Hite Ferry on Lake Powell.

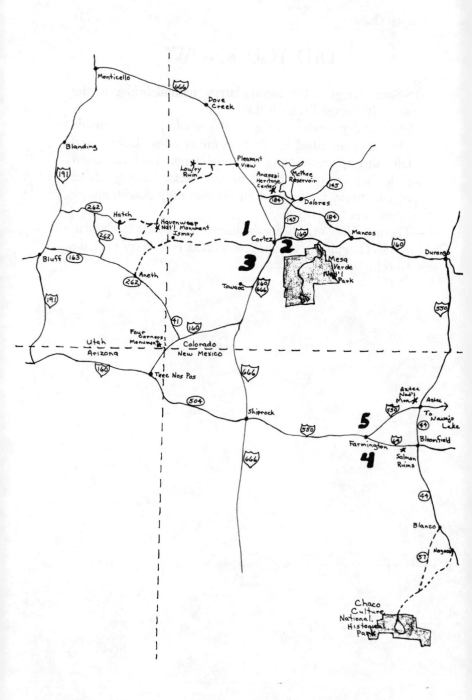

7

LAND OF THE ANCIENT ONES: The Four Corners

The Four Corners is the high plateau country around the spot where Colorado, Utah, New Mexico and Arizona meet. Archaeologists love it here.

Almost 2000 years ago it was the birthplace of an amazing prehistoric culture, the Anasazi. The people disappeared in a cloud of mystery, but the dry, desert air has preserved the remnants of their sophisticated civilization. Exquisite artwork, magnificent cities of stone, and thousand-year old furs and feathers have been found in the ruins of its abundance.

The nomadic ancestors of the Anasazi lived in the greater Southwest for thousands of years, gathering roots and berries and hunting with long spears and spear-throwing sticks called atl-atls. Then sometime around the birth of Christ, the people began settling in mountain caves and temporary shelters in the Four Corners area. From their southern neighbors, they learned to cultivate corn and squash.

A stable food supply provided an impetus for permanency and trade, as well as the time and energy to build a more complex society. Farming also brought new gods to worship, for now the rain, sun and soil held the sword of fate in their hands. The Anasazi became sky watchers, peering at the sun, moon and stars for clues to guide the rhythm of their agricultural lives. Complex ceremonies, religious rituals, and a way of life focusing on the cycle of seasons were the eventual result.

The need to store food also brought more demand for baskets, and weaving was transformed into a skilled craft of extraordinary proficiency. Burden baskets, trinket baskets, flat baskets, cooking baskets, and those so tightly woven they could be lined with pitch to store water were crafted by the people we now call The Basketmakers.

But baskets were only part of it. The expert weavers also used their craft to fashion yucca sandals, sacks without seams, carrying straps, and nets for trapping small animals.

As farming became more central to their lives, the people added other crops to their storehouses, including beans that brought protein to their diets and, later, cotton that could be woven into beautiful cloth. Wild turkeys were domesticated, too.

Anasazi woman grinding corn with stones

As the Anasazi became more sedentary, they moved to the mesa tops to be near their fields, where water was more available. At first, they built pit houses of mud and sticks to live in, exemplary for their energy efficiency and food storage capacity.

Somewhere around AD 750, the people began building aboveground houses of stone and adobe. This was the beginning of the Pueblo Period.

During the next few hundred years, the Anasazi continued to fish and hunt to supplement their food supply, but now they had the help of the bow and arrow. They also learned to make pottery, a skill that eventually became an art form expressed through intricately decorated pots.

Around AD 1100 the Anasazi entered what is called the Golden Age. Farming was at its most productive and efficient, with a system of terracing, irrigation ditches and check dams used to store moisture during dry spells. Craftsmanship was at its most masterful, with pottery, jewelry and ceremonial objects of exceptional beauty and durability adding an artistic touch to their lives.

By now, the Anasazi were using extremely fine masonry skills to build huge apartment complexes three and four stories high. Some were set exalted in the cliffs, others gracefully curved in a semi-circle around a plaza. Pueblo Bonito in Chaco Canyon is perhaps the most magnificent of these villages.

Then, suddenly in the 13th century, the complex civilization disappeared, leaving behind tens of thousands of relics. Mysteriously, throughout the Southwest, the people slipped away, as if they had merged with the earth.

By AD 1300, only the fragments of their story and the ruins of their once-great civilization remained. Many believe they migrated south and west to a more hospitable land, becoming the ancestors of the modern-day Hopi and other Pueblo Indians.

Why did they leave? Early theories claimed it was warlike nomads who entered the area and drove off the peaceful people, but no evidence of this has yet been found. Some say it was a terrible drought that lasted from 1276 to 1299. Modern-day Hopis say legends foretold their departure. It was not the chosen place, and, therefore, it was inevitable that they move on.

More recently scientists have added a new theory for their disappearance. They say a major factor was overcrowding and the depletion of natural resources, brought on by a burgeoning population that overused the fragile land and upset its delicate balance.

Vast amounts of timber were used constructing the wall and roof supports in the great pueblos, and the over-cutting of trees for this, as well as the burning of forests for new fields, left the land susceptible to erosion and flash floods. Years of intensive cultivation had exhausted the soil of its nutrients, leaving it far less productive. When drought came, there was no margin for error. The buildings remained, the people could not.

And in that theory may be the greatest lesson these ancient people have left behind for modern man. For if we treat the land the same today, where will we go?

DID YOU KNOW?

—Since the Anasazi left no written record, there are many things about them we will never know. Our primary source of information has come from archaeological excavations. Over the years, looters and vandals using bulldozers and even dynamite have destroyed countless sites and clues to the past in their ignorance and quest for profit.

—The Four Corners area supported a larger population during Anasazi times than it does today.

—The building craftsmanship of the cliff dwellings at Mesa Verde was not as skillful as that on the mesa tops.

—Archaeologists have found Anasazi food caches with seeds that will grow if planted.

—Anasazi history is divided into four approximate periods: Basketmaker from AD 1 to 450, Modified Basketmaker from AD 450 to 750, Developmental Pueblo Period from AD 750 to 1100, and Great Pueblo Period from AD 1100 to 1250.

—The Anasazi made tools out of bone, stone and wood, without using any kind of metal.

—The average pueblo had one kiva for every 12 rooms.

—Although the Anasazi had many dental problems, they had

fewer cavities than the average American.

Around the Four Corners

1. Cortez to Hovenweep and Lowry Ruins
2. Mesa Verde and the Anasazi Heritage Center
3. From Cortez to Farmington—Through the Four Corners
4. Farmington to Chaco Canyon
5. Farmington to the Southern Ute Reservation

1. CORTEZ TO HOVENWEEP AND LOWRY RUINS

Cortez, Colorado
Zip Code 81321   Area Code 303

The town of Cortez lies at the center of the land of the ancient ones, as well as of the modern-day Ute Indian. It makes a convenient place to stay while touring the Four Corners area.

Look west of town for the most visible landmark, Sleeping Ute Mountain. From certain angles, the outline of a sleeping Indian, arms folded on his chest, feathered headdress to the north, is easily distinguished.

One legend says the mountain was once a Great Warrior God who fought against Evil Ones. As they battled, their feet pushed in valleys and raised mountains. The Great Warrior God was wounded and entered a deep sleep, but one day he will rise to fight the enemies of the Ute people. When rain clouds gather, it is because the Sleeping Ute has released them from his pockets. It shows he is pleased with the people.

THINGS TO DO

Downtown is the **Cortez Center of the University of Colo-**

rado. A small museum has interpretive exhibits on natural history and archaeology. The center is also the working lab for the excavation at the Yellow Jacket site, a large Anasazi ceremonial center north of town. Illustrated talks on archaeology and Native American culture and history are offered some summer evenings. In addition, guided tours of archaeological sites, including the active dig at Yellow Jacket, the Anasazi Heritage Center near Dove Creek, and Mesa Verde, leave daily from the center in summer.

The Cortez CU Center, PO Box 1326, 25 N. Market, 565-1151. Museum hours are Monday through Saturday, 8:00 am–8:00 pm in summer. Winter hours vary. Admission is free.

Another excavation site is the **Crow Canyon Archaeological Center,** northwest of Cortez. Travel north about one mile on US Highway 666, then follow the signs about 2½ miles west to the center.

Crow Canyon offers a unique opportunity for adults and children elementary school age and older to participate in field seminars, archaeological digs and education programs from three days to five weeks. One of the more impressive digs is at Sand Canyon Pueblo, with over 400 rooms, kivas and towers, a complex some speculate was used as a major ritual center and not for habitation. The center also conducts evening lecture programs open to the public. It is not staffed for drop-ins, but if you call ahead, they will accept visitors.

Crow Canyon Archaeological Center, 23390 County Road K, 565-8975.

Cortez can be a good place to buy Native American arts and crafts. Try **Notah Dineh Trading Company,** 309 N. Broadway, or **Mesa Verde Pottery,** whose showroom has handcrafted pottery from the Pueblo Indians and crafts demonstrations such as weaving and pottery painting. Traditional ceremonial dances are also performed here in the summer. Mesa Verde Pottery is one mile east of Cortez on US Highway 160. The Cortez Visitor Center can give you a list of other area dealers.

The **Visitor Center** is in City Park. It has information on the area and dates of special events, as well as displays of

Anasazi artifacts and crafts by area artisans.

North of the center are two parks. Indian dances are held here in the summer, Monday through Thursday at 7:00 pm, and evening concerts are on Saturday. There is also a picnic area, children's playground, lake, lighted tennis courts, library, and the Cortez Municipal Pool, open daily from the end of May through Labor Day.

Hovenweep National Monument

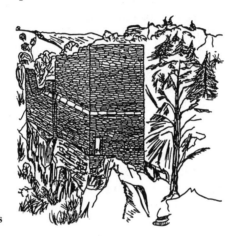

Holly Ruins

From Cortez take US 160 three miles south to the road through McElmo Canyon, and follow the signs 40 miles to Hovenweep National Monument. The road is paved, gravel and dirt.

To reach Hovenweep from Utah, take State Highway 262 east from US Highway 163 between Blanding and Bluff, Utah. Travel 14 miles to Hatch Trading Post. From here a paved and fair-weather dirt road travels about 16 miles to the ruins.

After heavy rains, the dirt roads are impassable. If in doubt about conditions, inquire at Mesa Verde, 303/529-4465. There are no phones at Hovenweep.

Hovenweep contains 700-year-old ruins of six Anasazi villages. The people here were farmers, planting their crops in the flat lands to the north. They were also excellent potters and skillful masons.

The ancient buildings are clustered in several canyons, possibly for protection from the elements. Of particular interest are the ruins of large towers—square, oval, circular and D-shaped. No one knows for sure their purpose, but some speculate they were used as forts, food storage bins, lookout towers, observatories to track the path of the sun for farming, temples for religious rites, or all of these.

Much of the beauty of Hovenweep is its remoteness. For children, the piles of tumbled masonry initially may not be as exciting as the restored ruins at Mesa Verde, but because fewer people are around, visiting will give them a chance to explore on their own, crawl inside the stabilized ruins, and travel back in time with their imaginations.

THINGS TO DO

Hovenweep has no regularly scheduled tours, but there is a ranger station with a few exhibits and a ranger on duty to answer questions. There is also a brochure for the **self-guided trail** through the best preserved and most impressive buildings, the Square Tower Ruins.

Look for Hovenweep House, standing at a cliff rim in the head of Square Tower Canyon. This large semicircular structure includes kivas, a large D-shaped tower and the ruins of living quarters for several families.

A trail from the campground leads to the Holly and Hackberry ruins, outstanding examples of Anasazi dwellings. It is a fairly level, though long, walk. Take into account that Hovenweep is hotter in summer than nearby Mesa Verde. You can also drive there on a dirt road.

Ask at the Ranger Station for information on visiting the other ruins in the monument.

The campground, $3 per night, has rest rooms, drinking water, picnic tables and cooking grills, but the nearest supplies and gasoline are at Hatch Trading Post 16 miles west in Utah or Ismay Trading Post 14 miles southeast in Colorado. The nearest lodging is in Blanding or Bluff, Utah or Cortez, Colorado.

Superintendent, Mesa Verde National Park, Mesa Verde, CO 81330, 303/529-4461 or 4465. The park is open daily year-round. The ranger station is usually open from 8:00 am to 5:00 pm. Admission is free.

DID YOU KNOW?

—Hovenweep is a Ute word meaning "Deserted Valley."
—Three of the buildings at Hovenweep have features to predict the summer solstice, winter solstice, vernal equinox and autumnal equinox.
—The separate groups of buildings may have been suburbs of a single city.

Lowry Ruins

A fair-weather dirt road leads from Hovenweep to **Lowry Ruins,** but a more reliable approach is through Pleasant View, Colorado, northwest of Cortez on US 666, then nine miles west on a gravel road. Hiking paths take you through fields to the partially excavated surface dwellings, constructed around AD 1090 by Anasazi farmers.

These remote ruins may have once been a religious or trade center. The great kiva is especially impressive, 45 feet in diameter, one of the largest ever found, and murals have been found in a smaller kiva. The self-guided trail tells about the main ruin and affords a spacious view that makes it seem like you can see forever.

Picnic facilities are available, but no camping, and there isn't always a ranger on duty.

Lowry is open 8:00 am to 6:00 pm., and admission is free. For more information, call the Anasazi Heritage Center, 303/882-4811.

2. MESA VERDE AND THE ANASAZI HERITAGE CENTER

Mesa Verde National Park

About 10 miles east of Cortez on US 160, midway between Cortez and Mancos, is the entrance to Mesa Verde.

Richard Wetherill and his brother-in-law Charlie Mason were looking for lost cows one snowy morning in 1888. They found something far different. Near a canyon rim, they greeted a stone city in the cliff with speechless wonder. It was the 217-room Cliff Palace, rising in dusty silence from a pile of rocks. Within 24 hours, they had added Spruce Tree House and Square Tower House to their discoveries. Although before this William Jackson had photographed and described other cliff dwellings in the Mancos River Valley just south of here, Wetherill's was an extraordinary archaeological find.

Less than three years after the discovery, a Swede named Gustaf Nordenskiold came to see the place for himself. It was early summer, and he planned to stay a week. He finally left in autumn, having busied himself for several months excavating ruins and collecting artifacts. The lure of Mesa Verde is still strong.

Mesa Verde is on a high plateau cut with canyons and green with pinyon pine and juniper. When the Anasazi first came here around AD 550, they lived on the mesa tops in pithouses covered with logs and a mud plaster mixture. Through several hundred years, their civilization progressed, until eventually they were building magnificent dwellings in the cliffs and using the mesas for farming their scattered plots with digging sticks. They flourished until the late 1200's, when they turned their backs on the home of their ancestors and migrated to the south.

For awhile, the Mesa Verdians were an active part of the Anasazi trade network, exchanging craft items for seashells, turquoise, and cotton from the south and west. They were also accomplished potters, decorating their vessels with personal designs probably passed from mother to daughter.

But it was their apartments in the cliffs that left such an impression. No one knows for sure why they originally abandoned the mesa tops for the cliffs. It was certainly less convenient to climb a rock face using hand- and toeholds than to walk a level path to the fields. Protection from the elements or their neighbors are two possibilities.

THINGS TO DO

Mesa Verde is to be savored slowly. Plan a full day or more to tour the ruins. From the entrance, it is 21 twisting miles to the park headquarters, museum and major ruins on Chapin Mesa.

Hiking is restricted to designated trails in the park. Most are self-guiding, but a few can be taken only with ranger guides. However, all of the major ruins can be viewed from overlooks. Be sure to watch the kids near the canyon rims.

Four miles from the park entrance is **Morefield Campground,** a refreshing place to stay. Private campsites are hidden in the oak, pinyon and juniper. There are also showers, an RV dumping station, and some utility hook-up sites. Evening campfire programs are conducted daily from early June to Labor Day. No reservations are taken, but the campground isn't usually full.

Visitor services in Morefield Village include a snack bar, general store, Native American crafts shop, service station, and laundry, open in the summer.

You won't need permits for the hiking trails originating in the Morefield area. Try the 1½ mile **Knife Edge Trail,** which leaves from the campground and affords vast views of Montezuma Valley. Part of the trail does cross a scree slope where footing can be unstable, so you may want to turn around at that point with young children.

The 7.8 mile round-trip **Prater Ridge Trail** climbs to the top of a mesa for a panoramic view and circles around the perimeter. The climb up is moderately steep.

From Morefield continue on the main road to a side road that travels ½ mile to **Park Point,** the highest point in the park, elev. 8572 feet. A short trail takes you to an impressive view of over 100 miles of Colorado, Utah, New Mexico and Arizona. The fire lookout station is staffed by rangers during the fire season.

Fifteen miles on the main road from the entrance is **Far View Visitor Center.** Stop to see the contemporary southwestern Indian exhibits and for an overview of the park. The center is open 8:00 am to 5:00 pm daily, Memorial Day through Labor Day, with plans to be open through September if the budget allows.

Lodging and guided tours of the park are available at the **Far View Motor Lodge,** open mid-May to mid-October. Sample the southwestern fare in the dining room, watch an Indian craft demonstration, shop for Native American crafts, or attend the evening multimedia programs on the Anasazi. For reservations, write the Mesa Verde Company, Box 277, Mancos, CO 81328, telephone 303/529-4421 in summer, 533-7731 in winter. Moderate.

Ask at the center about the ranger-guided or self-guided tours across **Wetherill Mesa.** This mountain road is 12 miles of sharp curves, and vehicles over 8000 pounds GVW and/or 25 feet long are prohibited, but roadside pull-outs offer super views of the park and the Four Corners area. A car tour takes about three to four hours. You can also walk or take a free tram to the mesa ruins. The road is open 8:00 am to 4:30 pm during the summer only.

Trails include a steep, ½ mile self-guided round trip to **Step House,** pithouses, petroglyphs, a masonry structure and prehistoric stairs; a level, ¾ mile self-guided trail to the **Badger House Community** of four mesa top ruins; and a ½ mile ranger-guided tour to **Long House,** the second largest ruin in the park.

The trail down to Long House is easy but does include a

200-foot vertical descent which you have to climb back up. Children will enjoy walking to the back of the ruins to feel what it was like to live in a cliff dwelling. A large central plaza is thought to have been used for ceremonies.

From Fair View, continue on the main road to **Chapin Mesa,** location of Spruce Tree House, Cliff Palace, and Balcony House. On the way, stop at **Far View Ruins.** The self-guided trail takes you to mesa top ruins. Three miles south is a prehistoric farming area around **Cedar Tree Tower.**

So the children can gain a full understanding of the time-sequence of Anasazi development, take the West Loop Road first, visit Chapin Mesa Archaeological Museum, and then visit the cliff dwellings.

Ruins Road Drive, open 8:00 am to sunset (but often closed in winter due to snow), has two six mile loops that will give you a closer look at many of the ruins.

Take the **right fork** first, past mesa top pithouses and ruins. Wayside exhibits and viewpoints highlight the sequence of architectural development in the area, beginning with the earliest pit houses of the Modified Basketmakers dating back to the 6th century AD.

Be sure to stop at **Sun Temple,** a multistoried building probably used for ceremonies. Since the ruins have been stabilized, it's a great place to let the kids explore the tiny enclosed rooms and walk around the top of the D-shaped walls. There is also a view of Cliff Palace. Sun Temple is open 8:00 am to sunset most of the year.

The **Chapin Mesa Archaeological Museum** covers every aspect of Anasazi life with exhibits and some of the finest artifacts of prehistoric people in the Southwest, many excavated from Mesa Verde. Children will particularly enjoy the excellent dioramas. Look for the Anasazi medicine man's bag.

The museum is open daily, 8:00 am to 6:30 pm in summer, and 8:00 am to 5:00 pm the rest of the year. Ask here about the schedule for the summer ranger-conducted tours through some of the ruins.

Snacks and souvenirs are available at Spruce Tree Terrace

from early spring through fall.

The high point of visiting Mesa Verde for the kids will be a tour through one of the cliff dwellings. The most easily accessible of the major ruins is **Spruce Tree House.** It is the third-largest cliff dwelling in the park, with around 114 rooms and eight kivas. The ½ mile paved self-guided trail begins near the museum and takes 45 minutes to an hour. It includes an optional climb down a ladder into a roofed kiva.

The trail is open 8:30 am–6:30 pm in summer, and rangers are on duty to answer questions. In winter, it is the only cliff ruin you can visit, and then only by guided tour.

Two trails leading into Spruce Canyon begin on the Spruce Tree Trail. **Petroglyph Point Trail** is 2.8 miles to one of the largest displays of rock art in the park, and ends at the parking area near the museum. The trail is fairly flat except for a scramble up the rocks to the top of the mesa for the return. **Spruce Canyon Trail,** 2.1 miles round trip to the canyon bottoms, is a little more strenuous and not as scenic. You must register at the Ranger Office to take either of these trails.

The **left fork** of Ruins Road takes you to Cliff Palace and Balcony House. **Cliff Palace** is the largest cliff dwelling in the Southwest. The ¼-mile, self-guided trail includes descending stone stairs. Climbing back, four 10-foot ladders parallel the ancient hand- and toehold trail to the top of the mesa. If the kids are old enough to handle the ladders, they'll love it!

Guidebooks are available at the ruin. There is also a ranger on duty, as well as picnic tables and rest rooms. The trail is open 9:00 am to 6:30 pm in summer.

The favorite for older kids may be the ranger-guided tour to **Balcony House,** which includes climbing a 32-foot ladder and crawling through a ten-foot long tunnel. The trail is ½ mile and takes about an hour. Tours begin every hour on the hour between 9:00 am and 5:00 pm, and every half hour between 10:30 am and 3:30 pm. They are limited to the first 50 people, so arrive early.

Superintendent, Mesa Verde National Park, CO 81330, 303/529-4461 or 529-4465. Admission is $5 per vehicle.

DID YOU KNOW?

—At its height, as many as 5000 people may have lived in the Mesa Verde pueblos.

—Mesa Verde is the only national park dedicated to the works of man.

—The Mesa Verde cliff dwellings were occupied for only about 75 to 100 years.

—Cliff Palace has four stories, 217 rooms and 23 kivas.

—There are an estimated 10,000 archaeological sites on the public land in Montezuma County (which includes Mesa Verde), between 60 to 100 per square mile.

—Much of our information about Anasazi daily life has come from the trash heaps at the bottom of the slopes in front of the houses, where the people often tossed their discards.

Anasazi Heritage Center

Take US 160 west of Mesa Verde eight miles to State 145. Turn north eight miles to State 184, then west and follow the signs to the Anasazi Heritage Center.

This Anasazi museum and research center opened with full services in the summer of 1988. In front of the museum is the 12th-century **Dominguez Ruin.** It was once home to between eight and ten people of the Northern San Juan Anasazi tradition, a more populous, agrarian, and less complex group than the Anasazi from Chaco Canyon. The ruins date from around AD 1 to AD 130.

A half-mile paved path up the hillside will take you to the **Escalante Ruins** and a lovely panorama of the mountains and Montezuma Valley. Escalante was a trade outpost for the Chaco Anasazi. The people here swapped timber, deer hide and farm produce for luxury items such as turquoise, parrot feathers, and shell ornaments from as far away as the southern California coast and Gulf of Mexico.

A self-guiding trail brochure will tell you about the ruins, as

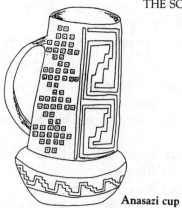
Anasazi cup

well as the natural history of the area. You can also make arrangements for guided tours by calling in advance. The trail is open 8:00 am to 5:00 pm daily.

Stop in the lobby of the **museum** to touch the artifacts. Museum displays depict Anasazi daily life, including a full-sized replica of an AD 800 pithouse. The test trench will give the children an idea of how modern archaeologists work.

Of particular interest to kids will be the hands-on exhibits in the **Discovery Area.** They include telling the age of a wooden beam using tree rings (this one may challenge you, too), grinding corn on a metate, weaving, computer games and microscopes to view seeds from the time of the Anasazi.

Most of the artifacts came from the Dolores Archaeological Program, which worked ahead of the equipment building McPhee Reservoir, and they represent the Northern San Juan Anasazi tradition from AD 1 to AD 1300.

Anasazi Heritage Center, 27501 Highway 184, Dolores 81323, 303/882-4811. The information hotline is 882-7600. Summer hours: 9:00 am–5:00 pm, Monday through Saturday, 10:00 am–5:00 pm Sunday. Call for winter hours.

State 184 continues to US 666. North is the town of **Dove Creek,** the "Pinto Bean Capital of the World." Using traditional dryland farming techniques, the people here grow an abundance of pinto beans. Recently, they have cultivated a bean grown by the Anasazi for over 1000 years. The bean is sweeter, mealier and cooks faster than the pinto. You can buy a package of these Anasazi beans from the museums or grocery stores in the area. Northeast of town is the **Dolores River Overlook,** with a view of the Dolores River and canyons.

DID YOU KNOW?

—The grave of a wealthy woman was found at the Dominguez Ruin. She was buried with 6900 beads and three mosaics of turquoise and shell, ceramic vessels, bone scrapers and many other items. Some archaeologists believe she was an influential visitor from the Chaco Canyon area.

—Escalante Ruins is thought to be the first recorded archaeological site in Colorado, the one mentioned in 1776 by the Dominguez-Escalante Expedition.

—Escalante is one of the northernmost outposts of the vast Chaco trade network.

—The Anasazi Center does not display human remains. Any that are found are returned to the proper Indian tribe for reburial.

—The Dolores Archaeological Program was the largest archaeological contract ever awarded in the United States. The project surveyed 1600 prehistoric sites, excavating 120 of these.

—Anasazi pottery was in demand by other cultural groups throughout the area and traded extensively.

3. FROM CORTEZ TO FARMINGTON—THROUGH THE FOUR CORNERS

Ute Mountain Tribal Park

Take US Highway 160 15 miles south of Cortez to the Ute Mountain Tribal Park. The park was established to preserve the 2000 Anasazi cliff dwellings found there and is part of the Ute Mountain Ute Indian Reservation. Twice the size of Mesa Verde and bordering it on three sides, the park has ruins just as intriguing, but far fewer visitors. It is still a primitive area, so visiting will be a different experience for the kids than seeing Mesa Verde, with the isolation and minimally reconstructed ruins adding to a sense of adventure and discovery.

To visit, you will need a guided tour. Full-day ground tours begin at 9:00 am from the **Ute Mountain Pottery Plant.** A Ute tour guide will give you and the children a personal perspective on Indian life and the history of the Anasazi and Ute Indians. Bring your own car, water, food, and enough gas for 50 miles of unpaved road.

Reservations are required. Contact Arthur Cuthair, Ute Mountain Tribal Park, Towaoc, CO 81334, 303/565-3751, ext. 282, or 565-4684.

You can also take a walking tour through the plant to see the pottery-making process.

The Tribal Park has a primitive campground along the Mancos River and evening slide programs. Day hikes and backpacking guided tours are also offered.

If you are at the reservation in June, you may have the opportunity to watch the annual **Bear Dance.** Marking the time the bear awakens from winter hibernation, the Utes celebrate with games, food, arts and crafts, and the Bear Dance.

Through the Four Corners

From Cortez take US Highway 160 38 miles southwest to **Four Corners National Monument,** on the Ute Mountain Ute Reservation and the Navajo Indian Reservation. This is the only spot in the U.S. where four states meet—Colorado, Utah, Arizona and New Mexico. It is marked by a concrete slab with the names of the states and by stalls of Ute Mountain Ute and Navajo vendors selling homemade Navajo bread and Indian arts and crafts.

Now that you're here, do what almost every other visitor does. Have someone take a picture of you with an arm or leg in each state. Don't be surprised if you're not alone!

Question: In what state is the Four Corners Monument? Answer: It's not in any state, it's on the Indian Reservation. Question: Which Indian Reservation? Answer: No one knows.

The controversy started with an 1868 survey that erroneously put the border between Colorado and New Mexico 100 yards too far south. Although other surveyors noted the mistake, in 1925 the Supreme Court made it legal by declaring the border was to be set by the 1868 survey.

Unfortunately, treaties with the Ute and Navajo depended on the placement of the border. The Navajo treaty established their northern reservation boundaries at the 37th parallel (100 yards north of the current border); the Ute treaty established their southern reservation boundaries at the Colorado-New Mexico border. The 100 yards had been given to both of them.

Continue southwest on US 160 to Teec Nos Pos, then turn east on State 504 to **Shiprock** on the Navajo Reservation. Shiprock is a lava plug (from the throat of a volcano) that rises 1700 feet from the desert floor. In Navajo, it is called Taebidahi, the "rock with wings," and it is sacred to them.

From Shiprock take US 550 around 25 miles to Farmington, New Mexico. You will pass two huge coal-fired generating plants, the **San Juan Generating Plant and the Four Corners Generating Plant.** Guided tours are available of the San Juan Generating Plant, telephone 505/599-5891, and the Four Corners Plant, depending on availability of manpower, telephone 598-6611.

Near the Four Corners Plant is **Morgan Lake,** a 150-acre lake where you can picnic, wind surf, and fish. For more information, contact the Navajo Tribal Office, 602/871-4941.

Farmington, New Mexico
Zip Code 87401   Area Code 505

Farmington is the largest city in the Four Corners area, with over 36,800 people. The town boomed with the discovery of oil and gas in the area and continues to benefit from the two nearby generating plants.

It is also a leading trade center for the eastern Navajo Reservation. The influence is obvious in the many Indian arts and crafts stores.

It's a good place to eat lunch (especially if the kids want fast food) or stay the night.

THINGS TO DO

Take the kids to the **Farmington Museum,** which covers the history, culture and geology of the Four Corners. Historical displays include a full-sized replica of a frontier business street and a time-line of the San Juan Basin. The Children's Gallery has hands-on exhibits, including a giant wall puzzle, television studio, and dress-up room. The museum also gets fine traveling exhibits.

Farmington Museum, 302 North Orchard, Farmington 87401, 327-7701. Hours: Tuesday through Friday, noon to 5:00 pm, and Saturday, 10:00 am to 5:00 pm. Admission is free.

Browse in the numerous outlets for **American Indian crafts.** The Foutz Indian Room at 301 West Main has Navajo jewelry and kachinas. Ask to see the rug room in the back of the store. Some of the trading posts west along Highway 550 are also good places to shop.

The town has several parks and swimming pools, and during the summer, the library has storytime hours. For more information, contact the **Convention and Visitors Bureau,** downtown at 203 West Main Street, 326-7602.

The children might enjoy a visit to the **Tom Bolack Ranch and Experimental Farm,** home of a former governor of New Mexico. The ranch has a herd of deer, a large flock of Canadian geese, coyotes, peacocks, guinea hens, and gardens that produce 400-pound pumpkins. Call ahead to ask directions and to make visiting arrangements, 325-7873.

Eleven miles east of Farmington on US Highway 64 is

Salmon Ruins, a pre-Columbian community of 600 ruins. In the 11th century it was one of the largest and most remarkably planned communities of the Chaco Anasazi. Although much of the original apartment complex is unexcavated and unrestored, a visit here can help you appreciate the overwhelming task of the archaeologist. However, kids fresh from Mesa Verde or Aztec ruins may be a bit disappointed.

The small museum has a slide show and some of the 1,500,000 artifacts taken from the ruins. A short walk or drive takes you to the ruins, where a booklet from the information center follows the self-guiding trail.

San Juan Archaeological Research Center and Library at Salmon Ruin, 975 US Highway 64, Farmington 87401, 632-2013. Hours: 9:00 am–5:00 pm daily. Admission is $1 for ages 16 and up, $.50 for ages 6-15.

4. FARMINGTON TO CHACO CANYON

Continue east of Farmington to Bloomfield, then turn south on the paved State 44 to Nageezi Trading Post. Turn southwest onto County Road 7800 for about 26 miles to the Visitor Center. You can also take State 44 to State Route 57 at Blanco Canyon Trading Post. Both roads are fair-weather dirt roads and can be impassable when wet, but the route from Nageezi is a better choice in the rain. Inquire locally if in doubt about conditions.

Chaco Culture National Historical Park

Chaco Canyon was a magnificent center of Pueblo Indian culture for over a century, an urban complex of stone rising from the desert. At its apex in the late 11th and early 12th centuries, it was the Anasazi leader in religion architecture, social organizations, politics and economics.

The Chacoan architects built multistoried pueblos with

over-sized rooms surrounding a plaza. Bustling cities like
Pueblo Bonito, Chetro Ketl, and Una Vida were examples of
their handiwork, and their pattern was widely copied by
others, including the unique masonry with two outer walls of
elaborate stonework filled with a core of rubble.

At one time, around 1000 people lived in the 600-plus
rooms of Pueblo Bonito, the largest of the towns. Terraced
streets bent in a crescent around the plaza, a long wall enclosed the front, and dozens of kivas dominated the city.

Life was bustling at the Chaco pueblos. In the plazas,
women ground corn, children played, men repaired buildings, dogs barked, and priests led colorful ceremonies. Traders
from exotic places mingled with the Chacoan farmers, craftsmen, and hunters, bartering salt from the Zuni Lakes, turquoise from Galisteo Basin, seashells from the Pacific Ocean,
and macaw feathers from Mexico for Anasazi pottery, turquoise jewelry and cornmeal.

Turkey

For years the Chacoans exerted a far-flung political, administrative and religious influence on the other Anasazi groups, and their elaborate network of 400 miles of roads, some as wide as 40 feet, linked them with outlier towns.

Eventually, like the other Anasazi settlements, those in Chaco Canyon were abandoned.

THINGS TO DO

Chaco Canyon is the gem of the Anasazi culture. It is uncrowded because of the bone-jarring dirt road you have to take to get there. In addition, services are extremely limited. It will not be as enjoyable for younger kids as some of the more accessible ruins, but older children will no doubt find it a fascinating place to explore.

Be sure to stop at the **Visitor Center** first for information and to plan your trip. A **self-guided tour** takes you through several of the ruins, or you can take a ranger-guided walk in summer.

The campground (no water) is about a mile from the center and has evening campfire programs in summer. Drinking water is available at the visitor center, but no other lodging, gas or food is available.

Chaco Culture National Historical Park, Star Route 4, Box 6500, Bloomfield, NM 87413, 505/988-6716 or 6727. Admission is $3 per vehicle. The visitor center is open 8:00 am to 5:00 pm; the ruins are open sunrise to sunset.

DID YOU KNOW?

—Chaco masonry is easily recognized by large sandstone blocks chinked with small stones, often in an attractive design, and the use of only a small amount of mortar.

—Great kivas may have been used as administrative and social centers, in addition to their religious functions. Only the Chacoan Anasazi built great kivas.

—Scientists can tell what kind of food the Anasazi ate when they were alive by looking at teeth in their skeletons.

—The pollution from the Four Corners generating plants was the only man-made thing seen by the first astronauts in space except the Great Wall of China.

5. FARMINGTON TO THE SOUTHERN UTE RESERVATION

From Bloomfield, turn north on State Highway 44 to the town of **Aztec**. Residents claim that "Six Old Soreheads" live here. Their names change daily, depending on who happens to be grumpy. Let's hope you don't run into them!

The **Aztec Museum**, 125 Main Street, has prehistoric artifacts, Indian arts and crafts, an early barber shop, and an outdoor display of pioneer farming and oil field equipment. It also has an extensive rock and mineral collection. Call 505/334-9829 for more information.

A fun stop for the kids might be the giant flea market, held every Friday, Saturday and Sunday throughout the year. Indians, Hispanics and whites bring their new and not-so-new goodies to sell at this cultural hodge-podge. The number of vendors varies with the weather.

Near the junction of US 550 and State 4 is Aztec Ruins.

Aztec Ruins National Monument

At Aztec you can see the remains of one of the largest prehistoric Anasazi towns in the Southwest, and it is one of the most accessible ruins for kids. Because it is smaller, it may be less overwhelming for the young than Mesa Verde. You can walk through the rooms, and kids will especially like the climb into the restored Great Kiva, where they can sit and listen to a tape of Indian chanting.

Aztec is over 65 miles north of Chaco Canyon, where the town's original builders probably had relatives. Construction began around AD 1110, with hand-quarried sandstone blocks hauled from over a mile away and timber dragged from the mountains 20 miles north. But the Chacoans abandoned the town almost as soon as it was completed, around AD 1200.

Twenty-five years later, a group of Anasazi related to the Mesa Verdians moved in, remodeled and built additions. Then, in only 50 years or so, they moved away, too, sealing the windows and doors and leaving everything in place as if awaiting their return.

Over 600 years later, Anglo settlers discovered Aztec and used it as a quarry for stones to build their own houses. Much valuable information was lost by the subsequent vandalism and stealing of artifacts.

THINGS TO DO

The tree-shaded, fenced park makes a pleasant place for a picnic. The **Visitor Center** has a video on the Anasazi and displays of prehistoric artifacts. Ask about the ranger badge children ages 6-16 can earn, and pick up a brochure for the **self-guiding trail** through the west pueblo, the Great Kiva, and the nearby Hubbard ruin.

As you walk through the ruins, look for the different architectural styles that distinguish the Chaco Anasazi from the Mesa Verde Anasazi (large sandstone blocks chinked with small stones for the Chacoan, T-shaped doorways for the Mesa Verdian). Look northeast of the main ruin near the cottonwood trees for the large mounds that indicate an unexcavated area, and see if you can count the kivas in the village.

When you reach the Great Kiva, tell the kids to climb inside and test the acoustics. You can easily hear a whisper from one side of the kiva to the other side.

Superintendent, Aztec Ruins National Monument, PO Box 640, Aztec, NM 87410, 505/334-6174. Hours: Monday through Friday from 8:00 am–5:00 pm, Saturday from 10:00 am–4:00 pm, and Sundy from 1:00 pm–4:00 pm, with extended summer hours. Admission is $1 per person or $3 per carload.

DID YOU KNOW?

—The roof of the Great Kiva at Aztec weighs 90 tons.

—The pioneers erroneously named the ruins "Aztec" because they assumed it had been built by the Aztec Indians of Mexico.

—Aztec was connected to Chaco Canyon by one of the Chacoan Anasazi's main roads.

—Many archaeologists believe the residents of Aztec eventually ended up at Taos, San Juan or Santo Domingo pueblos.

—The kiva here is the largest reconstructed kiva in North America, and the only great kiva that has ever been fully restored.

—Some archaeologists believe Aztec was the center for a new cult that eventually failed.

—Aztec was a popular place for a settlement because of the nearby Animas River that flows year round.

Navajo Lake

From Aztec, take State 173 to **Navajo Lake,** one of the best fishing holes in the state. Hiking, picnicking, fishing, camping, hunting, and a whole array of water sports are available at this 35-mile long reservoir.

Fed by melting snowpack, Navajo Lake abounds in cold and warm water game fish, ranging from rainbow trout and kokanee salmon to bass and crappie. Since the lake extends beyond New Mexico into Colorado, be sure to purchase the proper fishing license, depending on which part of the lake you plan to fish.

The lake itself is the principal source of water for the Navajo Indian Irrigation Project, quenching the thirst of 110,000 acres of land on the Navajo Reservation. The dam, an embankment filled with 26 million cubic yards of rocks and dirt, is almost three-quarters of a mile long.

Navajo Lake has four developed recreation sites. **Navajo**

Lake State Park, near the dam in New Mexico, includes the Pine River Site and Sims Mesa Site. Both sites in Navajo Lake State Park have a marina, store, camping, picnic area, and boat rentals. The small visitor center at the Pine River Site has interpretive displays of Anasazi life and of the dam, telephone 505/632-2278.

The **San Juan River Recreation Area,** also in New Mexico, is below the dam on the San Juan River and is accessible only by dirt road. It has camping, picnic areas and fishing access.

Navajo State Recreation Area, at the upper end of the reservoir, is near the town of Arboles (Spanish for "trees"), Colorado. Take State Highway 511/172 north to the town of Ignacio, Colorado, then turn east on State 151.

The area has a marina, restaurant, store, boat rentals, modern campgrounds, picnic areas, and a nature trail. Motels and restaurants are also available in nearby Arboles, two miles away.

The Visitor Center has a museum with displays of the dam and Anasazi exhibits excavated from the land that is now submerged under the reservoir. It is open late May to mid-August, 8:00 am–5:00 pm on Monday, Tuesday, and Friday, and 9:00 am–5:00 pm Saturday and Sunday. The center is closed on Wednesdays and Thursdays, and from noon to 1:00 pm daily.

Navajo State Recreation Area, Box 1697, Arboles, CO 81121, 303/883-2208. Day-use fee is $3.

Ignacio, Colorado
Zip Code 81137   Area Code 303

The town of Ignacio is the Consolidated Ute Agency Headquarters, and also the burial site of Chief Ouray in a small cemetery across the Los Pinos River. It was through his efforts that the Ute nation remained relatively peaceful, in spite of the numerous broken treaties that moved the Utes farther and farther from their mountain homeland. Ouray guided his people with a courage and persistence that undoubtedly saved them from the near annihilation other Indian tribes experienced at the hands of the invading white man.

If you need a place to stay, try the inexpensive **Sky Ute Lodge**, with its Cultural Center and displays of Indian arts and crafts and small museum. The center also has a swimming pool, a restaurant that serves southwestern, Indian and American food, and a gift shop. You can also make arrangements for tours and crafts demonstrations.

For reservations, write PO Box 550, Ignacio, CO 81137, or call 303/563-4531.

Sky Ute Downs is an arena in town where you can see Indian dances, horse shows and rodeos. Call 563-4502 for a schedule.

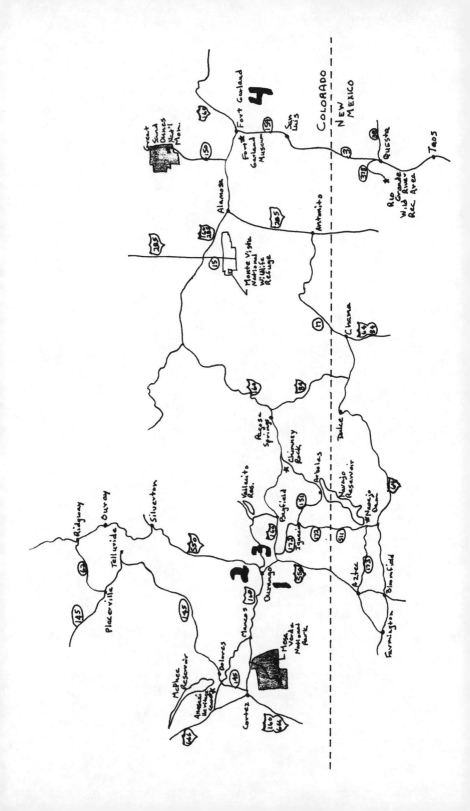

8

MOUNTAIN SPLENDOR: Southwestern Colorado

Most people think of mountains when they think of Colorado, and there's good reason behind it. If you squashed all the mountains in the state, the area of Colorado would be larger than Texas and Alaska combined.

But the southwestern part of Colorado is a transition zone, where the high desert of the Colorado Plateau meets foothills, lush farmlands, and grazing pastures. There, as the Plateau jams the lofty Rocky Mountains, it abruptly stops. Beyond is a rugged country that many say is the most spectacular in the state.

History whispers across the back roads here, and secrets ride the wind. Perched atop craggy peaks and hidden in deep crevasses, loose boards rattle in lonely spaces that once held dreams, whispering the legends that bind long-dead scoundrels and heroes to our time.

This is a place for the unhurried motorist to savor the

diversity and splendor of nature, where the next bend of the road leads to even more breathtaking scenery. And it's a place to ponder the works of man, where the remnants of his courage, audacity and persistence cling to Nature's jagged edge.

Indians came to the southern Colorado mountains first, and only recently did white man successfully invade these dizzying heights. Sometime after the Anasazi abandoned the area in the late 1200's/early 1300's, the semi-nomadic Ute Indians arrived. Living a life that left little mark on the land, they made their camps in the warmer, lower elevations, and visited the higher mountains to hunt and fish.

Their way of life ended with the coming of the white man. The first were the Spanish in the late 16th century, searching for gold, pelts, and Indian slaves. They explored the edges of the high country and later settled in the San Luis Valley.

Beaver

Trappers were next to discover these rich hunting grounds, spurred by the rise in popularity of the beaver hat in fashionable London in the early 1800's. Pitted against unfriendly Indians, unremitting loneliness, and the unforgiving land, these mountain men pushed into the wilderness. Men like Peg-leg Smith, Jim Bridger, Kit Carson, and Tom "Broken-Hand" Fitzpatrick, as rough and scraggly as the mountains they explored, came to know every crevice and ridge of this place. In fringed buckskin shirts and leggings, fur hats and moccasins, they trudged into the unknown searching for pelts and blazing the way for the armies and settlers that followed.

Then, in 1859, came the discovery of gold in Colorado, and two years later the discovery of silver. A new breed of man now invaded the hills. Lured by visions of fabulous wealth, the prospector burrowed ever deeper into the hills. As he stampeded over the land, his thoughts went little further than the latest rumor of riches just over the next hill.

The prospector possessed the same hardiness, courage and stubborn tenacity that enabled the mountain man to survive, but his dreams were built of thinner castles in the air. Confident and brazen, he declared "The Rockies or Bust." More often than not, it was bust.

Gold, by nature, is hard to find. Once found, it's even harder to get out, usually sealed together with other metals deep inside a mountain. Every so often, the earth heaves upward, exposing the gold-bearing rock to wind and rain, leaving "free gold" on the hillsides and in the streams after the rock erodes away.

When one of these nuggets was found, the next gold rush had begun. Overnight, the mountains crawled with miners, and hastily-built camps of tents, saloons and stores were born. The surface gold was gone almost immediately, picked by a lucky few. A fortune remained in the maze of veins underground, but to extract it meant an investment of hard work, time and money.

Most preferred to grab their pick and gold pan and follow the call to another strike. They abandoned or sold their claims to large companies, leaving behind the litter of their shoddy shanties and the scattered insides of the earth.

Boisterous camps that mushroomed overnight were suddenly lifeless. Many of them died a sudden death, akin to their birth. Others faded slowly and painfully, their barren remains still dotting the hillsides. Some, like Silverton, Ouray and Telluride, survive to the present and have brought the flavor of the Gay Nineties with them.

But there's always been more than "gold in them thar hills."
Primitive wilderness laced with crystal-clear streams; flashing
waterfalls cascading into narrow chasms; silent forests of towering pines; and bony peaks that reach heavenward like the
petrified fingers of ancient giants—these make up the magnificent Rocky Mountains. And these are the treasures waiting to
be discovered in mountain splendor.

DID YOU KNOW?

—Colorado has over 1000 peaks at least two miles high, and
  53 peaks over 14,000 feet.
—A good beaver pelt was worth between $6 and $10 in the
  1800's.
—Indians called gold "the yellow metal that drives the white
  man crazy."
—More capital to develop Colorado came from discoveries of
  silver than gold.
—Silver miners found rich deposits of silver carbonate in the
  tailings of abandoned gold mines.

Durango to Northern New Mexico

1. Durango, Colorado
2. San Juan Skyway—A Loop of Silver from Durango
3. East from Durango to the Great Sand Dunes National
   Monument
4. Fort Garland to Northern New Mexico

1. DURANGO, COLORADO
Zip Code 81301/81302   Area Code 303

Durango was built by the Denver & Rio Grande Railroad in 1880-81 as a smelter and freight center for the mineral boom in the nearby San Juan Mountains. Like a proud father, the railroad incorporated its initials (DRG) into the name of the town.

Durango grew quickly, and by 1881 the population exceeded 1,000, with a saloon for approximately every 17 people and one church to be shared by all. Violence came easily in the rowdy town, as gamblers, cowboys, prospectors and railway workers jostled each other amid the mud, tents and shanties.

Aided by a moderate climate and easy access to both the desert and nearby mountains, the town has grown from the early nucleus of the southwest Colorado rail system to the hub of southwestern Colorado.

THINGS TO DO
Downtown Durango is a slice of the Old West, with cowboy boots, Stetson hats, and bolo ties on parade. Lining Main Street are Victorian taverns, honky-tonk saloons, and shops filled with Indian crafts and railroad memorabilia. To add to the mood, pile the kids into one of the **horse-drawn carriages** for a tour.

Many of Durango's original buildings were destroyed in the 1899 fire, but some remain. One of the most elegant is the red sandstone **Strater Hotel** on the corner of Seventh and Main. Large, durable and lavish, this is one of the West's grand old hotels, its original 1880's elegance restored by several face lifts.

When druggist Henry Strater built the hotel, it had 50 rooms, each individually decorated with Victorian furniture and wallpaper. Don't worry, the commodes have been replaced by private baths.

Older kids will enjoy an evening at one of the melodramas—rated by Time Magazine as some of the best in the country—in the hotel's **Diamond Circle Theater.** They are performed Monday through Saturday evenings, May through September.

The Strater Hotel, 699 North Main Avenue, Durango 81302, 247-4431, out-of-state 800/626-4886. Moderate to expensive.

Another place to stay downtown is the stately **General Palmer House,** established 1898. It is on the same block as the narrow gauge train depot. The lobby and a few of the guest rooms are restored as originals, but the majority are more modern.

The General Palmer House, 567 Main Avenue, 247-4747, or toll free 800/523-3358 outside Colorado, 800/824-2173 inside Colorado. Moderately expensive.

If the children (or you) have a sweet tooth attack, run, don't walk, a few doors down to the **Rocky Mountain Chocolate Factory** for homemade fudge or a caramel apple rolled in chocolate candies.

If you spend the night downtown, don't be surprised if your early morning is disturbed by the mournful whistle of one of the **Durango & Silverton Narrow Gauge Railroad's** engines. Every day in summer, one of these tiny coal-fired locomotives pulls out of town, sighing, coughing and belching black soot, and trailing behind her authentically restored coaches filled with eager tourists.

Her 90 mile round trip up the Animas River Canyon to the old mining camp of Silverton follows the original route built for ore trains bringing gold and silver down from the hills. The train travels through scenery that can only be described as breathtaking. Along the way, it stops to let off backpackers and fishermen heading for the back country and guests of the Tall Timber Resort, telephone 259-4813. After a few hours in Silverton for lunch and browsing, the train returns. Round-trip time is eight hours.

Although a fire recently destroyed the original roundhouse, the train chugs on. Several depart daily between early May and late October.

Riding the train is a thrilling experience, however, the round trip is crowded, noisy, and cinder-sprayed, and may be too long for younger children. Consider an overnight layover in Silverton, with a return trip the next day, or make arrangements to ride the train one way, traveling the other half by car or bus.

For information on riding the bus from Silverton to Durango, call the Silverton Depot, 387-5416. You can also take a shorter trip on the Animas River Railway that leaves from Rockwood (see under San Juan Skyway for more information).

For train reservations, contact the Agent, Durango & Silverton Narrow Gauge Railroad, Rio Grande Depot, 479 Main Avenue, 247-2733. Be sure to reserve early. The train is booked several months in advance. Round trip tickets start at $32 per adult and $16 for ages 5-11.

The **La Plata County Historical Society Museum,** in the old Animas City schoolhouse, is a small museum with nature and historical exhibits, some of them hands-on.

The museum is at Thirty-first Street and West Second Avenue, telephone 259-2402. Museum hours are now sporadic, but future plans include daily summer hours. Admission is $1 for adults, children are free.

Take the kids to the **fish hatchery.** At any one time, there are thousands (seems like millions) of trout here, living the first few months of their lives so they can be freed into the nearby streams and reservoirs for you to catch for supper. The museum visitor center will tell you about the Colorado fishing industry. You can also pick up a fishing map and watch the fish feeding themselves. There is one pool with very large fish (as in "the one that got away") that you can feed yourself. Next to the hatchery is a park that makes a great place for a picnic.

Colorado State Fish Hatchery, Seventeenth and Park Avenue just off Main, 151 E. 16th, 247-4755.

The kids can cool off at the municipal pool, 2400 Main Avenue, or walk the nature trail that follows part of the course of the Animas River.

Four miles west of town on Highway 160 is **Canyon Collec-**

tors, a commercial operation with an interesting collection of early Indian goods, cowboy items, and antique firearms. Where else can the kids walk through an arch of over 3,000 deer antlers?

If you're hankering for western fare, visit the **Bar D Ranch** for an authentic chuckwagon supper followed by western entertainment, or a morning horseback or jeep ride and cowboy breakfast. If you arrive early, browse in the shops at the ranch or ride the train. Bar D is nine miles north of town on County Road 250.

Bar D Ranch, 8080 County Road 250 North, 247-5753. For a cowboy breakfast or horseback ride only, call the stables at 247-5755. It is open May through September.

Another uniquely western experience is staying at a **dude ranch,** where you can ride, swim, fish and hike to your heart's content. Some have special children's programs.

Try Colorado Trails Ranch, PO Box 848W, Durango 81302, 800/332-DUDE, or Wilderness Trails Ranch (next to Vallecito Reservoir), 776 County Road 300, Box A, Durango 81301, 247-0722.

The **Durango Chamber Resort Association** is a good place to ask about other lodging and restaurants in town, as well as the numerous seasonal events in the area. It is located at 111 S. Camino del Rio, 247-0312. For central reservations, call 800/358-8855 in-state, 800/525-8855 out-of-state.

Around 20 miles northeast of Durango is **Vallecito Reservoir.** Take either Highway 240 (the Florida Road) for a leisurely drive, or Highway 160 to Bayfield, then north on Highway 501 to the lake.

This beautiful mountain valley reservoir has 22 miles of shoreline and is a popular spot for water sports, camping, hiking and horseback riding. Boat rentals, lodging, and food are all available at the lake and in nearby Bayfield. Try your fishing luck and see if you can top the lake records—a 30-pound 1-ounce northern pike and a 24-pound 10-ounce German brown trout.

DID YOU KNOW?

—The railroad to Durango hauled the last gold ore in the 1950's.

—A few of the famous people who have stayed at the Strater Hotel are Will Rogers, Wiley Post, President Kennedy and President Ford.

—Louis L'Amour wrote many of his books about the Old West in Room 222 of the Strater Hotel.

—In the early days of the town, court was held in a large room above the general store. During one murder trial, the spectators cleared the floor to dance while the jury deliberated. They stopped long enough to hear the verdict, "guilty," then resumed their fun.

—The narrow gauge railroad track was necessary because of the steep climbs and tight turns to the mountain mines. The 3' track was also cheaper to build than the 4'8½" standard gauge.

2. SAN JUAN SKYWAY—A LOOP OF SILVER FROM DURANGO

For a stunning 232 mile circle journey through the San Juan Mountains, also known as the "American Alps," take Main Avenue to US Highway 550 north from Durango. Part of your journey will follow the famed **Million Dollar Highway,** a feat of remarkable engineering.

There are several stories about how the highway got its name. One version says it came from the huge amount of low-grade ore used in the roadbed, worth over $1,000,000. Another says it was because the cost to build the road in 1922 was $1,200,000. Still another version contends the scenery is worth a million dollars. Whichever account you like best, this strip of pavement will take you through spectacular country where superlatives fall short.

Columbine

Along the way you will pass the shells of silver boom towns and hillsides gophered with mines. Most were abandoned when the repeal of the Sherman Silver Purchase Act in 1893 sent the price of silver plummeting. Mining had a brief revival in the late 1890's with the discovery of gold, but although it remains a large part of the economy of the San Juans today, the boom is obviously over.

Leaving Durango, US 550 parallels the narrow gauge railroad tracks through the **Animas River Valley.** Dotted with small ranches and summer homes, these fertile meadows serve as grazing ground for horses and sheep against a vivid backdrop of green pine and the red rock walls of Hermosa Cliffs.

Six miles north of Durango is **Trimble Hot Springs,** a natural mineral springs with an outdoor swimming pool, therapy pools, and private tubs. Cost is $4.75 per adult and $2.75 per child under 12. It is open daily 7:00 am to 10:00 pm, telephone 303/259-0314.

A few miles farther is **Honeyville,** where the kids can watch bees making honey under glass.

Turn left from US 550 about 16½ miles from downtown Durango to Rockwood and the **Animas River Railway,** which shares the Durango and Silverton Railroad's tracks. The Railbus, a motorized coach and gondola, carries 80 passengers through the Animas River Canyon to spots for fishing, hiking, picnicking, and sightseeing. It's a good alternative if you don't have the time or money to take the train to Silverton. It operates early May through October. Call 247-9349 for reservations.

Twenty-five miles north of Durango is **Purgatory Ski Area,** with a mild climate that locals brag translates to "the hottest skiing in the West." In summer, take your children for a rollicking ride on the alpine slide, or rent mountain bikes to ride down from the top of the scenic chairlift.

On the other side of **Molas Pass,** 10,910 feet, is a zigzag downhill into the town of Silverton, nestled in the mountains on the flattest piece of land in San Juan County. The valley, one mile wide by two miles long, is called Baker's Park.

DID YOU KNOW?

—The area between Lake City, Silverton, Ouray and Telluride is called the Silver Triangle. The earth here has yielded over half a billion dollars of rich ore.

—San Juan County is one of the few counties in the United States where not even one acre is devoted to agriculture.

—Navajo legend claims that near the town of Silverton is a hole in the ground that was the entry for the Dine (The People) into this world.

Silverton
Zip Code 81433   Area Code 303

An unbelievable amount of mineral wealth has been taken from the hills around Silverton by the nippers (operated the elevators), shushers (took the buckets of ore from the stope inside), and trammers (pushed the ore carts). Story has it the town was named when an early mine-operator bragged, "We may not have gold here, but we have silver by the ton."

By 1879, the 3000 residents had 35 saloons to choose from. At one time, Silverton boasted three railroads spiraling into town and connecting it to the rest of the world—that is, when there wasn't too much snow. In 1884 the rails were blocked for 73 continuous days by avalanches.

This is the "mining town that never quit." Although the population has dwindled to about 800 residents, the town is still largely supported by mining, and the wide streets, quaint churches, wood-plank sidewalks, and false-fronted buildings remind one of its exciting frontier past.

THINGS TO DO

The Grand Imperial Hotel on Main Street was built in 1882 and has been restored to its original Gay Nineties character with a mahogany bar that is the oldest in the region. It also has a restaurant and some historical items on display. It is, however, open only in summer.

The Grand Imperial Hotel, 1219 Greene Street, P.O. Box 97, 387-5527. Moderate.

North on Main Street is **The San Juan County Museum,** next to the county courthouse in the former San Juan county jail. The museum has a fine collection of antique mining equipment and historical exhibits of the area.

San Juan County Museum, 1567 Greene Street, 387-5838. Hours: daily, mid-May through mid-September, 9:00 am–5:00 pm; mid-September through mid-October, 10:00 am–3:00 pm; and closed in the winter. Admission is $1.25 for adults, children under 12 are free.

The **Teller House Hotel,** 1250 Greene Street, is in a renovated 1890's Victorian building. Once a fashionable boardinghouse, it is now an affiliate of American Youth Hostel and offers inexpensive dormitory lodging, as well as European-style private rooms. The cost of lodging includes breakfast, and the room comes with a bonus. Downstairs is a French bakery where you can buy delicious pastries. (See Appendix C for more information on American Youth Hostel.) Call 387-5423 for rates and reservations.

A 2½ mile long trip on **Scenic Drive** takes you to the Christ of the Mines Shrines, an overlook of the town, and through a lovely grove of aspen trees. To reach this dirt road, travel north on Greene Street to the courthouse, then turn left onto 15th Street. When the road intersects with US 550, turn left back to town.

Take the kids to one of the nearby mining ghost towns. Follow the main road through downtown (State Highway 110) northeast along the Animas River. You'll pass the **Hillside Cemetery,** where rotted wooden markers, the occasional aspen growing from a sunken grave, and modern gravestones blend past and present.

Farther on is the boardinghouse entrance of the **Garry Owen Mine,** 12,000 feet high on the nearly vertical slope of Galena Mountain. The tramway was the only access to the mine and boardinghouse. Today, it remains as a monument to the courage of the miners who swayed up to the mine in ore buckets on Monday morning, then back down at the end of the week for "R and R" in **Howardsville.** The town is now ruins, but the tiny log county courthouse still stands.

Continue on to the **Shenandoah Mill,** with its 10,000 foot tramway that ends high on the mountainside at King Solomon Mine, which first produced silver in the 1870's.

Mine

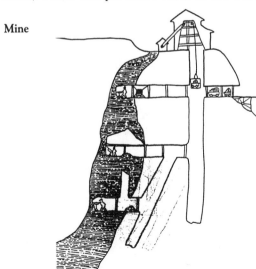

The pavement ends in **Eureka,** 8.7 miles, where you can see remnants of the gigantic **Sunnyside Mill.** From here the road becomes four-wheel drive, passing various ghost towns such as Animas Forks en route to Lake City.

Back in Silverton, **rent a horse, jeep, or mountain bike** to explore the gorgeous countryside. Or take a hike into the **Weminuche Wilderness,** the largest wilderness area in Colorado. If it's winter, sledding, cross-country skiing, ice skating and snowmobiling are popular pastimes. The **Silverton Chamber of Commerce,** south of downtown on Highway 110, has maps and more information on the area.

DID YOU KNOW?

—Silverton is the oldest continuously inhabited community in southwestern Colorado.

—The Hub Saloon was the first floor bar in Silverton (1883). The words to the song "There'll Be a Hot Time in the Old Town Tonight" were written here (although the town of Cripple Creek, Colorado claims the same distinction).

—A miner sometimes used his scoop shovel as a sled. When it snowed, he would sit on the scoop and hold the shovel handle between his legs, streaking down the mountains to town.

—Old Blair Street has been used as a setting for many movies. Some of these include "Across the Wide Missouri," "Night Passage," and "Around the World in Eighty Days."

—Burros used by miners were also called Rocky Mountain Canaries.

The Million Dollar Highway from Silverton to Ouray

The 24 mile stretch of US 550 from Silverton to Ouray is one of the most spectacular drives in Colorado, the **Million Dollar Highway.** Hanging like a shelf from the sheer walls of the narrow Uncompahgre Canyon, the road was constructed in the 1920's.

The highway follows much of the original bed of the toll road between Silverton and Ouray, hacked out of the mountainside in 1881 by Otto Mears. In those days, the road was traveled only by the brave, with a roadbed grade described by a local newspaper as "four parts vertical and one part perpendicular."

As you leave Silverton, the road parallels the rich redness of **South Mineral Creek** for a few miles. Look for the numerous old mines hugging the faces of steep rocky cliffs.

On the other side of Red Mountain Pass, 11,018 feet, is the Idarado Mine, at one time one of Colorado's leading copper producers. Almost 350 miles of underground tunnels connected this mine and others in the area, extending all the way to Telluride. Ironton Park, a grassy valley where the stream runs orange through the marshy meadow, was once the site of the thriving mining camp of Ironton.

In a few more miles the road becomes a widened ledge, originally blasted out of the vertical side of the mountain by Mears. He called this part of his road the "Rainbow in the Sky Highway," with a pot of gold at both ends of the rainbow. The original 21% grade has been diminished to 6% by modern highway engineering, and the ledges that were once only slightly wider than a stagecoach have been widened. The corkscrew turns remain.

Two miles before the town of Ouray is roadside parking to view **Bear Creek Falls,** plummeting 227 feet into the canyon below. This is where Mears had his toll booth. The charge was $5 for a stagecoach and horses, $2 for horse and rider.

Ouray
Zip Code 81427   Area Code 303

"The Switzerland of America," as the town is nicknamed, snuggles in an astonishingly beautiful alpine valley surrounded by a 13,000 foot, multicolored amphitheater of rock.

In spring these red, grey and orange mountains cascade with waterfalls flowing from high country snowfields.

Before the white man came, elk, deer, and Rocky Mountain sheep roamed freely throughout this lush mountain valley. But when silver was discovered in the surrounding mountains in 1875, the pristine land sprouted the rough and tumble mining town of Ouray. Today, this small town of about 800 exudes a pleasant warmth and ambience mixed with the character of the Old West.

THINGS TO DO

In downtown Ouray is the **Old Opera House,** 5th Avenue and Main Street. Stop by at 8:30 pm for the nightly showing of "The Odyssey," an excellent slide show about the area using five screens, 15 projectors, and the music of Aaron Copeland to create a dramatic effect.

For the kids to learn more about the mining and history of the region, visit the **Ouray County Historical Museum** in the old St. Joseph's Hospital, built 1887. The museum contains period rooms, such as an assayer's office, children's room, and doctor's office. It also contains collections of antique guns, mineral specimens, Ute Indian artifacts, and old hospital equipment, including what the curator claims is the greatest bedpan collection in the world. The museum also offers evening lectures in the summer.

Ouray County Historical Museum, corner of Fifth Street and Sixth Avenue, is open in summer, 9:00 am–5:00 pm daily.

If the kids want to be entertained, send them to **Chipeta Enterprises.** This movie theater, ice cream parlor, electronic game room, and gift shop is next door to the post office on Main Street.

At the southwest end of town is **Box Canyon,** a gorge 221 feet high and only 20 feet wide. Take the short hike into the rocky crevice that ends at the foot of roaring Box Canyon Falls, where the deafening boom and the spray in your face will convince you of the tremendous power of water. A longer, more strenuous walk leads to the top.

Abandoned mill

The trail begins across the bridge at the south end of First Street, or off US 550 south of town. Turn at the sign for Box Canyon Falls, then left across the bridge. The right fork of the road leads to Box Canyon Falls Park, where there are rest rooms, picnic tables and parking.

Box Canyon Falls is open from mid-May to mid-October. Admission is $1.25 per adult and $.75 for children.

The left fork of the road (the sign reads Yankee Boy Basin) takes you to the **Camp Bird Mine** five miles away, the mine that saved Ouray from oblivion after the silver crash. Story has it that Thomas Walsh, the flamboyant Irish carpenter who discovered gold there in 1886, named it after the large Rocky Mountain jays that stole his lunch one day while he was prospecting. Before he sold it, the Camp Bird Mine was earning for Walsh between $3,000,000 and $4,000,000 a year. Inquire locally about the condition of the rough dirt road.

The children can take a guided tour of a real mine at the **Bachelor-Syracuse Mine,** a silver and gold mine in operation since 1884. The mine train will take you over 3,300 feet into the side of Gold Hill. You can also pan for gold, eat at the outdoor cafe, or walk the nature trail. Take US 550 one mile north of town, then turn right onto County Road 14 and travel one mile to the mine.

The mine is open daily, late May through mid-September from 10:00 am to 4:00 pm; from mid-June through August from 9:00 am to 5:00 pm. Tours are hourly, and reservations are recommended. Write PO Drawer 380W, Ouray, telephone 325-4500.

A hike will take you to **Lower Cascade Falls,** on the northeast end of town. The trail begins at the upper east end of 8th Avenue. This ½ mile steep, but short, trail climbs over and around the rocks to the bottom of the falls.

For other hiking trails, contact the **Visitor Information Center** in the park on the north end of town, 325-4746. The park also has playground equipment, a railroad caboose, tennis courts, a jogging track, goldfish pond and picnic tables.

But the best thing in the park is the **Radium Springs Swimming Pool,** a huge mineral hot springs pool 250 feet long by 150 feet wide. If you are used to smelly hot springs, this one will be a pleasant surprise. The 156-degree water is odorless and cooled to a comfortable temperature of between 85 and 95 degrees.

The pool is open daily in the summer and several days a week in the winter. Admission is $3.75 per adult, $3.25 ages 13-17, and $2.50 ages 5-12. Call 325-4638 for hours.

Several of the motels also have hot springs pools for use by their guests. One of the oldest is **Wiesbaden Hot Springs Spa and Lodgings,** with subterranean natural grottoes filled with hot springs water. When the spa was built in 1879, it was known to the miners as "Mother Buchanan's Bath House." Today, lodging has been added, as well as an outdoor hot spring pool and numerous testimonials from past patrons who have enjoyed the healing waters.

Wiesbaden Hot Springs Spa and Lodgings, PO Box 349, corner of Sixth Avenue and Fifth Street, 325-4347. Lodging is moderately priced, but if you don't want to spend the night, you can bathe in the hot springs for $9.

In addition to several other motels in town, you can also stay at the Amphitheater Campground at the south end of town.

If your kids are adventurous, take a **pack or jeep trip** across the glacial terrain and rocky canyons to visit ghost towns. Several places in town offer vehicle rentals and guided tours. Ask at the Visitor Center for a listing.

For a taste of the West, try the **Bar C** chuckwagon supper, with western entertainment by the Bar C Wranglers.

Bar C, located 4½ miles north of Ouray just off US 550, is open daily in the summer. For reservations call 325-4423.

DID YOU KNOW?

—The first church services in town were held in the unfinished saloon. The unwashed congregation sat on boxes of liquor and beer kegs.

—The water for Radium Springs Swimming Pool is piped from Box Canyon.

—The town was named in honor of Ouray, Chief of the Ute Indians, who used this valley as a hunting ground and considered the hot springs magical healing places.

—The Camp Bird Mine is the second-richest gold property in Colorado.

—Tom Walsh bought the Hope Diamond for his daughter, Evalyn Walsh McClean. You can read more about their story in her book *Father Struck It Rich.*

Ouray to Telluride

Leaving Ouray, continue on US 550 to the town of Portland. Left of the river is the horse thief trail used by outlaws in the early mining days to drive stolen horses to Utah and bring stolen cattle back (you can see the other end of the trail near Moab, Utah).

Ten miles from Ouray at Ridgway turn west onto State 62

through the magnificent Uncompahgre Mountains. Several miles past the town of Placerville, turn southeast on State 145 to visit the town of Telluride, three miles from the highway on a spur road. Although a straight line between Ouray and Telluride is only six miles, the road distance is closer to 50.

Telluride
Zip Code 81435   Area Code 303

Telluride is cupped at the headwaters of the San Miguel River, where it breathes in remote stillness in a beautiful hanging valley over a mile and a half high. Bordering the town on three sides are precipitous granite walls rising to 14,000-foot peaks. In the past, many residents lost their lives in this box canyon, where the annual 300 inches of snow sometimes crashes down in spring avalanches.

In 1889 the San Miguel County Bank in Telluride was the target for the first bank robbery by Butch Cassidy and his "Wild Bunch." They escaped with around $30,000. Obviously encouraged by success, Butch Cassidy went on to become one of the West's most notorious outlaws.

When the promise of silver beckoned to Telluride in 1878, the prospector followed. Like the other silver cities in the San Juans, the town almost died in 1893 when the Sherman Silver Purchase Act was repealed and the price of silver dropped from $1.29 to $.50 an ounce. The town rallied with the discovery of gold, then languished again.

Today, the hint of boom is again in the air, and this picturesque town with antique street lights offers history, nostalgia, outdoor adventure, spectacular scenery and an array of exciting festivals throughout the summer.

THINGS TO DO
Downtown next to the courthouse is **Galloping Goose #4**, a train engine built in the 1930's by the Rio Grande Southern Railroad. This is one of eight such contraptions made from Cadillac or Pierce Arrow bodies with old truck beds. They

once chugged their perilous way from Ridgway to Durango, wobbling, stinking of gasoline fumes, and puffing clouds of oily smoke.

The scenery wasn't the only part of the ride that was breathtaking. The track was laid on a narrow shelf hundreds of feet above deep gorges that were crossed and recrossed on shaky wooden trestles of loops and horseshoe curves. Most passengers agreed with the stationmaster, who greeted them with "To Hell you ride."

In front of the **Sheridan Hotel,** rivaling the Brown Palace when it was built in 1895, William Jennings Bryan made his famous "Cross of Gold" speech to an enthusiastic audience, urging the United States to maintain the silver standard. In modern times, hang gliders have landed here after tempting fate with a jump from the 12,785-foot **Ajax Mountain** in the east. The historic hotel has been refurbished and is a comfortable place to stay.

For reservations, contact The New Sheridan Hotel, PO Box 980, 231 West Colorado, 728-4351. Moderate.

From the hotel, look to the east for **Bridal Veil Falls,** a breathtaking cascade that is Colorado's highest waterfall. At the top of the falls are remnants of a hydroelectric power plant for the Smuggler-Union Mine. In the distance north of town you can see **Ingram Falls** plummeting several hundred feet down Ingram Mountain.

The **San Miguel Historical Museum** has a collection of pioneer and mining memorabilia. Built in 1895, the three-story stone building was once a miners' hospital.

Currently, the museum is open only during summers (10:00 am to 5:00 pm daily), with plans to open on selected weekends in winter. The museum is located north of Fir Street, telephone 728-3344. Admission is $3 for adults, children 12 and under are free.

Fun places for children include **Underdawg,** 121 W. Colorado Avenue, a hamburger and ice cream parlor with video games, and **Teen Center,** Columbia and Townsend, which conducts special programs once a week that are open to visitors.

Telluride Town Park, two blocks east of town near the San Miguel River, has limited public camping, an outdoor heated pool, playground, and kid's trout pond.

In the winter, **Telluride Ski Area** offers some of the most challenging ski runs in the state. In the summer, board the chairlift a few blocks south of Main Street for a ride to a great view. Cost is $5 for adults, $3 ages 7-12, 6 and under free.

You can also take a hike in the surrounding mountains. A word of caution: Keep children away from abandoned mines and mine shafts. Poisonous gas, rotting wood, and water-filled tunnels make them extremely dangerous to explore!

One of the most popular trails is the **Bear Creek Canyon Trail,** beginning at the end of South Pine Street and leading to Bear Creek Falls two miles out of town. The **Wasatch Trail** leaves the Bear Creek Trail to the right just before the falls and passes many abandoned mining sites. East of town is a trail to the base of **Bridal Veil Falls.**

For more information and a map of hiking trails, contact the **Telluride Chamber Resort Association,** which also serves as the Chamber of Commerce. The Association can also tell you about the string of summer weekend festivals, beginning in May and lasting through early October. Two of the most popular are the Bluegrass Festival in June and the Jazz Festival in July. They also have information about camping, jeep tours, gold panning trips, hot air balloon flights, and horseback rides.

DID YOU KNOW?

—The town of Telluride was originally called Columbia, but a California mining town had the same name. After numerous letters were misdirected, the U.S. Post Office asked the town to change its name.

—Otto Mears was the engineer who built the railroad to town. Mears rode the first train from Telluride to Durango down the part of the route called the Ophir Loop and declared he would never ride it again. He ordered a horse and wagon to take him back to Telluride!

—Telluride has been the home of several colorful characters. Among them are Nikola Tesla and L. L. Nunn, the first people to generate electricity using alternating current; Dr. George G. Balderston, the first (and possibly only) person to take out his own appendix; and trend-watcher John Naisbitt, author of the book *Megatrends*.

—Thanks to L. L. Nunn, by 1894 most of the mines in Telluride were lighted by electricity.

—During the spring of 1914 a downpour swept mud and rocks through the town, depositing them halfway to the ceiling in the Sheridan Hotel.

—J. B. Ingram became owner of the Smuggler Mine, one of the most profitable in town, in a novel way. He discovered that two adjoining mines, the Sheridan and Union, had each claimed about 500 feet more than legally allowed, so he staked the extra footage for his own.

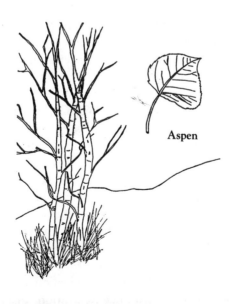

Aspen

Telluride to Durango

Return to State 145 and turn south through green forestland thick with groves of aspen, called "quakies" by the cowboys because of the way their leaves move in the wind. The land is in its prime in fall, when the aspen leaves turn brilliant yellow and gold.

Take a picture at **Trout Lake,** the base of an ancient caldera circled by snowy peaks. This private lake is open for fishing and boating.

At the crest of the San Miguel Mountains is **Lizard Head Pass,** 10,250 feet. **Lizard Head Peak,** the remains of an ancient volcano, is a grotesquely-shaped rock formation resembling a giant reptilian god.

Near the highway, in the town of **Dolores,** is a monument marker detailing the Dominguez-Escalante expedition that passed through here in 1776. You can also see **Galloping Goose #5** with a hot 1928 Pierce Arrow engine, sibling to Goose #4 in Telluride.

Take the kids to watch the **Village Blacksmith,** one of the few remaining working blacksmiths in the country, on the north side of Highway 115 between 11th and 14th streets. **Old West Antiques,** 315 Central, has an interesting small museum of old printing equipment and historical items.

For a ranch-style meal and western show, try **Dolores River Line Camp** outside of town. Call 303/882-4158 for reservations.

South of Dolores is **McPhee Reservoir,** the second largest in Colorado, stretching 13 miles along the Dolores River. This is a popular place for water sports such as boating (including sailboating and houseboating) and water skiing. In addition, fishing in this "two-story" lake is excellent, both for cold water and warm water fish. See if you can catch one of the eight to ten-pound rainbow trout living here. For the energetic, try jet skiing and sailboarding. For the more sedate, canoe in the "wakeless zones."

The area has two full service recreation complexes and fisherman access points. **McPhee Recreation Area** on the west side is the largest complex. To reach the area, take State 184 past the **Anasazi Heritage Center** (see Chapter VII) to the access road, then two miles east. **House Creek Recreation Area,** on the east shore of the reservoir, is accessed 15 miles north of Dolores on Norwood Road.

Southwest of Dolores turn left on State 184 to the town of **Mancos,** the first town in Montezuma County. Outside of Mancos is a lumber mill where most of the matchsticks in the United States are split from aspen wood.

If you want to stay in the area, the **Lake Mancos Ranch** is a guest ranch with separate children's program and a casual atmosphere. Write 42688A CR-N, Mancos 81328, or call 303/533-7900.

Turn west on US 160 outside of Mancos seven miles to Mesa Verde National Park (see Chapter VII). Or turn east to return to Durango.

3. EAST FROM DURANGO TO THE GREAT SAND DUNES

To continue your journey through southern Colorado, take US 160 east from Durango. State 172 branches southeast through the **Southern Ute Indian Reservation** (see Chapter VII).

Near the junction of US 160 and State 151 is **Chimney Rock,** two freestanding pinnacles of rock. For part of the time between AD 925 and 1125, Indians of the Chaco culture lived here. They left behind a great kiva and a pueblo on top of the mesa.

Living 1000 feet above the valley floor wasn't easy, and there must have been compelling reasons they chose this place. The masons who left palm and fingerprints in the clay fragments used tons of rock and soil for building, all of which had to be carried to the top of the mesa. Water was scarce and was probably transported daily from the river valley below, a round trip of over a mile. Soil on top of the mesa was poor, so part of the population no doubt lived in temporary camps on the valley floor, farming with digging sticks and stone hoes. Some archaeologists think part of the food supply grown here was periodically shipped to Chaco Canyon.

There are many theories about Chimney Rock and its inhabitants. Some believe the people who lived in the high mesa ruins were an elite class supported by a working class in the valley. Some claim the Indians chose the mesa as their home because the elevation aided in defense or in sending messages to Chaco Canyon. Others believe the two rock pinnacles are a shrine to the Twin War Gods. Strong evidence also points to the use of Chimney Rock as an astronomical observatory.

Why did the people move here? Why did they leave? What was life like in this isolated, dramatic place? We may never know the answers, but you and the kids can visit the ruins and formulate your own theories.

A free daily (weather permitting) tour begins 9:00 am weekdays, June through mid-September, and is led by the U.S. Forest Service. Call 303/264-2268 for more details.

On Friday, Saturday, Sunday and Monday during the summer, tours are offered with Indian guides from Lake Capote Park at 10:00 am. Daily tours at 6:00 pm are also available. Adults are $2, children under 12 are free. Reservations are required. Contact Chimney Rock Archaeological Tours, PO Box 81, Chimney Rock, CO 81127, 303/731-5256.

Lake Capote is a spring-fed lake well-stocked with trout. Since it is on the Southern Ute Reservation, you will need a tribal fishing permit, $5 per day, rather than a Colorado fishing license. Permits can be purchased at the Lake Capote store, where you can also rent fishing gear, rowboats and campsites. In the evening at the campground, Southern Utes give cultural demonstrations, including flute-playing, dancing and storytelling.

Pagosa Springs
Zip Code 81147   Area Code 303

Pagosa Springs, at the base of Wolf Creek Pass, is renowned for the mineral springs it uses to heat the town courthouse and schools. The Indians called the water "Pagosah," which means healing waters. According to legend, the hot springs appeared one night in answer to prayers for a cure to a terrible plague that afflicted them.

For years after, the Utes and Navajos fought over the possession of this powerful medicine. One day they decided to settle the matter with a fight to the death by champions. The Utes appointed an Indian agent named Pfeiffer as their representative. At the onset of the fight, Pfeiffer hurled his bowie knife at his Navajo foe, killing him instantly and winning the hot springs for the Utes.

THINGS TO DO
You can see the **original hot spring** near downtown. It is just south of the Pagosa Spring Inn Motel over the bridge on 4th Street.

More exciting might be a dip in a pool fed by the legendary hot springs. **The Spa Motel and Pool,** at the corner of San Juan Street and Light Plant Road, is a resort with men's and women's bathhouses, indoor mineral pools, and an outdoor public swimming pool. Admission to the pool is $3.00 for adults, $2.25 for ages 13-18, $1.50 for ages 5-12. Several other motels in the area have spring-fed hot tubs.

Let the kids get rid of excess energy at the playground in **Town Park** (just south of the stoplight) while you listen to the San Juan River flow by. On summer evenings, enjoy a picnic and free entertainment.

The **Pagosa Springs Area Chamber of Commerce** is in a log cottage in the park. In addition to information about the area and a listing of special events, the chamber offers nature walks and tours conducted by residents.

The **San Juan Basin Historical Society Museum** has pioneer memorabilia and Indian artifacts from the late 1800's. Period rooms include a dentist's office, general store, schoolroom, and barber shop. The museum is three blocks east of the stoplight on US 160.

The museum, telephone 264-4424, is open June through August, Monday through Saturday, 10:00 am–5:00 pm. Admission is $1 for adults and $.50 for children.

The most lavish—and expensive—place to stay in town is the **Fairfield Pagosa Resort,** three miles west of town on US Highway 160. The resort has lodging (including condominium rentals), two restaurants, a golf course (which is open for cross country skiing in the winter), a health spa and indoor pool, tennis courts, an equestrian center, six lakes, aerial tours, a championship miniature golf course, and a children's day camp.

Even if you don't stay there, let the kids climb to the top of the swaying tower in front of the lodge and look through the telescope to the surrounding mountains. Or walk inside the tiny Six Mile Ranch cabin and try to imagine living there with your whole family.

For reservations, contact Fairfield Pagosa Resort, PO Box 4040, 731-4141 or 800/523-7704.

Also west of town is **Astraddle a Saddle,** which offers barbecue hayrides and horse-drawn sled rides, pulled by Belgians, Clydesdales and draft mules. Write PO Box 1216, telephone 731-5076, for information.

Take US Highway 160 east of town and turn south on US 84. **Echo Lake State Park,** about five miles from town, is a small lake for trout and bass fishing. Nearby is a sawmill where the kids can watch the journey of a log becoming a board.

Be sure to stop at **Rocky Mountain Wildlife Park** for kids to see the indigenous animals of the area. Wolves, elk, coyote, black bear, mountain lion, and others are exhibited in natural settings to help you forget this is a zoo.

Rocky Mountain Wildlife Park, Rt. 2 Box 9A, Pagosa Springs, CO, 264-4515. Hours: 10:00 am to 6:00 pm daily.

Admission is $4 for adults, $2 for children under 12.

DID YOU KNOW?

—The Pagosa Spring is the largest and hottest known hot spring in the world, with 1,000,000 gallons of 160-degree water bubbling up daily.

—In the late 19th and early 20th century, many Americans believed mineral hot springs could cure a wide range of ailments, including arthritis, heart disease, kidney stones, and obesity.

—Theodore Roosevelt, Thomas Edison, and Sarah Bernhardt were some of the famous health-seekers that came to Colorado to bathe in the hot springs.

From Pagosa Springs to the Great Sand Dunes

Sixteen miles northeast of Pagosa Springs on US 160 is the parking area for **Treasure Falls.** A short walk takes you to the foot of this beautiful 100-foot waterfall where legend says a treasure in gold bars is buried.

Wolf Creek Pass, elevation 10,850 feet, crosses the Continental Divide, which means water going west from here ends up in the Pacific Ocean and water going east heads for the Atlantic Ocean. Wolf Creek Pass Ski Area gets more snow (an average of 465 inches a year) than any other ski area in Colorado.

At the top of the pass, take the dirt road left to the scenic viewpoint, **Lobo Overlook.** The view over the top of the Rockies extends in all directions, and if you bring your picnic, you can eat lunch with the clouds. Keep the children's jackets handy. It's often chilly at this elevation.

From the mountain peaks you descend into the **San Luis Valley,** a high park surrounded on all sides by mountains. On most days it's easy to see why the Ute Indians who lived here called themselves "the Blue Sky People." Chamber of commerce brochures still use the term "sun drenched."

The first permanent settlers were Spanish, and since the rim of mountain ranges surrounding the valley formed a natural barrier to the outside, many early traditions are still observed. Until recently, the people spoke a dialect similar to that of the Conquistadors, and Spanish influence is easily seen in the adobe churches and buildings, the pink and turquoise homes, and the flocks of sheep.

In Monte Vista, turn south five miles on State 15 to the **Alamosa-Monte Vista Wildlife Refuge,** the 13,000-acre home or flyway for a variety of birds and other wildlife. The self-guiding Avocet Trail is a loop drive which takes you past habitats of many marsh birds.

In early spring and fall, thousands of sandhill cranes descend on the refuge in their migratory journey. Sometimes a few whooping cranes straggle along with them. An innovative program to help this endangered species involves a foster parent program between the sandhills and the young whoopers.

For more information, write Refuge manager, Alamosa-Monte Vista National Wildlife Refuge, PO Box 1148, Alamosa, 81101, 719/589-4021.

Young railroad buffs may enjoy a stop at the **Alamosa Train Shop** to see the model railroad operating layout in Alamosa. The shop, 2051 Main Street, 714/589-4643, is open most days except Sunday, 10:00 am to 1:00 pm and 2:00 pm to 5:00 pm.

Take the kids to **Splashland,** a swimming pool filled from a natural hot springs in the area. There is also a toddler wading pool, and you can rent swimsuits and towels. It is one mile north of town on State 17, telephone 589-6307.

Splashland is open Thursday through Tuesday, 10:00 am to 6:30 pm (Sunday from 12 noon to 6:00 pm). Cost is $3 per adult, $2.50 for ages 13-18, $2 for ages 6-12, children under 6 free.

For more information on the area, visit the Chamber of Commerce in the old railroad depot in the park. Out front is a narrow gauge engine and car.

From Alamosa, US 285 takes you to New Mexico, passing through Antonito, Colorado, one end of the line for the Cumbres-Toltec Scenic Railroad (see Chapter IX).

Continue on US 160 east of Alamosa to the junction with State 150. Turn north for 16 miles to the Great Sand Dunes.

Great Sand Dunes National Monument

Nature's sandbox is a mysterious and wonderful place. "Singing Sands," the Indians called it, and you can still hear strange sounds when the wind blows. Colors here can be startling, especially when sunrise or sunset changes the dunes from pink to red to orange. And with the relentless shifting of the sand, a ghost forest of skeletal trees appears and disappears.

The dunes were formed by water and wind. For thousands of years streams carried sand, silt and gravel into the San Luis Valley and deposited it. Because little vegetation grows to hold down the sandy soil in this arid place, the sweeping wind picks it up, skipping and rolling the grains of sand toward the barrier of the Sangre de Cristo Mountains.

When it gets there, the only way to go is up, over the mountains. As the wind climbs this steep wall, it loses velocity and drops all but the lightest of its load. Over thousands of years, the wind has dropped trillions of tons of sand, piling the dunes over 700 feet high.

Stories tell of a herd of strange horses living deep in the 150 square mile dune field, their webbed feet perfectly adapted to running over the sand. More frightening tales tell of whole wagon trains disappearing under the sand without a trace.

THINGS TO DO

If you are a child or young-at-heart, this is a place to labor to the top of a sand mountain and jump as far as you can, or to bury something small you don't care about and try to find it again. It's a place to try to roll down a dune in a straight line; to try to leave a perfect footprint; to look for patterns of shadows, animal tracks, and traces of wind; to stick your hand in the sand and have a friend try to find it to shake; to pretend you're exploring a strange new land or lost, crawling across the barren waste mumbling "water."

It is not a place to come in the heat of the day, when the temperature of the sand can reach above 140 degrees Fahrenheit, or in a windstorm when abrasive grains are sent scouring like sandpaper. Nor is it a place to wander off by yourself. Keep landmarks and your children in sight, be sure to wear shoes, get off the dunes when storms approach, and expect to need a shower when you leave. See Chapter XIII for more activities.

The **Visitor Center** has information and exhibits, as well as the schedule of ranger programs. Ask for the leaflet to help you identify animal tracks in the sand and about the Junior Ranger program. The center is open 8:00 am to 8:00 pm from Memorial Day to Labor Day, 8:00 am to 5:00 pm during the winter.

A general store sells provisions and gasoline, but the only accommodations in the area are campsites in **Pinyon Flats Campground,** which operates April through October. Since no reservations are taken for campsites, it is wise to arrive early. Cost is $6 per night.

Superintendent, Great Sand Dunes National Monument, Mosca, CO 81146, 719/378-2312. Admission is $3 per vehicle.

DID YOU KNOW?

—There are only five different plants that grow in the Great Sand Dunes.
—Two types of insects that live here are found nowhere else in the world.
—One of the insects here is called the giant sand treader camel cricket. His tracks are often seen on the dunes.
—"Petrified lightning," called fulgurites, are formed when a lightning bolt hits sand and melts it into glass. One of the largest of these rare silica cylinders ever found was nearly nine feet long.
—The Great Sand Dunes are the highest dunes in the United States.

—The San Luis Valley has the earliest European settlements in Colorado.

—A higher water table once made the San Luis Valley Colorado's breadbasket.

4. FORT GARLAND TO NORTHERN NEW MEXICO

Twenty-five miles east of Alamosa on US 160 is **Fort Garland,** an adobe military outpost established in 1858 to protect the settlers of the San Luis Valley from the Ute Indians. The fort is now a historical museum, complete with a re-creation of the headquarters of one-time fort commander Kit Carson. Also on display is folk art of Hispanic life in the valley.

For more information or for off-season tours, contact Fort Garland, PO Box 368, 81133, 719/379-3512. Summer Hours: Monday through Saturday, 10:00 am–5:00 pm, and Sunday, 1:00 pm–5:00 pm. Admission is $2 for adults, $1 for children 6-16, children under 6 are free.

From Ft. Garland, take State 159 south to Taos, New Mexico. In San Luis, the oldest town in Colorado, stop at the **San Luis Cultural Center** to see their pioneer and Indian artifacts, including collections of home remedies, butterflies, barbed wire, and comic books.

San Luis Cultural Center is open in summer, weekdays 8:00 am–4:30 pm, weekends 11:00 am–4:00 pm. Admission is $1 for adults, $.50 for ages 6-12.

Just north of Questa, New Mexico, turn west on State Road 378 towards Cerro. The visitor center for the **Rio Grande Wild and Scenic River Recreation Area** is eight miles.

This BLM recreation area contains 40 miles of the Rio Grande, a roaring white water of a river that has cut its way through the land, ending up at the bottom of a 650 foot chasm. You and the kids can camp, fish, hike, picnic and float on the wild river.

The Visitor Center has displays, a video, maps, and wildlife and geological information. It is also the best place in the area to find environmental education publications. Rangers conduct a two-mile guided nature hike on Saturday and Sunday at 10:00 am and an evening campfire program on Saturday in the amphitheater.

For more information, contact the Bureau of Land Management, PO Box 1045, 224 Montevideo Plaza Building, Taos, NM 87571, 505/758-8851. Camping is $6 a night. There is no charge for day-use.

Return to State 3 and travel south toward Taos. About 15 miles before town, a marked gravel road on the left travels six miles to the **D. H. Lawrence Ranch and Shrine,** where the ashes of this famous author rest in a shrine built by his wife, Frieda. The shrine is open year-round; admission is free.

State Highway 3 continues to Taos.

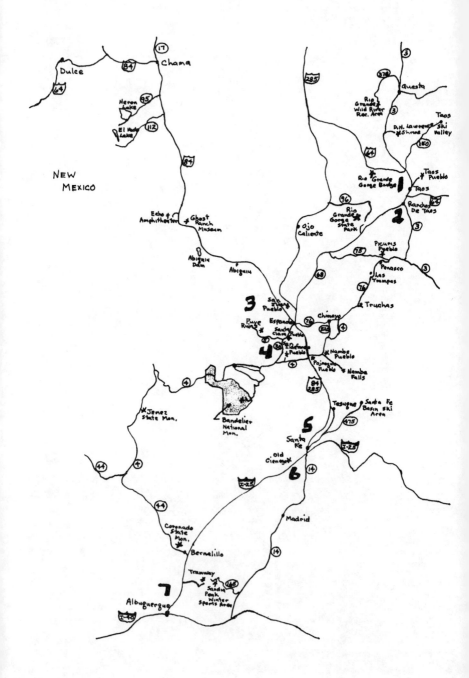

9

A THREE-CULTURE SALAD: New Mexico

New Mexico is an enchanted land, with mountains, high desert mesas and wilderness of enduring beauty. There is plenty of the outdoors to explore here, but there is also a unique culture you won't find anywhere else in the world, an eclectic blending of old and new, and of Hispanic, Indian and Anglo.

Like a salad, these three peoples have mixed, while each retained its individuality. Rural Hispanic Catholics seek their miracles in chapels of red adobe, while in kivas Native Americans beat the ancient rhythms of the land. Albuquerque, a national leader in high tech, bustles with Anglo pride. Quaint Spanish colonial Taos, its narrow, winding streets clogged with 20th-century automobiles, is bordered by 900-year-old Taos Pueblo, where some residents continue to live without electricity and indoor plumbing.

Ancestors of the Pueblo Indians were the first permanent inhabitants in the area. A scattered group of people living in self-sufficient adobe villages, they worshiped the gods of their ancestors and tilled their fields in relative peace.

Then came the conquerors, carrying the banner of Spain. They came seeking adventure and souls to convert, but more than that, they came for gold. Francisco Vasquez de Coronado was the first, in 1540, searching for the legendary Seven Cities of Cibola. He led a clanking, clamorous procession of live-stock herds, a thousand friendly Indians recruited from Mexico, dozens of foot soldiers and over 250 horsemen. All he found were cities of mud, so he moved on.

The first Spanish came to stay in 1598 with Don Juan de Oñate, almost 10 years before the English founded Virginia. They did not come as guests. Rather, they sought to proclaim their religious and cultural dominion.

Priests were among these first colonists, and with sanctimonious fervor, they attacked the pagan natives. Sacred kivas were destroyed and religious leaders executed. The situation was exacerbated by the discovery that the Indians were a cheap source of human labor. By the thousands, they were enslaved and forced to work in the mines, fields, and missions, where cruelty and brutality were common.

After 80 years, the Indians, who outnumbered the Spanish ten to one, fought back. Under the leadership of a man named Popé, and in an unprecedented feat of Pueblo Indian organization and unity, the cry of freedom was heard in every village on August 10, 1680. Runners were sent to each with a knotted cord marking the date for the bloody rebellion to begin.

Within days, the land was purged and every Spaniard either killed or driven south towards Mexico. The churches were sacked and burned, and the mines sealed, their treasures hidden forever.

Twelve years after the Great Pueblo Revolt, the Spanish, under Don Diego de Vargas, returned. Before long, life was much as it had been before the rebellion. Many protested the inhumane treatment of the Indians, but even the demands of King Carlos of Spain to abolish the slavery were ignored.

The trickle of settlers widened, and by 1695, 1500 settlers had immigrated. They came on El Camino Real, the Royal Highway, a 1500 mile link between Santa Fe and Mexico City.

Supplies, colonists, and soldiers streamed north on this royal road; the gold, silver, and turquoise of the new colony streamed south, and was then loaded on ships bound for the Royal Vault in Seville, Spain.

The hemorrhaging of wealth from the New World was staggering. Between the mid-1500's and 1820, the Americas (including Mexico) lost approximately $20 billion, more wealth than the rest of the world possessed at that time.

Meanwhile, the settlers kept coming—adventurers, noblemen, convicts, religious zealots, and humble farmers, all seeking a new life. Some were courageous pioneers, others greedy opportunists.

The Spanish reigned until 1810, when the Mexican and Indian residents revolted. In 1846 the Mexicans were displaced by the Americans when General Stephen W. Kearny and the Army of the West sauntered into Santa Fe and, without a single shot being fired, declared the territory part of the United States.

Around the turn of the century, northern New Mexico saw a new influx of settlers: the artists. They were attracted by the air of Native American mystery, the unique artistic tradition of the Spanish settlements, and the scenery washed in vibrant colors and bathed in brilliant light, a light that changes with the time and seasons to create a steady stream of new images.

Today, you can spend thousands of dollars for their works of art. You can also visit an Indian pueblo, where life goes on much as it has for the past millennium; explore a museum commemorating the nuclear bomb; watch the Christian religion honored in dances taught to Native Americans by the Spanish; or, like the artists that still come here by the hundreds, seek creative inspiration and try to capture the ever-changing, ever-constant face of the land and life of New Mexico in a moment of time.

DID YOU KNOW?

—Ristras, often seen hanging from porches in New Mexico,

are strings of vegetables, either onions, garlics or chilies.
—Chilies, high in Vitamin C, have been used as a digestive aid, herbal medicine, food preservative, wound disinfectant, and to cure hangovers.
—Many of the early Spanish settlers in New Mexico were Jews fleeing the Spanish Inquisition.

Visiting the Nineteen Indian Pueblos

Visiting the Indian pueblos is like stepping into the past. Although the pueblos may be open to visitors, there are certain rules to keep in mind. People's homes and kivas are off-limits, as are cemeteries. Barricades or signs will usually inform you of restricted areas. Most pueblos also have photography restrictions, and alcoholic beverages are forbidden. For complete information, contact the Governor's offices. Addresses are listed in Appendix B.

If your timing is right, you can attend one of the public dances. Many have been performed for hundreds of years, and serve as celebrations of thanksgiving or supplication. As with all earth-based rituals, the dates are geared to the seasons and may change at a moment's notice. Others, like the Moorish Matachina dances at Christmas, were taught to the Indians by Spanish missionaries, and dates are more predictable. The dates of the feast days also never vary. They follow the Roman Catholic calendar and honor the individual patron saint of each pueblo.

If you do attend a public dance, remember these are religious as well as social occasions. Do not talk or applaud during the ceremonies or walk across the dance plaza. Some pueblos allow photography of the ceremonies with a permit, some under no circumstances.

From Taos to Albuquerque

1. Taos

Horno oven and Pueblo structures

2. From Taos to Santa Fe
3. Española to the Apache Reservation—Heading to The Four Corners
4. Española to Albuquerque
5. Santa Fe
6. From Santa Fe to Albuquerque—The Turquoise Trail
7. Albuquerque

1. TAOS
Zip Code 87571   Area Code 505

The Spanish arrived at the stacked adobe Taos Pueblo in 1540 and established a mission and trade network shortly thereafter. By the early 1800's, the town of Taos had become a headquarters for western frontiersmen and an important branch on the Santa Fe Trail. Kit Carson was one of the early residents, and when he wasn't scouting, trapping, or soldiering, he lived here with his wife and family.

During the Civil War, Southern sympathizers tried to remove the United States flag that flew from the plaza flagpole. Kit Carson and a group of Taoseños took it upon themselves to stop this outrage. Patrolling day and night, they managed to keep the flag aloft 24 hours a day, until it finally wore out.

Ansel Adams said of Taos, "This is the most completely beautiful place I have ever seen." Ernest Blumenschein and Bert Phillips, two artists, would have agreed with him. Almost a hundred years ago, the wagon they were traveling in to Santa Fe broke down nearby. They became enamored with the area and settled here. They were followed by Mabel Dodge Luhan, a wealthy socialite who invited her famous artist and writer friends to visit. Since then, the town has been a mecca for the professional and amateur alike.

Except for traffic-clogged Main Street, Taos remains reminiscent of an earlier time. Winding narrow streets meander past remnants of Spanish colonial times, historic homes and shops. Among them are almost 80 art galleries. Adobe buildings, more horizontal than vertical, cluster around placitas. And in Taos Plaza, the American flag, through a special Act of Congress, still flies 24 hours a day, replaced once a year with a new one.

THINGS TO DO

Downtown Taos is best seen on foot, with your car parked in one of the nearby municipal lots. The town centers around **Taos Plaza,** site of the original 1790's Spanish settlement, although frequent fires have destroyed all buildings older than the 19th century.

Shopping in Taos is a popular pastime. A store the kids might enjoy is Tiovivo, a toy shop one block from the plaza on State Highway 68 (Paseo del Pueblo Sur).

Around the corner from Tiovivo is the **Kit Carson Home and Museum,** bought by Carson in 1843 as a wedding present for his bride, Josefa Jaramillo. The original house, built in 1825, had 12 adobe rooms with 30"-thick walls. The museum is filled with Carson memorabilia and other artifacts from 19th-century Taos and the Old West. (See Chapter XIII for an activity.)

Kit Carson Museum, East Kit Carson Road, 758-3063. Summer hours: 9:00 am–5:00 pm daily. Winter hours: 10:00 am–4:00 pm daily. Admission is $2.50 adults, $1.50 children, under age 6 free. If you plan to visit the other two museums administered by the Kit Carson Foundation—the Ernest L. Blumenschein Home and the Martinez Hacienda—a discount ticket for all three is available.

Nearby is the **Taos Book Store,** telephone 758-3733, where you and the kids can find a wonderful array of books on the Southwest, as well as a fine selection of children's books.

If you missed their booth on the Plaza, continue south a few blocks on Paseo del Pueblo Sur/State 68 to the **Chamber of Commerce.** They have maps, a guided walking tour of the town, and information on Pueblo ceremonies and the numerous festivals.

For information and maps of **outdoor activities** in nearby Carson Forest, call the Taos Ranger District Office, 758-2911.

Two blocks west of Taos Plaza on Ledoux Street is the **Ernest L. Blumenschein Home** (take Ranchitos to Ledoux). Blumenschein was one of the co-founders of the Taos Society of Artists, and his old adobe home is filled with paintings by early Taos artists, Spanish colonial furnishings, and European antiques.

Ernest L. Blumenschein Home, 13 Ledoux Street, 758-0505. Summer Hours: 9:00 am–5:00 pm daily. Winter hours: 10:00 am–4:00 pm daily. Admission is $2.50 adults, $1.50 children, under 6 free. Family rate is $6.00.

Next door is the library and the **Museum of Taos Art.** If the kids are old enough, let them visit the **Children's Library** while you go to the museum, which is dedicated to the art and art history of Taos County from the late 19th century to the present. Storyteller Hour at the library is Saturday, 11:00 am.

The Harwood Foundation Museum of Taos Art, 25 Ledoux Street, PO Box 766, 758-3063. Hours: Monday through Friday, 10:00 am to 5:00 pm, Saturday until 4:00 pm. Suggested donation is $1.

Downtown ½ block west of the Taos Inn is the **Charles Bent Home.** Bent was trader, trapper, mountain man, co-builder of Bent's Fort, and first governor of New Mexico. His tenure as governor lasted less than a year, from 1846 to January of 1847, at which time he was killed during the Indian Pueblo Revolt. The old adobe home has a small museum, with a mishmash of frontier and Bent family artifacts that range from the historical to the bizarre. You can still see the hole in the wall that was carved by family members trying to escape the Indian attack in 1847.

Have the kids look for the skull with the arrowhead, the ostrich egg, doctor's tools, calliope and disks, pre-Civil War leg splint, baby shark, iguana, and dual spigot coffee pot.

Governor Bent House and Museum, Bent Street, 758-2376. Summer hours: 9:00 am–5:00 pm daily. Winter hours: 10:00 am–4:00 pm daily. Admission is $1.00 for adults, $.50 for ages 8-15, under 8 free with adult.

If it's a nice day, stop at the nearby **Apple Tree Shanty** for an award-winning meal under the shade of the apple trees (or in the dining room if you prefer).

If you are an art lover and the kids aren't, let them swim at **Coronado Swimming Pool** on Armory Street while you visit the nearby galleries.

Less than a block north of the Taos Inn on State 68 is **Kit Carson Park and Cemetery.** The lawn and playground make this a refreshing stop for children. The Old Indian Trail, used for years to travel between Taos Pueblo and the Spanish settlement, cuts through the park. Kit Carson and his wife Josefa are buried in the cemetery, as well as other notable early Taoseños.

Just north of the park is the **Nicolai Fechin Home.** Fechin was a painter and wood-carver from Russia, and his Russian country-style home is filled with fine wood carvings.

The home, 227 North Pueblo, is open in summer, Saturday and Sunday, 1:00–5:30 pm, and by appointment, 758-1710. Suggested donation is $3.

You'll want to drive to **La Hacienda de Don Antonio Sever-**

Spanish adobe archway

ino **Martinez,** two miles west of the plaza on Ranchitos Road/
Highway 240. Martinez, a prominent merchant and politi-
cian, lived here with his family between 1804 and 1827. The
sprawling hacienda, with 21 rooms and two courtyards, was
built like a fortress and served as an important trade center.

A visit will give you and the children an interesting glimpse
into life in Spanish colonial New Mexico. During the summer, weaving and blacksmith demonstrations are occasionally
conducted. (See Chapter XIII for an activity.)

*Martinez Hacienda, Highway 240, 758-1000. Summer
hours: 9:00 am–5:00 pm daily. Winter hours: 10:00 am–5:00
pm daily. Admission is $2.50 adult, $1.50 children, and $6.00
for families.*

Be sure to visit **Taos Pueblo,** home of the Taos Indians for
perhaps 900 years. North of Taos Plaza on State 3/US 64
(Paseo del Pueblo Norte), turn right (east) at the Mobil station.
The Pueblo is about two miles from town.

Legend says the Indians were led here by an eagle, which
dropped a feather to indicate the spot where they were to build
their multistoried adobe village. Electricity and indoor
plumbing have still not made their mark at some parts of the
pueblo, and it seems the only change since the turn of the
century has been the year and model of tourists' automobiles.

As the Indians sit and watch, visitors amble from shop to
shop through the dusty plaza. St. Jerome Chapel, built by

Spanish missionaries, stands in quiet contemplation at one end of the plaza, dogs bark, screen doors slam, and the smell of home-baked bread for sale lingers over all. Look for the signs by doorways indicating an artisan has work for sale inside.

Ask at the information center for guided tours, dates of public ceremonial dances and powwows, and crafts demonstrations.

Taos Pueblo is open every day until sundown. Admission is $5 per car, and there is a fee for photography, sketching and painting.

North on State 3/US 64 approximately four miles from Taos Plaza is the **Millicent Rogers Museum.** Just before the blinking light at the junction with State 150 (between the junction and the service station), turn left onto the dirt Museum Road.

This interesting museum has one of the best collections of Native American and Hispanic arts and crafts in the Southwest. Jewelry, textiles, kachinas, paintings, craftsmen's tools from the 17th and 18th centuries, agricultural implements, baskets, and changing exhibits are all included, as well as one of the most important collections of the life work of Maria Martinez, famous potter from San Ildefonso Pueblo. The gift shop has an excellent selection of Native American crafts and Spanish wood carvings.

Millicent Rogers Museum, just off State 3, telephone 758-2462. Hours: open daily, May through October, 9:00 am–5:00 pm, and November through April, Tuesday–Sunday, 10:00 am–4:00 pm. Admission is $3 for adults, $1 for ages 6-16, and $6 for families.

Continue to the junction and bear left (west) on US 64 to the **Rio Grande Gorge Bridge,** a steel arch bridge that offers a distant view of the river 650 feet below. The height of the Washington Monument would easily fit inside, with about 100 feet to spare!

If you turn right on Highway 150 at the junction, you will come to the European-style **Taos Ski Valley,** eighteen miles northeast of town. It is well-known for deep powder and the challenging expert slopes (vertical drops of 2600 feet) that make up just over half of its available runs. The resort has children's programs, ski lessons and childcare available. For ski information, call 776-2291; for lodging information call 800/992-7669, or contact the Taos Chamber of Commerce.

Four miles south of Taos on State Highway 68 is Ranchos de Taos, with art galleries and the **Church of San Francisco de Asis (St. Francis of Assisi),** one of the Southwest's most famous churches. The beauty of its massive four-foot thick walls and sloping buttresses make it one of the most painted and photographed churches in the world.

Inside hangs the mysterious "Shadow of the Cross," a painting first exhibited at the St. Louis World's Fair in 1904. At certain times of day, a haloed Christ appears to be carrying a cross; at other times the cross and halo disappear. The church is open to visitors, 10:00 am–2:00 pm and 1:00–4:00 pm on weekdays. Stop first at the parish office next door for a 15-minute film presentation on the church and painting.

If you want ambience in a place to stay, try the **Taos Inn.** This historic hotel, one block north of the plaza on State 68, is restored with the rustic charm of antiques, fireplaces in the rooms, and southwestern furniture. Local artists, writers and musicians are said to hang out in the hotel library, and Doc Martin's, the hotel restaurant, serves innovative southwestern food.

Taos Inn, 125 Paseo del Pueblo Norte, 505/758-2233 or 800/ TAOS-INN. Moderate to expensive.

If you want to spend the night away from downtown, try the **Sagebrush Inn,** where Georgia O'Keefe once lived and painted. This adobe inn reminds one of a Spanish hacienda, with a pleasant tree-shaded setting, swimming pool, and comfortable atmosphere, although some of the rooms are a bit time-worn.

Sagebrush Inn, PO Box 1566, 758-2254. Moderate to expensive.

DID YOU KNOW?

—In the 1800's, mountain men traveled for miles to the Simeon Turley distillery, ten miles north of town, to stock up on Taos Lightning whiskey.

—Taos Pueblo is the largest occupied multistoried pueblo in the United States.

—When the Spanish conquistadors first saw Taos Pueblo in 1540, they thought it was one of the fabled Seven Cities of Gold.

—Taos has its share of ghosts and strange happenings—consider the Spanish and Indian ghosts of the Navajo Gallery (owned by well-known artist R. C. Gorman) that don't speak English; the sounds of children playing that residents of Ranchitos Road insist they hear; the clip-clop of horse hooves on Bent Street; the apparition of Arthur Manby in his old house, the Stables Art Center; the blue spheres the 17th-century Taos Indians saw floating down the mountainside.

2. FROM TAOS TO SANTA FE

Taking the High Road

The High Road from Taos to Santa Fe will take you to an earlier time of ancient Indian pueblos and Spanish settlers.

From Ranchos de Taos take State Highway 3 south to **Ft. Burgwin Research Center Museum.** Ft. Burgwin, built in the 1850's to protect the main road to Santa Fe from Apache and Comanche raids, is now part of Southern Methodist University.

The research complex has been built on the original foundations, and a museum is to open soon that will cover the prehistory and history of the area, including military exhibits, a nature trail, pit house, and kiva. The pueblo site being excavated here is one of the largest prehistoric sites in the northern Rio Grande Valley.

Fort Burgwin Research Center, PO Box 300, Ranchos de Taos, NM 87557, 505/758-8322.

Turn right (west) at State 75, through Penasco to **Picuris Pueblo.** The pueblo, settled about AD 1130, was once a link between the plains and pueblo tribes. You can still see the remains of the original plaza and pueblo, the only above-ground kiva to survive in the modern pueblos, and Spanish churches.

Picuris pottery, some of the most durable around, sparkles from the micaceous clay (clay with mica in it) from which it is fashioned. Although not many potters remain, you can visit four of them in their homes in the pueblo.

The Visitor Center has a restaurant, general store, and tribal museum, and sells camping and fishing permits. You can also make arrangements to drive through the pueblo for a small fee, either on a self-guided or guided tour.

For information on camping, recreation, road conditions, maps, and wilderness permits for Pecos Wilderness area, stop at the ranger station just outside of Peñasco.

Take State 76 southwest to the town of **Las Trampas,** founded in 1751 by 12 families from Santa Fe. The town has one of the finest surviving 18th-century churches in New Mexico. To see the inside, get a key from the caretaker in the store across from the church.

Eight miles farther on State 76 is **Truchas** (elev. 8,600 feet). This small farming community was built around two plazas for protection from Comanches and offers a beautiful view of the Rio Grande Valley. It is known for its excellent weavers and as the movie location for "The Milagro Beanfield War."

In **Cordova,** the superb wood-carvers sell their art from their homes. If the church of San Antonio de Padua is open, you can see the carved religious figures and altar screen.

The town of **Chimayo** was built around an old Indian pueblo. This late 1500's Spanish outpost is now famous for traditional weavers who often work on looms passed to them by their ancestors. For demonstrations by seventh-generation weavers, stop at the Ortega Weaving Shop or the Centinela Traditional Arts Center (the Trujillo family).

Follow the signs one mile south to **Santuario de Chimayo,** where thousands have come to be healed by the miraculous dirt at "The New World Lourdes." This early Spanish chapel blazes from the light of hundreds of candles left on the altar with the prayers of countless pilgrims. Look for the small bulto of Santo Niño, who is said to walk through the countryside at night healing the sick and performing good deeds.

In a room beside the altar is a hole in the ground filled with the dirt that has drawn the travelers here. Indians were the first to believe the dirt in the area was healing. When the Spanish settlers arrived in the early 1800's, they built a chapel and began to use it themselves. Today, pilgrims flock here in search of the miraculous, although it is no secret the hole is periodically refilled by the priests. The anteroom is a monument to their faith, with cast-off crutches and braces lining walls covered with scribbled prayers and letters of thanksgiving.

Down the road, **Rancho de Chimayo** offers ambience and an ample meal of mild Mexican food for $10 or less, Tuesday through Sunday from noon to 9:00 pm. Call 505/351-4444 for reservations. Across the road is the charming **Hacienda Rancho de Chimayo,** a small bed and breakfast, telephone 351-2222.

Continue on State 520 to **Nambe Pueblo.** At the Bureau of Reclamation sign for Nambe Falls, turn east on State Highway 4 to visit the pueblo, recreation area, and BLM reservoir.

According to legend, the beautiful Nambe Falls was formed from the tears of a maiden mourning for her lover, who had been killed by a jealous suitor. When she prayed for revenge for her beloved, the two warriors were swallowed by the earth.

For more information about Nambe Recreation Area and Dam, contact Nambe Ranger Station, 505/455-2304.

At US 84/285, turn south to Santa Fe; north to Espanola; or continue straight on State 4 to Bandelier and Los Alamos.

If you turn south on US 84 to Santa Fe, you can camp and picnic at Camel Rock at **Tesuque Pueblo.** The campground has RV hookups, groceries, picnic tables, and a heated pool.

DID YOU KNOW?

—Between 1696 and 1706 the Picuris Indians deserted their pueblo to avoid the Spanish and lived with the Apaches.
—Picuris was the last pueblo to be visited by the Spanish, 1591. They have never signed a treaty with the United States and exist as a sovereign nation.

State Highway 68 from Taos to Santa Fe

If you take State 68 southwest from Taos, you will pass **Rio Grande Gorge State Park.** The park is open all year, with camping, rafting, kayaking and great fishing from the banks of the Rio Grande.

Farther on at Embudo, once an Indian pueblo, the river funnels through the gorge. The Embudo Gauging Station, built by John Wesley Powell to measure the depth of the river, is still used today.

Continue to **San Juan Pueblo,** main office for the Eight Northern Indian Pueblos Council. It is famous for its pottery, interesting carved wood, and the San Juan Crafts Cooperative, where you can often watch the many artisans at work. The cooperative is open 9:00 am–5:00 pm, Monday through Saturday. There is also a restaurant that serves traditional Indian food, including fry bread, Tewa burgers, Indian teas, posole and Indian fruit pies.

You can visit the plaza and purchase a tribal permit for fishing and picnicking at San Juan Tribal Lakes, just south of the pueblo. In the evening you can play bingo.

The town of **Española** is filled with fast food, motels, and low-riders, customized cars with welded chain steering wheels and crushed velvet. On weekends an informal parade cruises town. They are punctuated by hop and scrape contests, where hydraulic pumps propel one end of the car over two feet in the air and then to the ground in a cloud of sparks.

About 25 miles from Española is **Ojo Caliente,** a natural mineral hot springs made into a resort in 1869. This is a casual, inexpensive resort—definitely not up-scale. Take State 68 north, then turn west on US 285, telephone 505/583-2233.

3. ESPAÑOLA TO THE APACHE RESERVATION—HEADING TO THE FOUR CORNERS

To travel north toward Colorado, take US 84 from Española past the village of **Abiquiu,** built on the site of a 16th-century Pueblo Indian ruin and once the home of the late Georgia O'Keefe. For water sports, stop at Abiquiu Dam a few miles farther north, developed for year-round recreation.

Continue on US 84 to **Ghost Ranch,** an adult study retreat of the Presbyterian church and a research center for desert farming. It is worth a visit to see the two small museums, the **Florence Hawley Ellis Museum of Anthropology** and the **Ruth Hall Museum of Paleontology,** where the kids can view the first complete skeleton of coelophysis, a small dinosaur found here in 1947. You can also walk the Chimney Rock Trail, a 45 minute self-guided trail that explains the geology of the area.

Ghost Ranch Conference Center, Abiquiu, NM 87501, 505/685-4333.

Continue on US 84 to **Ghost Ranch Living Museum,** a southwestern wildlife zoo funded by the National Forest Service. In addition to the animals, the kids will enjoy the interesting exhibits on geology and soil and water conservation. A nature trail takes you through a miniature watershed, and you can look through an Osborne Fire Finder in the ranger tower.

Ghost Ranch Living Museum, US Highway 84, Abiquiu, NM 87510, 505/685-4312. Hours: daily except Mondays, 8:00 am—6:00 pm, May through September, and until 4:30 pm,

October through April. Admission is by donation; recommended $2 per adult, $1 per student and children under 12 free.

A few miles farther on US 84 is **Echo Canyon,** an amphitheater carved by wind and water from a box canyon. Take the ten minute walk down the Trail of the Echo to play with your own echoes. The Little Echo Trail, an interpretive ¼ mile nature trail, leads to a small canyon where a new natural amphitheater is in the making. There is also a national forest campground with water and a picnic area that is open year-round.

You can take a pleasant break at **El Vado State Park,** where the kids can water ski, or down the road at **Heron Lake Dam and State Park,** popular for fishing and sailing because of the no-wake policy. A lovely hiking trail, Rio Chama Trail, connects the two lakes, and both make a good place for camping and picnicking.

Around 38 miles from Ghost Ranch is the town of **Chama,** once a supply town for ranchers and a shipping point for lumber. Today, it is home to the narrow-gauge **Cumbres & Toltec Scenic Railroad,** built in 1880 and revived as a scenic ride over Cumbres Pass. Not as well-known as the train ride from Durango to Silverton, the trip is every bit as scenic. You can almost hear the sound of the Gandy Dancer's hammers as the narrow track cuts through the steep granite cliffs in places where it couldn't go around them.

The train operates June to mid-October, with the most spectacular rides in September and early October, when the aspen are in their glory. Be sure to book ahead.

Cumbres & Toltec Scenic Railroad, PO Box 789, Chama, NM 87520, 505/756-2151, or PO Box 668, Antonito, CO 81120, 719/376-5483. Round trip is $27 for adults, $10 for children under 12.

DID YOU KNOW?

—The Cumbres & Toltec railroad line was used for filming

the circus train scene in the movie "Indiana Jones and the Last Crusade."

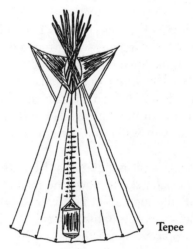

Tepee

Jicarilla Apache Reservation

West from Chama on US 64 is the Jicarilla (hick-a-REE-yah) Apache Reservation, a pristine land of mountain forests, rolling hills, and sagebrush flats edged by sandstone canyons. It's easy to lose yourself here in the deep forest and forget about civilization. Sportsmen especially revel in the abundant big game and the lakes stocked with trout. For tribal permits, contact the Game and Fish Department, PO Box 546, Dulce, 87528, 505/759-3255.

The Apache were once nomadic, like the Navajo, and the men were ferocious warriors, while the women excelled in basketry. The kids can still see their traditional wickiups, homes of poles covered with grass and brush, blending with the landscape.

The center of the reservation is the small town of **Dulce.** You and the children can watch the expert craftsmen weaving baskets at the **Tribal Arts and Crafts Shop and Museum.** As on all Indian reservations, be sure to ask first if you want to take pictures.

A good place to stay in town is the inexpensive **Best Western Jicarilla Inn,** PO Box 233, Dulce 87528, 759-3663. This comfortable motel has a restaurant, gift shop, and a tepee in front the kids can sit inside. The motel is also the visitor center and has maps and information about the area, as well as package tours that include the Chama train ride and a cultural presentation.

The other place to stay in town is **Arnold's Apache Haven Motel,** PO Box 401, 759-3348, which also has a restaurant.

4. ESPAÑOLA TO ALBUQUERQUE

State Highway 5 from Espanola will lead you to several modern-day pueblos, ancient ruins, and the high-tech town of Los Alamos.

Española to Bandelier

Santa Clara Pueblo is about three miles southwest of Española on State 5. The pueblo is open daily, with no charge for either visiting or photography. As you walk or drive through, stop at the shops for pottery demonstrations of the famous Santa Clara pottery, shiny red and black.

Singing Water Pottery and Tours beside the highway has information and tours, Native American crafts for sale, and a cafe that serves traditional food.

You can also make arrangements for tours and meals with senior members of the tribe, and for pottery and bread baking demonstrations and traditional dances from the tribal office.

The main attraction of Santa Clara is their ancestral home, **Puye (Poo-yay) Cliff Dwellings,** where Anasazi from the Four Corners originally settled between the 13th and 16th centuries.

Approximately two miles west of the pueblo turn on State Highway 30 toward the cliff dwellings and **Santa Clara Canyon,** a recreational area with fishing, hiking, picnicking, and camping for a nominal fee.

The Indians originally lived in caves hollowed in the tuff cliffs, moving later to pueblos on the upper slopes and atop the 7000-foot mesa. Maybe they got tired of the roofs caving in as freezing water cracked and collapsed the soft volcanic rock. The cave-like rooms of Puye extend over a mile, and the original inhabitants used stepping places and finger holds cut into the cliffs to climb between the mesa top and cavate rooms.

The Visitor Center has information and guided tours, and pottery demonstrations are sometimes given in the adjacent Harvey House. The self-guided trail leaves from behind the Center. If the children aren't up to the climb, take the road to the top of the mesa to see the pueblo.

Puye is an exciting place for kids because they can explore the caves and see petroglyphs, then climb to the mesa top via a trail and wooden ladders to the partially restored pueblo, kiva and "Great Community House."

Puye Cliff Dwellings are open 9:00 am–6:00 pm daily, April through October, depending on weather. Admission is $4 for adults, $3 for children 7-14.

At the junction with State Highway 4, turn east a few miles to **San Ildefonso Pueblo,** where black on black pottery has been made famous by potter Maria Martinez. Dusty streets edged with barbed wire and wooden fences lead to the village plaza, where a huge 200-year-old cottonwood flourishes.

The Visitor Center sells crafts and has information on guided tours and craft demonstrations, and the small tribal museum has historical, cultural and traditional exhibits. You can also purchase a permit to fish for rainbow trout and catfish in the pool, open April to October, and there are picnic facilities.

The pueblo is open 8:00 am–5:00 pm weekdays, 9:00 am–5:00 pm weekends. There are small admission and photography fees.

Bandelier National Monument

Continue southwest of Santa Clara on State Highway 4 and follow the signs to Bandelier.

In this area of volcanic ash compressed to a rock called tuff, hundreds of ruins dot the hillside. The settlement began as small, independent farms, but by 1450, the people had banded together into several large pueblos on the basalt mesa.

Stop to take the interesting self-guided nature trail to **Tsankawi Ruin,** a large unexcavated ruin. This scenic two mile round-trip has several steep climbs, so be sure to carry water. And remind the kids to leave the pottery shards for others to enjoy.

Continue several miles to the **Visitor Center** and museum, which has exhibits, a slide program, snack bar, checklists of plants and animals in the area, and information on the guided walks and campfire programs at the campground, open March to November.

A good hike for children is the self-guiding trail into **Frijoles Canyon,** where cliff ruins are strung about two miles along the north side of the canyons. The flat, easy walk leads to Tyuonyi ruin, once a four-story circular pueblo that was home for around 100 people.

At the cliff ruins, encourage the kids to climb into the cave rooms, letting the entrance frame the view of Frijoles Canyon, and imagine themselves 500 years back in time. Ceremonial Cave is where most visitors stop. Then the canyon narrows, and the trail continues six miles to the northern boundary of the monument.

You can also take the bit more strenuous, but excellent, **self-guided nature trail** down lower Frijoles Canyon.

Ask at the center for information on the numerous back-country trails and camping possibilities (90% of the Monument is wilderness), horseback riding in the summer, and cross country skiing in the winter.

Bandelier National Monument, Los Alamos, NM 87544,

505/672-3861. Hours: daily, 8:00 am–7:00 pm in summer, until 5:00 pm in winter. Admission is $5 per car.

DID YOU KNOW?

—The houses at Bandelier were built on the east side of the canyon to take advantage of extended sunlight.
—You can tell the different rooms by different colors of plastered walls and by the regularly spaced holes which once held vigas (roof beams).
—Underneath the shiny patina of the tuff cliffs, the rock is soft and crumbly, and was easily dug away by the Indians using stone and wooden tools.

Los Alamos
Zip Code 87544   Area Code 505

From State Highway 4, take the turnoff to Los Alamos. A word of advice—stay away from State Highway 4 after 3:00 pm on weekdays to avoid rush hour traffic. It can be remarkably slow at that time.

Los Alamos, the Atomic City, began in secrecy as the base for the Manhattan Project that developed the atom bomb. Today, it is the center for advanced Star Wars research, and frequent signs remind visitors of "no admittance" and "danger—explosives."

Enola Gay

THINGS TO DO
If the children are older, be sure to visit the **Bradbury Museum of Science,** part of the Los Alamos National Labora-

tory. This excellent hands-on museum documents the history of nuclear power, weapons development, alternative energy sources, biomedical research, and computer technology. Many of the sophisticated exhibits let you interact with computers, microscopes, lasers and Geiger counters.

The Bradbury Museum of Science, Diamond Drive, 667-4444. Hours: Tuesday–Friday, 9:00 am–5:00 pm, and on Saturday, Sunday and Monday, 1:00 pm–5:00 pm, except for laboratory holidays. Admission is free.

The kids will also enjoy a dip in the **Larry Walkup Aquatic Center,** 2760 Canyon Road, a large indoor swimming pool.

Near downtown, the **Los Alamos Historical Museum** has a bookstore, diorama of prehistoric man on the Pajarito Plateau, local history exhibits, and World War II memorabilia.

Los Alamos County Historical Museum, 1921 Juniper, 662-6272. Hours: 10:00 am–4:00 pm Monday through Saturday, 1:00 pm–4:00 pm Sunday. Admission is by donation.

Next door in the Fuller Lodge is the **Chamber of Commerce,** and across the street is a picnic area by the small lake.

Los Alamos to Albuquerque

Take State Highway 4 south of Los Alamos toward Albuquerque. West of Bandelier the highway squiggles to one of the world's largest calderas, **Valle Grande,** about 15 miles from Los Alamos. In winter, this 175 square miles looks like a mountain-ringed frozen lake dotted in the middle with an island. A stream meanders on the valley floor where sheep graze in summer.

Thirty miles southwest of Los Alamos is the village of Jemez Springs, an old resort with hot springs. North of town look for **Soda Dam,** built up over the centuries from the calcium deposits of Soda Spring. The river flows under the 300-foot long, 50-foot high and wide dome that is still building. Nearby is the Jemez Ranger Station for information on the campgrounds and trails in the national forest.

Jemez State Monument contains the impressive ruins of

the Jemez Pueblo village of Giusewa (Gee SAY wah) and its mission church, established in the 1620's. The small museum has interesting exhibits that interpret the history of Jemez from the point of view of the native inhabitants, and includes hands-on artifacts.

Jemez State Monument, Jemez, NM 87024, 505/829-3530. Hours: Thursday through Monday, May to mid-September, 9:00 am–6:00 pm; from 8:00 am–5:00 pm the rest of the year. Admission is $2 for adults, $1 for ages 6-16.

Connect with State Highway 44 and turn left to **Coronado State Monument,** near the town of Bernalillo, where you can see the partially reconstructed ruins of Kuaua Pueblo on the west bank of the Rio Grande. The pueblo was once a meeting-ground for the Anasazi and Mogollon cultures. Coronado may have spent the winter of 1540 here with his entourage of 1200 people and stockyard of pigs, chickens and cattle.

There is an interpretive trail through the ruins, a restored kiva with mural reproductions, a small museum, and a room displaying some of the outstanding original paintings from the kiva. Kids will enjoy trying on the conquistador armor and playing the drum in the museum, and climbing into the kiva on the ladder through the smoke hole.

Nearby is **Coronado State Park,** which has camping and picnic sites and is also the headquarters for Bernalillo State Forest.

Coronado State Monument, State Highway 44, Bernalillo, NM 87004, 505/867-5351. Winter Hours: daily 8:00 am–5:00 pm. Summer Hours: 9:00 am–6:00 pm during the summer. Admission is $2 for adults, $1.00 for children 6-16.

5. SANTA FE
Zip Codes 87501-87506   Area Code 505

Santa Fe brings Old World charm to the present. The town was officially settled in 1610 by the Spanish, and it is their mark that is most evident.

Many of the buildings are "the oldest" this or that in the

country. The architecture is low and flat, with softly rounded lines in muted earth tones. Here and there, a vibrant mural splashes color. In the churches, angular wood carvings with elongated features decorate the sanctuary, and the chiming bells could have come from a day 200 years ago.

The drivers seem to be in no great hurry. Maybe it's because most of them are tourists like you and trying to figure out the maze. Will Rogers once said of Santa Fe, "Whoever designed this town did so while riding on a jackass backwards and drunk." Between the adobe buildings, streets wind in a pattern all their own, once ancient trails that connected fields and homes. Now that the open spaces are filled with buildings, any logical pattern is hidden from modern eyes.

The residents live at a south-of-the-border pace, so adjust your own gears down a notch or two and delight in the "City Different."

THINGS TO DO

Many of the attractions in Santa Fe hold little appeal for the younger child, but older kids and those with an historical bent will find a charming city of the past.

Santa Fe is a walking town, even during times when the streets around the Plaza aren't closed to traffic. Start your tour at the Plaza in **Old Town,** heart of the city. In the 1800's the Santa Fe Trail ended here in what was described as a "sea of mud."

The U.S. customs office, the ring for bullfights and the adobe wall are gone now, but the kids can still see watering troughs in the northwest corner and a clock that's been here since 1916. Browse in the unique art galleries (over 125 of them in town) and shops, watch the people, or just sit and try to figure out the city's street system.

On the north side of the Plaza is the **Palace of the Governors,** the oldest public building in continuous use in the United States. Criminals were once jailed, whipped, and hanged here, and military supplies were stored in two towers that have since disappeared. Today, it houses the state's history museum, a library and photo archives. Out front, colorful Indian men and women display their wares in an open-air market under the portico.

The museum, telephone 827-6483, is open 9 am–4:45 pm daily, and closed Mondays in January and February. Cost is $3 per adult and $1.25 per child. If you also plan to visit the Museum of Fine Arts, the Museum of International Folk Art and the Museum of Indian Arts and Crafts, you can purchase a two-day pass for all four for a reduced price.

The **Museum of Fine Arts,** also on the Plaza, was built in 1917 on the site of the old Ft. Marcy military headquarters and contains over 8,000 art objects, mostly regional works.

The museum, telephone 827-4455, is open 9 am–4:45 pm daily, closed Mondays in January and February. Admission is $3 per adult and $1.25 per child.

Walk through the lobby of the **La Fonda Hotel.** When it was built in 1846, it had one story centered around a patio and stables where horses and travelers short on cash could spend the night. Billy the Kid is said to have washed dishes in the kitchen.

If you want to stay in this venerable old hotel, call 982-5511 or write 100 East San Francisco Street, Box 1209, Santa Fe 87501 for reservations well in advance. Rates are expensive, but children under 12 stay free.

East one block on San Francisco Street is **St. Francis Cathedral,** begun in 1869 by Bishop Lamy on the site of a 1622 monastery. On East Palace Avenue, across the street from the cathedral, is **Sena Plaza.** Endless details were built into what was originally a 33-room hacienda for Don Juan Sena's 23 children. Look for typical features of mid-1800's Spanish homes, rest on a bench in the shady plaza, eat lunch, or browse in the small shops and galleries. (See Chapter XIII for shopping activities.)

Loretto Chapel is the opposite direction from the cathedral. Wind to Water Street, then turn right. Its Gothic design was inspired by Bishop Lamy's home chapel in Paris.

Legend has it that Lamy's nephew killed the architect when

he discovered him in an affair with his wife, leaving the stairway to the choir loft unfinished. The sisters prayed, and a mysterious carpenter appeared and built the ornate winding stairway 23 feet high with no side or center supports, using only a hammer, saw, T-square, and buckets of water to soak the wood so he could bend it.

You and the kids can watch the ½ hour multimedia presentation "**Footsteps Across New Mexico**" for an overview of the state and its history. It is shown daily between 9:30 am and 4:30 pm. Admission is $3.20 for adults, $2.40 for ages 6-16.

Four blocks south of the Plaza (401 Old Santa Fe Trail, near Old Santa Fe Trail and De Vargas Streets) is a building billed as the oldest inhabited house in United States, although ceiling beams date it no older than the mid-1700's. Walk through the gaudy curio shop to the thick walled rooms in back. The adobe construction is an old technique called "puddled adobe," which used poured mud rather than bricks.

Across the alleyway is **San Miguel Mission,** the oldest Christian church in continuous use in the country. Churches have been in this spot since as early as 1626. The original was destroyed in the Pueblo revolt, then rebuilt in 1710 partially on the old foundation. You can see the remains of the original chapel through peepholes near the altar.

Again, there are conflicting claims. The mission church at Isleta Pueblo was built around 1613, and the one at Acoma in 1629, and both are still essentially intact.

The oldest shrine to the Virgin Mary in the United States is **Santuario de Guadalupe.** Built in the late 1700's with a blend of Spanish and Indian architecture, it has art and religious exhibits. The color of the wall behind the altar comes from oxblood. The church is four blocks from the Plaza at Guadalupe and Agua Fria streets. The shrine is open to visitors except on Sundays, telephone 988-2027.

If the kids are tired of old buildings, take them for a picnic and walk in **Santa Fe River Park,** which follows the Santa Fe River through town.

Canyon Road, one of the oldest streets in Santa Fe, is a few blocks southeast of the Plaza. Here, art galleries, historical buildings, gardens, and unique shops cluster together. The road was once walked by Pueblo Indians and padres following the Santa Fe River through the mountains to Pecos pueblo. Even if they aren't interested in shopping, children may enjoy exploring the back alleyways and placitas.

Cristo Rey Church (Canyon Road and Camino Delora), one of the largest adobe buildings in the United States, was built in 1939 with almost 200,000 handmade adobe bricks. Inside is a 32 foot high, hand carved stone altar screen from 1760.

Cabezon, New Mexico

Keep right to Upper Canyon Road and follow the signs to the **Randall Davey Audubon Center.** Don't be daunted by the "No Trespassing" signs. They are to remind you to stay on the road. This 135-acre Audubon Society wildlife sanctuary is a pleasant place for kids. Pick up a brochure in the office for the self-guiding nature trail.

The Center is open Monday–Friday, 9:00 am to 5:00 pm, or by appointment, telephone 983-4609. Admission is $1 per adult, $.50 per child.

A ten-minute drive from the Plaza will take you to three more museums. Take Old Santa Fe Trail Road to Camino

Lejo Street and turn left to the Museum Complex.

Children will particularly enjoy the **Museum of International Folk Art**, which has objects from over 100 countries, including the Girard collection, one of the largest groupings of ethnic crafts and folk art miniatures in the world. Costumes, textiles, toys, religious art, ceramics and decorative art objects are just some of the things you will find here.

Museum of International Folk Art, 706 Camino Lejo, 827-8350. Hours: 9:00 am–4:45 pm daily, closed Mondays in winter. Admission is $3 per adult, $1.25 per child ages 6-16.

The **Museum of Indian Arts and Culture** houses one of the world's finest collections of Southwest Indian artifacts, although not always displayed in an interesting way for children. Kids will, however, enjoy the resource center, open afternoons, which has touch displays, books, and occasional craft demonstrations. The restaurant serves Native American dishes, and Fridays in summer, Youth Gallery Talks are offered.

Museum of Indian Arts and Culture, 710 Camino Lejo, 827-8941. Hours: daily 10:00 am–5:00 pm, closed Mondays in January and February. Admission is $3 per adult and $1.25 per child.

The privately owned **Wheelwright Museum of the American Indian** was built to preserve Navajo ceremonies. Originally called the House of Navajo Religion, its entrance faces the rising sun, and five logs symbolize the five worlds of the Navajo.

Today the museum contains some exhibits of historic and contemporary Native American arts. In summer, let the children listen to well-known Joe Hayes tell stories near the tepee outside while you shop at the Case Trading Post in the basement.

Wheelwright Museum, 704 Camino Lejo, 982-4636. Hours: Monday through Saturday, 10:00 am–4:45 pm, and Sunday 1:00 pm–4:45 pm, closed Mondays in winter. Admission is by donation.

Most people come to Santa Fe to shop, and the town is

loaded with quaint shops. A store the kids will particularly enjoy is **Enchanting Land Children's Bookstore,** 303 E. Alameda, which sells books, gifts, and learning toys, and offers special events and programs such as art demonstrations and storytelling. Call 988-2718 for more information. **Trespassers William Children's Bookstore,** 330 Garfield, 982-4100, is another fun store for kids.

Santa Fe has numerous festivals and special events, but perhaps the most famous is the **Santa Fe Summer Opera Festival.** For over 30 summers, the repertory opera company, the only outdoor one in the nation, has been delighting audiences. Try it with the older kids.

You won't have trouble finding a good place to eat in Santa Fe, but one with an atmosphere that might appeal to kids is the **Super Chief Diner,** 531 Guadalupe, which offers typical diner meals in an old railroad car. For a fancier meal, try **La Tertulia Restaurant,** across the street from Santuario de Guadalupe in what was once the convent. The picturesque restaurant serves moderately priced southwestern meals for lunch and dinner, Tuesday through Sunday.

Santa Fe has a central reservations number for lodging to meet your special needs, whether it involves a room with a water bed or one that allows pets. In-state call 983-8200, out-of-state 800/982-7669. You can also write or call the Santa Fe Convention and Visitors Bureau, Box 909, Santa Fe 87501, 800/528-5369 or 984-6760.

For information on guided tours of the town and dates of special events and festivals, contact the Chamber of Commerce on the southwest corner of Sheridan and Marcy, 983-7317.

If your timing is right, you can take the kids to **El Rancho de las Golondrinas (Old Cienega Village),** 15 miles south of Santa Fe. Take I-25 south to exit 271, then turn west. This living history museum covers 400 acres and depicts life in Spanish Colonial New Mexico. Over 20 restored structures from the 16th and 17th centuries are authentically furnished, and an outdoor walking tour takes you through them, including grain mills, a blacksmith shop, and weaving areas. There are also outstanding summer festivals that depict the lives of the early settlers.

Old Cienega is a great place for kids. The only drawback is the short visiting hours. It is open on the first weekends, May through October, from 10:00 am to 4:00 pm. Admission varies depending on special events, but is generally around $2 per adult and $1 per child. To arrange guided tours at other times and to encourage them to extend their hours, contact Old Cienega Village Museum, Route 2, Box 214, Santa Fe, NM 87501, 471-2261.

Hyde Memorial State Park is eight miles from downtown. Take Bishop's Lodge Road (an extension of Washington Avenue) northwest to Artist Road (State Road 475) and turn right. The road becomes Hyde Park Road. The Park has a visitor center, playground, restaurant, general store, hiking trails, fishing and campground.

Further on is **Santa Fe Ski Basin,** where you can ride the chairlift in summer and ski in winter.

If you are feeling extravagant, consider staying at **Bishop's Lodge,** 1000 acres that was once the private retreat of Archbishop Lamy, and later, Joseph Pulitzer. This luxurious resort is a complete vacation within itself, offering swimming, golfing, fishing in the stocked trout pond, skeet shooting, riding and more. There are special summer programs designed for ages 4-12 and special activities for teens.

Bishop's Lodge, PO Box 2367, Santa Fe 87501, 983-6377.

A few miles farther on Bishop's Lodge Road is **Shidoni Foundry,** which has a small park with interesting metal sculptures. Every Saturday the kids can watch bronze being poured between 12:00 noon and 4:00 pm and during the week they can walk through the foundry between 10:30 am and 10:45 am, noon and 1:00 pm, and 3:00 pm and 3:15 pm. Admission is free.

At **Glassworks Studio and Gallery** next door, the children can watch glass being blown every day except Sunday.

DID YOU KNOW?

—Santa Fe was the seat of government for Spain, Mexico, the Confederacy and the Territorial United States. Today it is the state capital of New Mexico and the oldest capital city in the United States.

—The full Spanish name for the town is La Villa Real de la Santa Fe de San Francisco, which means "The Royal City of the Holy Faith of St. Francis."

—Las Fiestas honors the memory of Don Diego de Vargas and celebrates the return of Spanish colonialists to New Mexico. This week of festivities begins after Labor Day with the burning of Old Man Gloom (Zozobra).

—Billy the Kid was once chained in the plaza on public view.

—Burro Alley was named because woodcutters used to leave their burros here loaded with firewood from the mountains, while selling their wares to Santa Fe citizens.

—The paved loop of the Paseo de Peralta roughly follows the line of the walls around the original Spanish colonial outpost of 1610.

—The Cross of the Martyrs on a low hill off Paseo de Peralta was erected to remember the 21 Franciscan missionaries killed in the Pueblo revolt.

—The main character in Willa Cather's "Death Comes for the Archbishop" was based on Bishop Lamy of Santa Fe.

6. FROM SANTA FE TO ALBUQUERQUE—THE TURQUOISE TRAIL

The Turquoise Trail (State Highway 14 between Santa Fe and Albuquerque) travels through the mesas and mountains past ghost towns and mining camps.

The village of **Cerillos** began with the discovery of lead in 1879. Turquoise from the mine near town was once traded as far away as Mexico and Canada. You can visit the small

Rusting steam engine—New Mexico

museum and petting zoo in town.

The rows of company houses in **Madrid** once rented for $2 a month per person, with an extra $.50 if you wanted electric lights. In the 1880's, the town had 21 saloons and four hotels. Guests included General Grant and Sarah Bernhardt.

Stop in town at the **Old Coal Mine Museum,** a railroad repair yard with a restored locomotive and coal mine shaft.

Hours: daily, Memorial Day through Labor Day, 10:00 am– 5:00 pm, and during the winter from 10:00 am–4:00 pm on weekends only. Admission is $1.50 adults, $.50 for children ages 6-12.

In summer, take the kids to the melodrama and buy a packet of marshmallows to throw at the villain.

Golden was the site of the first gold rush west of the Mississippi. It is now a collection of crumbling structures.

Turn west at the junction with State Road 165 toward Sandia Crest. **Tinkertown Museum** has animated wood carvings depicting a western town and a three-ring circus that children will find interesting.

The museum is open daily 9:00 am–6:00 pm, April to November, telephone 505/281-5233. Admission is $2 for adults, $.50 for children under 5.

Hiking and camping are popular pastimes in the Sandia Mountains, and numerous side roads will lead you to lovely picnic spots.

At **Sandia Ski Area** you can take the 15 minute chairlift ride 7000 feet up the side of the Sandia Mountains. From the top is a view 100 miles in all directions. A hiking trail from the Sandia Crest House Restaurant and Gift Shop leads 1½ miles to Sandia Peak. If the kids are hungry, purchase a box lunch at the restaurant to take with you.

Sandia Crest, telephone 505/243-0605, is open 10:00 am to 9:00 pm daily, May to October, and 10:00 am to one hour after sunset the rest of the year. Cost for the chairlift in summer is $4.

Return to State Highway 14 and continue to Albuquerque through Tijeras (Spanish for "scissors") Canyon, the route used by Comanche raiders, 49ers and settlers. For more information, contact the Turquoise Trail Association, 505/281-1384.

7. ALBUQUERQUE
Area Code 505

Albuquerque, the geographical center of New Mexico, bustles with 450,000 people. The town was formed by early Spanish settlers who had originally lived in scattered ranches and farms. To minimize the threat from hostile Indians, the Santa Fe authorities ordered them to come together around plazas in the early 1700's. The resulting settlement had 252 residents and was named after the Duke of Alburquerque (the first "r" was later dropped). Their church, San Felipe de Neri, still lends its charm to Old Town.

The plaza was the center of activity until 1880, when the railroad bypassed the area. Downtown then grew up along the tracks two miles east, while Old Town remained suspended in time.

Santa Fe may be the capital, but Albuquerque is the hub of activity. It's a city in spirit and deed, the most metropolitan place you'll find in New Mexico.

THINGS TO DO

Old Town, off Rio Grande Boulevard NW, will give you a dose of Spanish colonial times. Quaint shops, galleries, and restaurants in historic adobe cluster around the plaza and give it a special ambience not found in many other places in town.

Many of the old buildings come with stories. At least one comes with a ghost. The 1880 Armijo home, in the 200 block of San Felipe, reportedly boasts the spirit of a servant girl who died here. Employees in the current restaurant have been known to hear her call their names.

A walking tour is the best way to catch the sights and surprises of Old Town—hidden patios and winding alleyways, the smells of roasting chilies and burning pinyon, the sounds of street musicians. Let the kids take a ride in a horse-drawn buggy, watch an Old West gunfight, climb the Civil War cannons, or attend a puppet show.

The **Visitor Information Center** on the plaza, 243-3215, will provide more information on the special events and entertainment.

After exploring Old Town, take the kids to the nearby museums. The **Albuquerque Museum,** one block from the plaza, has historical, art and science exhibits. Included is the largest collection of Spanish conquistador artifacts in the world, as well as other Spanish colonial artifacts (see Chapter XIII for an activity). The Gem Theater has a multi-image show on the history of the city, and interesting changing exhibits are in the gallery. You can also join a tour here for Old Town.

Albuquerque Museum of Art, History and Science, 2000 Mountain Road NW, 242-4600. Hours: Tuesday through Friday, 10:00 am–5:00 pm, and Saturday and Sunday 1:00 pm–5:00 pm. Admission is $2 for adults, $1 for children and seniors.

New Mexico Museum of Natural History, just north of the Albuquerque Museum, is a 4.5 billion-year time capsule of the universe. This is a must-see for the kids! Exhibits will take them into a frigid Ice Age cave, a seething volcano, the seacoast of 70 million years, or back to the age of dinosaurs, complete with a flying quetzalcoatlus boasting a 38-foot wing span. They can also watch an active beehive, use a video microscope and explore the other numerous hands-on exhibits.

If you see only one museum in the Southwest, make it this one. Your kids will thank you!

New Mexico Museum of Natural History, 1801 Mountain Road NW, PO Box 7010, 87194, 841-8837. Hours: daily, 10:00 am–5:00 pm with slightly extended hours in the summer. Admission is $2.00 for adults, $1.50 for seniors, $1.00 for children 3-12.

The **Indian Pueblo Cultural Center,** operated by the All-Indian Pueblo Council, was built to resemble Pueblo Bonito in Chaco Canyon. It's a good place for the children to learn about the history and culture of the 19 Rio Grande Indian Pueblos and to gather information about visiting them.

Pottery and crafts from each pueblo are exhibited, as well as a replica of a pueblo home. Murals decorate the walls of the central courtyard, where authentic dances are held at 11:00 am and 2:00 pm on weekends in the summer. Films and craft demonstrations are also held periodically. The Pueblo Kitchen Restaurant, open 7:30 am to 3:30 pm, serves traditional Pueblo Indian food, and the gift shop offers arts and crafts for sale.

Indian Pueblo Cultural Center, 2401 12th Street NW (one block north of I-40), 843-7270. Hours: daily in summer, 9:00 am–6:00 pm, closed Sunday mid-October to mid-May. Admission is $2.50 for adults, $1.00 for students.

Take the kids to the **Rio Grande Zoo,** New Mexico's largest. Many of the animals are displayed in natural habitat enclosures, and the zoo is noted for its hoofed animals and herpetology (those slithery animals your kids probably love and you probably hate) displays. The prairie dog village near the center of the zoo and the tropical birdhouse are also popular. A children's zoo is open all year and in summer includes a petting zoo and storytellers performing animal tales.

Rio Grande Zoological Park, 903 10th Street S.W., 843-7413. Hours: 9:00 am–5:00 pm daily in winter, with extended summer hours. Admission is $4 for adults, $2 for children ages 3-11 and seniors.

Another interesting place for kids is the **Rio Grande Nature Center,** which displays the history, ecology and geology of the Rio Grande Valley. Many native animals are protected in this 270-acre reserve where land and water come together in a desert climate. The nature center building is partially underground, so the plants and animals in the huge artificial pond can be viewed from both above and below the water. You can also follow nature trails through the bosque (the meadow, marsh and forest along a river in the desert).

The Rio Grande Nature Center is at Candelaria Road on the east bank of the Rio Grande, telephone 344-7240. Hours: daily 10:00 am–5:00 pm. Admission is $.25 per person.

Indian Petroglyph State Park has several trails to the top of an extinct volcanic cone and along the edge of a lava flow etched with hundreds of petroglyphs. A loop drive has turn-offs to other trails, and picnic tables are also available. From I-40 take Coors Boulevard north to Montano, west to Unser, then north to the park.

Indian Petroglyph State Park, 6900 Unser Boulevard NW, 823-4016. Hours: daily, weather permitting, 9:00 am–5:00 pm in winter, 10:00 am–6:00 pm in summer. Admission is $1.00 per car.

Give the kids a thrill and take the 2.7 mile ride to the top of Sandia Peak (elev. 10,678 feet) on **Sandia Peak Tramway,** the longest in the world. At the base of the tram is a nature trail, the Firehouse restaurant with an 1873 steam power fire engine, and a gift shop. At the top are hiking trails and the High Finance restaurant, open Easter through Thanksgiving. The incredible panorama seen from the top of Sandia Crest takes in thousands of square miles. Sunsets can be particularly stunning.

Sandia Peak Tramway is open daily with varying hours

during the day and evening. Call 298-8518 for information. Tram rates are $9 for adults, $7 for ages 5-12. Special rates are available after 4:30 pm for those with reservations for dinner at the High Finance (243-9742) or Firehouse (292-3473) restaurants.

To get there, take I-25 north to the Tramway exit, then follow Tramway Boulevard 4½ miles east, or take I-40 to the Tramway Boulevard exit, then north for 10 miles.

Elena Gallegos, Albert G. Simms Park, 1700 Tramway NE (1½ miles north of Montgomery), is a 640-acre mountain picnic area popular for hiking and sightseeing. Call 291-6224 for more information. Cost is $1.00 per vehicle.

The **University of New Mexico,** on University Boulevard and Ash NE, has a lovely campus with a duck pond, several interesting museums and special events held throughout the year.

The anthropology department of the University has a world-wide reputation, and you can see its public displays in the **Maxwell Museum of Anthropology.** The collection emphasizes native cultures of the Southwest, but also features others from around the world.

The newly-remodeled museum is on the west edge of campus on Redondo Drive just off University, telephone 277-4404. Hours: Monday through Friday 9:00 am–4:00 pm, Saturday 10:00 am–4:00 pm, and Sunday 1:00 pm–5:00 pm. Admission is free.

The **Geology and Meteorite Museum** has extensive fossil and mineral collections that range from dinosaur bones to moon rocks, and includes one of the largest meteorite collections in the United States.

The museum is in Northrup Hall, 200 Yale NE, room 107, telephone 277-4204. Hours: Monday through Friday, 8:30 am–4:30 pm, and on weekends 9:00 am–12 noon and 1:00 pm–4:00 pm. Admission is free.

University Art Museum houses the largest collection of fine arts in New Mexico.

The museum, on Cornell Street, telephone 277-4001, is

*open in the summer, Tuesday through Friday, 10:00 am–4:00
pm, weekends 1:00 pm–4:00 pm in summer. Winter hours,
Tuesday through Friday, 10:00 am–5:00 pm and 7:00 pm–
10:00 pm, weekends 1:00 pm–5:00 pm. Admission is free.*

The Manhattan Project which developed the first atomic
bomb was centered in New Mexico, and the **National Atomic
Museum** commemorates New Mexico's role in this development. In addition to nuclear weapons, a B-52 airplane and

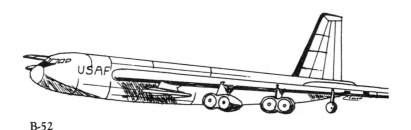

B-52

full-scale missile systems, there are displays emphasizing the
peaceful use of atomic energy, as well as alternative energy
exhibits. A documentary film with newsreel clips from the
1930's and 1940's is shown several times daily. Just south of the
museum is the "Power Tower," gigantic solar collectors. Call
844-8443 for movie and guided tour times.

*The National Atomic Museum, Kirtland Air Force Base, is
open daily 9:00 am–5:00 pm. Admission is free. To reach the
museum, take Central Exit from I-40 and turn west to the gate
on Wyoming Boulevard.*

If you're in town on a weekend, check for special events at
the **State Fairgrounds.** Two especially fun events are the New
Mexico State Fair (the third largest in the country) in September and the International Balloon Festival in October. People
come from as far away as Australia to participate in the
Balloon Festival, a race of bobbing colors that is the largest
balloon festival in the world. Organizers claim it is photographed more than any other event, including the Rose
Bowl parade.

As in most cities, there are several commercial enterprises that are fun for kids. **Uncle Cliff's Familyland,** 4800 Osuna NE, is an amusement park with roller coaster, log flume, bumper cars, kiddie rides and others. The park is open evenings and weekend afternoons, spring through fall. **Photon** is a high tech entertainment center with laser games in the Montgomery Plaza Mall, 5001 Montgomery NE, Suite 147. **The Beach,** Montano at I-25, has water slides, a wave pool, a lazy river for older children, and a 40-foot water-breathing dragon. It is open daily in the summer, weather permitting, 11:00 am–8:00 pm.

A favorite place to eat with locals and tourists alike is **Garduno's of Mexico,** 5400 Academy Road Northeast, 821-3030. This large, upbeat restaurant is inexpensive to moderately priced and is a good place to sample authentic New Mexican cuisine. Take exit 230 off I-25, then ¼ mile south on San Mateo and one block east on Academy.

The kids might enjoy sampling the green chile cheeseburgers or blue corn enchiladas at **Monroe's.** Two locations: 1520 Lomas Northwest, 242-1111, and 6021 Osuna Road Northeast, 881-4224.

DID YOU KNOW?

—Albuquerque was part of the Confederacy for two weeks in 1862.

—Until 1821, the only legal trade in Albuquerque was with official Spanish caravans,

—Sandia Tram was built with the aid of a helicopter.

—It requires 640 acres (1 square mile) to graze a cow in this area.

—Nearby Mt. Taylor is an 11,000-foot volcano.

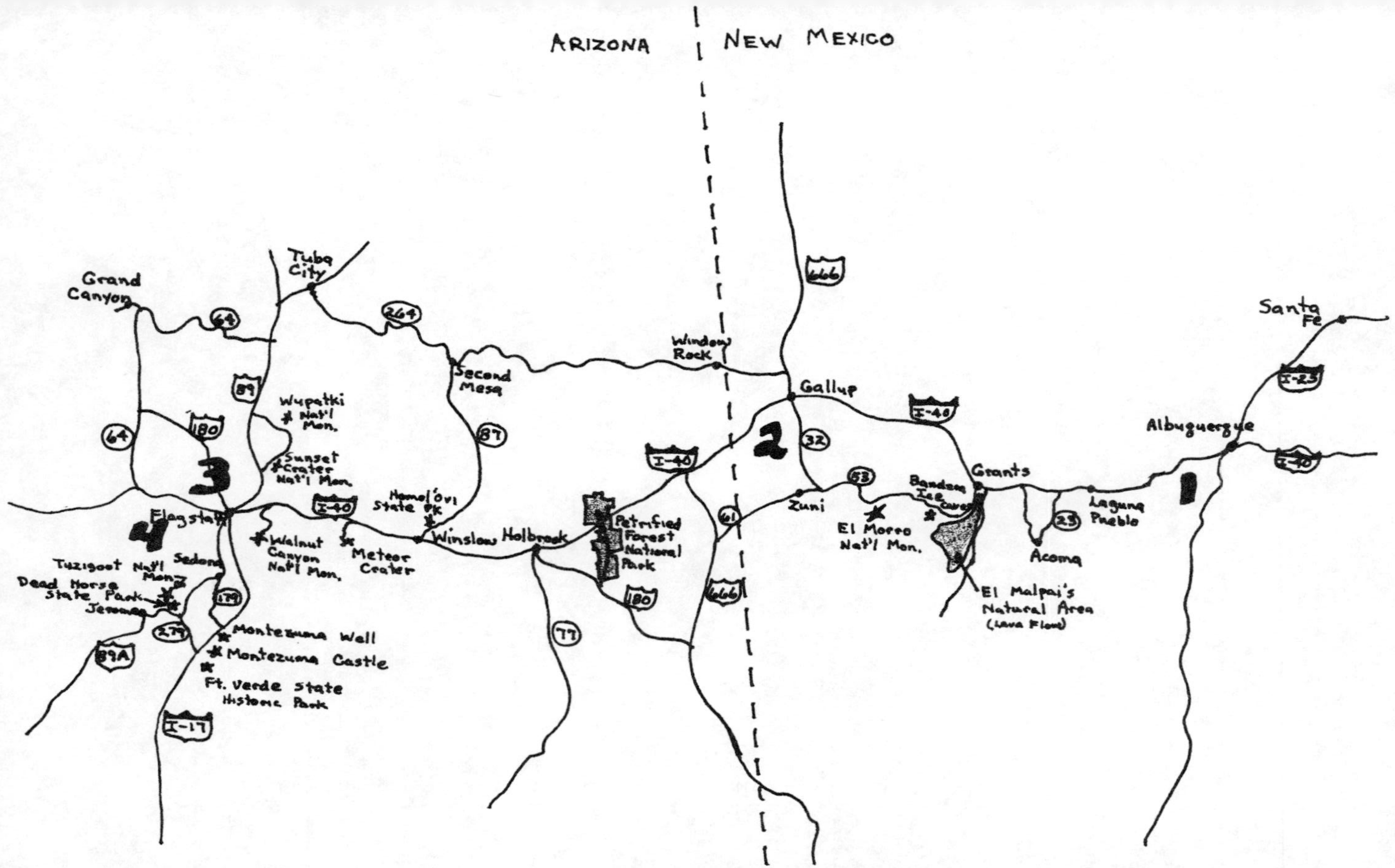
ARIZONA
NEW MEXICO
Grand Canyon
Tuba City
Second Mesa
Window Rock
Gallup
Santa Fe
Albuquerque
Wupatki Nat'l Mon.
Sunset Crater Nat'l Mon.
Homol'ovi State Pk
Winslow
Holbrook
Petrified Forest National Park
Zuni
El Morro Nat'l Mon.
Bandera Ice Caves
Grants
Acoma
Laguna Pueblo
El Malpai's Natural Area (Lava Flow)
Flagstaff
Walnut Canyon Nat'l Mon.
Meteor Crater
Sedona
Tuzigoot Nat'l Mon.
Dead Horse State Park
Jerome
Montezuma Well
Montezuma Castle
Ft. Verde State Historic Park
64
180
89
264
87
I-40
I-17
179
279
89A
77
666
61
32
53
23
I-25
1
2
3
4

10

GATEWAY TO THE UNUSUAL: Albuquerque, NM, to Flagstaff, AZ

What would moo, squeak, clank, neigh, bleat, and have the appearance of a medieval pageant? If you said a Spanish conquistador expedition—Coronado's, to be exact—you're right.

By some accounts, Francisco Vasquez de Coronado was a handsome, spirited young man, and a courageous leader who inspired confidence in his followers. It was in February, 1540, that he saw his finest day of glory.

Imagine the noise and commotion when this bold adventurer left Compostela, Mexico to pursue the illusionary Seven Cities of Cibola, leading one of the most elaborate and ostentatious armies imaginable. It is estimated that it would cost over a million dollars today to duplicate his expedition. The roll call of the day included 225 mounted men, 62 armed foot soldiers, around 700 Indian camp tenders, herdsmen, and warriors in padded cloth body armor, and three women. They were accompanied by hundreds of pack mules loaded with supplies, an array of weapons (including bows and arrows, halberds, javelins, crossbows, harquebuses, shields, swords, lances and six light artillery pieces), extra horses (23 for Coronado alone), and herds of cattle, sheep and oxen.

At the head of the procession were Fray Marcos and four other Franciscan friars, shod in sandals and wearing loose gray robes. Behind rode young noblemen from Spain, many of whom had paid for the privilege of dividing the sought-for treasure. They were dressed in bright silks, shiny armor, plumed helmets and capes embroidered with silver and gold. Even the cloths which hung over their horses and almost swept the ground were brilliantly colored.

It was the hottest, driest time of year when the expedition traced a tortuous path through 300 miles of rugged Arizona. As accidents and lack of food took their toll, the survivors were buoyed by Fray Marcos' assurances that riches awaited them at the Zuni town of Hawikuh. Since he had supposedly seen the place on an earlier journey, the adventurers had full faith in the good father's word.

When they finally reached Hawikuh in July, they realized the riches existed only in the friar's mind. "All crumpled together," is how one disappointed expeditioner described the dusty adobe village—not to mention their hostile greeting of arrows and stones hurled by the 150 residents.

After a brief battle, the Spanish marched into the village and found corn, beans and turkeys. For the exhausted, starving men, at the time it was a better prize than silver and gold.

After they recovered, they cursed Fray Marcos and moved their headquarters east to Tiguex Pueblo (near the current Bernalillo, New Mexico), where their hopes were rekindled by fresh tales of riches told by a captive Plains Indian named El Turko. His stories included golden eagles adorning the prows of huge canoes, common people eating from plates of gold, and a ruler who napped under a tree with golden bells that lullabyed him to sleep.

The Spanish followed El Turko all the way to Kansas, where

he finally confessed he was leading them on a wild goose chase in hopes of abandoning them to die. El Turko was garroted, and the dejected Spaniards headed towards home.

On the way, Coronado was seriously injured in a horse race. This disillusioned young dreamer, who once wrote in his expedition journal "God knows what I have suffered," was doomed to spend the rest of his life a broken man and semi-invalid, just as a gypsy fortune-teller in Spain had predicted years earlier. The reward for many of the daring nobles who had followed him was equally grim—an old age of poverty, their resources depleted by the great journey.

Although Coronado failed to find gold, he did lay claim to a vast new land for Spain, which included what is now Arizona. Many think it is a place synonymous with desert. Even the state flower, the giant saguaro, calls forth visions of hot, dry and barren. But just as this prickly cactus blooms wax-white and fragrant with spring rains, so the vastness of Arizona blossoms with a wild, rugged beauty.

It was this same wide-open-spaces-to-get-lost-in that attracted murderers and thieves in the late 1800's, when the place gained a reputation for lawlessness. One of Arizona's towns, Jerome, was dubbed the "wickedest town in the West" by a New York City newspaper. Many of the early residents were proud of their rough and tumble image, bragging that it was common for businesses to install stone shutters to keep out the gunfire.

The Wild West outlaws are gone today, but nature's handiwork still predominates, and many of the landmarks are as striking as when Coronado saw them. Peering across the Painted Desert at dusk, or traveling a back road through the mesa pines, you might feel you've found a treasure even more precious than the mythical Cibola.

DID YOU KNOW?

—Only 10,000 years ago, much of Arizona was covered with

lush forests. Then, a permanent drought afflicted the area, and within a few hundred years the forests had disappeared.
—Indian women grind seeds of the saguaro cactus into flour.
—One theory about petroglyphs is that they were made by the same people who carved rock art in Spain, Crete and Sumatra.
—The battle at Hawikuh was the first authenticated armed conflict between Europeans and Indians in what is now the United States.

From Albuquerque to Flagstaff

1. Albuquerque to Gallup—Land of the Conquistadors
2. From Gallup to Flagstaff—Route 66
3. Flagstaff, Arizona
4. Circle South from Flagstaff—Stories from the Past

1. ALBUQUERQUE TO GALLUP— LAND OF THE CONQUISTADORS

West of Albuquerque on I-40 is **Acoma Pueblo,** the oldest continuously inhabited city in the United States. To visit, take Laguna exit 108 to State Road 23 and the Visitor Center, or take Laguna exit 102 south to Acomita Lake and the tribal offices.

Acoma, the Sky City, is perched on the huge rock of Enchanted Mesa, jutting 400 feet above the surrounding desert. The location makes for an ideal defense. When the Spanish conquistador Alvarado came here in 1540, he found a village situated in the strongest position in all the land.

The visitor center has a museum with pottery and history exhibits, a crafts shop and a restaurant that serves native food. You can also make arrangements to tour the Sky City, where a few people live much as their ancestors did in AD 1150, and the original Spanish mission. Every bit of the dirt used to build the mission between 1629 and 1640 was carried up from the plains.

For more information, contact Box 309, Pueblo of Acoma, NM 87034, 505/552-6604. Summer hours are 8:00 am–7:00 pm, spring hours until 6:00 pm, and winter hours until 5:00 pm. Cost is $4 for adults, $2.50 for ages 12-18, and $2 for ages 6-11.

Continue on I-40 west to exit 89 and travel south on State Road 117 to **El Malpais National Monument.** A Navajo legend says this immense lava flow is the blood of a giant killed in the Zuni Mountains by the Twin War gods. The surrealistic landscape comes complete with a jumble of cinder cones, ice caves, lava tubes, and sculpted sandstone.

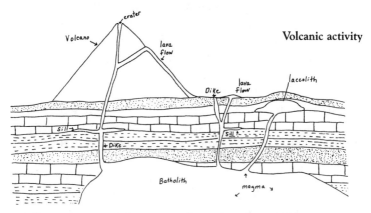

The most recent flow spewed out less than 1000 years ago. When the first Spanish came through in 1540, they crossed El Malpais, cursing their difficulties. Future expeditions wisely skirted around it.

Have the kids look for the gray-green lichens that cover much of the lava. Also look for spatter cones, piles of lava blobs in the shape of cones formed when lava is squeezed out of a crack in the hardened top of the lava flow.

From Sandstone Bluffs Overlook is a view in the distance of the cinder cones that stretch 20 miles from Cerro Brillante to Bandera Crater and make up the Chain of Craters. You can camp, picnic and hike here.

Farther south State Road 117 takes you past **La Vieja,** an old woman's face nature carved in stone; a trail to **La Ventana,** the largest sandstone arch in New Mexico; and **The Narrows,** where the lava ends in front of the sandstone cliffs. You can hike and rock climb at the Narrows. A little over three miles farther on is a camping and picnicking area. Retrace your route 21 miles back to I-40.

The 360,000-acre park is managed jointly by the National Park Service and the Bureau of Land Management. Stop at the information center, 620 East Santa Fe Avenue in Grants, or call 505/285-5406. The center is open 8:00 am to 5:00 pm. There are no campgrounds, water or toilets in this as yet undeveloped park.

Continue on I-40 to the town of **Grants,** which boomed in the 1950's as the "Uranium Capital of the World."

The New Mexico Museum of Mining, the only uranium mining museum in the world, will give you a glimpse into the mining boom. The museum includes historical displays, the richest uranium ore in the U.S., and Indian artifacts.

Kids will enjoy a tour into a simulated mine guided by a former miner. As you take the elevator down the mineshaft, try to imagine what it would be like to spend day after day in this underground world.

The New Mexico Museum of Mining, 100 Iron Street, 505/287-4802. Admission is $2. Tour hours: Monday through Friday, 10:00 am–12:00 noon and 1:00 pm–4:00 pm, Saturday 10:00 am–4:00 pm and Sunday 1:00 pm–4:00 pm.

For camping and water sports, stop at **Bluewater Lake State Park,** open year-round with 25 miles of shoreline. There is also a children's playground and grocery store. The lake is 26 miles northwest of Grants on I-40 and State Road 412.

State 53 south of Grants was once part of the Ancient Way, the trail used by the Indians between the Hopi Mesas and Acoma. Later, the Spanish and American pioneers called it the Zuni-Cibola Trail, and traveled this way for the reliable water source at El Morro (see below).

Bandera Crater and Ice Caves, a part of the El Malpais lava flow, is around 25 miles south of Grants on State 53, then ½ mile on a dirt road. Bandera is the area's most accessible ice cave. Hundreds of years ago, Coronado visited this natural ice-box, led by Zuni tour guides. Later, ranchers used it as a source of ice in the summer.

Ice caves exist inside collapsed lava tubes that were formed when the outside rock cooled and hardened over a river of molten lava. When the lava later drained out, tunnels were left behind, some several miles long and over 50 feet wide.

Since the top layer of lava acts as insulation, the temperature in the cave (below freezing) remains relatively constant. Over time, the lava roof cracks and water oozes down from above, forming stalagmites of ice and crystallized water on the ceiling.

As you enter the cave, notice the temperature, direction of the wind, and shape of the cave. The blue-green color is from algae in the water. Try to find the different layers that show alternate freezing and thawing.

The Trading Post has Indian artifacts, many found in the lava, and local Indian arts and crafts. Behind the post is an easy 1½ mile trail to Bandera Crater, an 800-foot deep volcanic cone.

Bandera Crater and the ice caves are operated by the privately-owned Ice Caves Resort, 505/783-4303. Hours: daily, 8:00 am to 7:00 pm. Admission is $4 for ages 12 and over, $2 for ages 5-11.

El Morro National Monument

Southwest of Bandera on State Highway 53 is El Morro National Monument, 43 miles from Grants.

El Morro is a buff-colored bluff, a prominent landmark that was named by Spanish conquistadors in the 17th century. As they followed the ancient Acoma-Zuni Trail, the spot became a convenient place to pitch camp that offered a constant supply of water.

Prehistoric Indians made their home on top of the 200-foot

El Morro

high mesa, and they left their marks in the form of petroglyphs and pictographs. In less than two centuries, they abandoned their mesa-top homes for the more hospitable valley floor. Their descendants are the modern Zuni.

Many travelers have stopped at El Morro, and like the Indians before them, have left etchings in the sandstone mesa. The first European to carve his name on Inscription Rock was Don Juan de Oñate on his way to colonize the new Mexico in 1605, 15 years before the Pilgrims landed at Plymouth Rock.

Numerous others have added to the record you see today— Spanish, American, Mexican, Indian—leaving behind a cultural hodge-podge of graffiti that tells an abbreviated history of the area.

THINGS TO DO

Start at the **Visitor Center,** open 8:00 am to 8:00 pm daily. The museum has interpretive displays, including a touch table and some of the numerous artifacts excavated from the pueblo ruins. Ask for handouts on the flora, fauna and geology of the area, as well as a trail guide.

The **trail to Inscription Rock** and the mesa top begins directly behind the visitor center. Before you begin, let the kids carve their names on the stone placed in front of the museum so they won't be tempted to do it later.

As you study the numerous inscriptions, ask the kids to imagine what happened to the people who left their names and part of their stories here. Compare the Spanish inscriptions with the petroglyphs you will see later. When you look at the petroglyphs, can you recognize any of the symbols? What do you think they mean?

Also look for Indian footholds, notches in the sandstone about 12 feet above the ground. This short-cut from the mesa to the pool was used by Indians who couldn't wait to slake their thirst by taking the longer path.

The trail is open 8:00 am–5:00 pm in the winter and until 7:30 pm in the summer. A hike to Inscription Rock takes a round trip of about 30 or 40 minutes. The trail becomes steep and continues to the ruins on top of the mesa.

The monument also has a small campground and picnic area, and several national forest campgrounds are nearby.

Superintendent, El Morro National Monument, Ramah, NM 87321, 505/783-4226.

DID YOU KNOW?

—El Malpais is Spanish for badlands.
—Bandera Crater is one of the youngest craters in the United States.
—The lava flow from Bandera created the longest known lava tube in the Southwest—almost 17.5 miles long!
—The largest ruin at El Morro is Atsinna, which is Zuni for "writings on the rock." Some archaeologists have estimated that it contained as many as 1000 rooms.
—The latest Spanish inscription at El Morro was carved in 1774.

—Wall niches in the pueblo at El Morro were probably used for personal items like jewelry and for religious objects.

—Women of Acoma carried water to their homes by balancing 3-5 gallon tinajas on their heads.

Zuni Indian Reservation

West of El Morro is Zuni Pueblo. Europeans first saw the pueblo in 1539, when the Spaniard Fray Marcos de Niza is said to have mistaken the sun's reflection on the adobe for a city made of gold. Coronado came several years later to Hawikuh expecting to find riches and found a mud village instead. Today the pueblo is a mixture of old and new, with horno ovens and red sandstone houses from the past capped by television antennas.

The Zuni, like their relatives the Hopi, live a daily life filled with religious devotion and punctuated by ceremonial dances to give thanks for their blessings. The masked Kachina dances are the most sacred of these.

With an empathy for nature, the Zuni learned to farm this arid place, developing an elaborate system of check and diversionary dams that takes advantage of the sudden, but infrequent, thunderstorms. This same system also acted as an effective erosion control in areas of heavy runoff, so that when rain fell, canals carried water to thirsty plants.

The Zuni also built "waffle gardens," fields divided by low mud walls into small squares and rectangles that could be individually watered. With these methods, they had spectacular success, cultivating up to 10,000 acres at a time, almost the entire Zuni Valley.

By the end of prehistoric times, the pueblo was a center of trade for a region ranging from the Colorado River to the Great Plains to northern Mexico. When the early white settlers came, the Indians continued in this role, supplying tons of corn to the military. The commander of Ft. Defiance at one time said the fort could not survive without the Zuni corn.

THINGS TO DO

The Zuni are noted for their handsome inlay jewelry, decorative pottery, and weaving, so stop at the **village cooperative** if you want to shop for these. You can also contact individual craftsmen through the cooperative. It is located on the left of the road as you enter from the east, and is open Monday through Saturday.

Nearby, and across the street, is the **tribal office,** next to the post office. Stop here for directions, hours the mission is open, and permission if you want to take photographs or visit the older villages, including the unrestored Hawikuh. You can also buy a fishing permit here. Blackrock, Ojo Caliente and Nutria lakes have abundant northern pike, trout, bass and catfish, as well as camping and hiking.

West of tribal headquarters take the first street to the left and wind up to the **Old Mission Church** (turn right at the crossroads). Recently restored, this adobe church is one of the oldest in the United States. Although it was originally built in 1629, it was partially destroyed in the Great Pueblo Rebellion of 1680. The walls have been decorated by two Zuni Indians with murals that combine their Indian culture and Christian faith. Visitors are welcome at Mass at 10:00 am Sundays.

If you visit in late November or early December, you may witness a **Shalako** ceremony, one of the most colorful of the Kachina dances. This ceremony marks the end of the religious calendar, with the cycle beginning again with the winter solstice.

For more information, contact Zuni Tribal Headquarters, PO Box 339, Zuni, NM, 87327-0339, 505/782-4481.

DID YOU KNOW?

—To the Zuni, the colors of corn represent the six directions. Yellow is north, blue is west, red is south, white is east, multicolored is above and black is below.
—The tribe mined copper and turquoise from tunnels and

open pits.

—Some believe the Zuni had the most sophisticated system of smoke signals of any tribe.

—In 1970 they became the first Indian community to administer their own affairs.

Gallup, New Mexico
Zip Code 87301   Area Code 505

The town of Gallup is on I-40. Before 1880 it was called the Blue Goose and was a combination way station, saloon and store. When the railroad came in 1881, the stop became a town.

Coal mining soon became an important part of the economy, as well as trading between the settlers, ranchers and Native Americans. At one time the town was the major trade center for the Navajo Reservation.

With the rise in popularity of the automobile, a new road was built, and Route 66 (now 66 Avenue) went smack through the middle of town, bringing with it the first influx of tourists.

Tourists are still an important part of the economy, and the town is still a crossroads for Indian trade, especially for the nearby Hopi, Navajo and Zuni.

THINGS TO DO
Northeast of town (Exit 33 on I-40) is the road to **Red Rock State Park,** once home to Anasazi Indians and now a center for modern-day Indians. Dances are performed nightly at 7:30 pm from Memorial Day through Labor Day, with a traditional Indian feast served before. Cost for the dances only is $3 per person, with children under 6 free.

Red Rock Museum covers the history and culture of the Navajo, Hopi and Zuni, including a waffle garden of corn, beans and squash. The museum is open Monday through Friday, 8:30 am–4:30 pm. Admission is by donation, suggested $1 per adult, $.50 per child.

The park also has a trading post, full service camping

facilities and nature trails. Major annual festivals are held in the large arena, including the largest inter-tribal gathering in the world. For four days in August, 20 Indian tribes come together for dances, crafts, rodeos, pole climbing, flute solos, Indian food, and an all-Indian parade through downtown Gallup. Call 800/242-4282 out of state or 722-2227 in state for festival information.

Red Rock State Park, PO Box 328, Church Rock, NM 87311, 722-3839.

Ask at the **Chamber of Commerce,** 103 West Highway 66, for a list of reputable Indian arts and crafts dealers in Gallup, as well as for an historic walking tour of town and directions to the swimming pool.

The **El Rancho Hotel,** built by movie mogul D. W. Griffith, has been enjoyed by famous actors such as Ronald Reagan, Spencer Tracy and Katherine Hepburn. They left behind their autographed photos in the art gallery. *Phone 863-9311, or write 1000 East 66 Avenue, Gallup, NM 87301 for reservations. Inexpensive.*

DID YOU KNOW?

—The town of Gallup was named after David L. Gallup, paymaster for the railroad. It came from the phrase "going to Gallup," which meant going to get paid.

—Rodeos like the one at Gallup are popular among the Indians.

—The Inter-Tribal ceremony has been held every year since 1922. In 1923 one performance had to be canceled after a downpour followed a Hopi rain dance. The organizers collected $1,000 insurance money from their rain policy.

2. FROM GALLUP TO FLAGSTAFF—ROUTE 66

Petrified Forest National Park

Fifty miles west of Gallup off I-40 is the entrance to the Petrified Forest National Park and the Painted Desert.

Legend has it the Petrified Forest was turned to stone by an Indian goddess, enraged when the wood in the area was too wet to start her fire. Scientists, on the other hand, claim it took millions of years to petrify.

Around 225 million years ago an ancient forest grew here in a stream-crossed valley. The air was hot and humid, and those strange creatures we call dinosaurs roamed freely. Over time, both dinosaurs and forests disappeared. Repeated stream flooding ripped up the pine-like trees, blanketing them with dirt that was saturated with silicon-rich water.

Sealed in a sediment tomb, the logs were slow to decay, giving time for the silicon to combine with oxygen to form quartz crystals in the plant tissue, sometimes even replacing it. Other trace minerals interacted with the plant residue, too, and the trees were transformed into petrified rainbows.

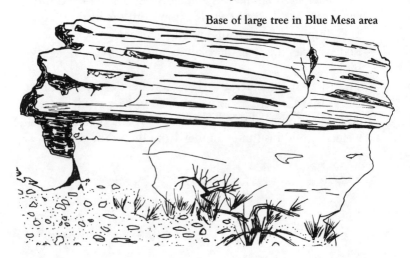

Base of large tree in Blue Mesa area

When, 60 million years ago, the land rose from 8,000 feet below sea level to almost a mile above, the dirt around the forest started to wash away, uncovering what is probably the largest area of petrified wood in the world. The process continues today, and every year erosion exposes new jeweled logs that have been buried for millennia.

North of I-40 from the petrified wood sites is the Painted Desert, colorful bands of eroded shale and sandstone stretching all the way to the Grand Canyon. With the right amount of heat, light and desert dust, the very air seems to shimmer with color. Early morning and evening, and following a rain, the colors are most vivid.

THINGS TO DO

Stop at the **Painted Desert Visitor Center** so the kids can watch the film showing the process of wood petrifying. The center also has exhibits, information on camping and hiking trails, and maps of the area.

The 27 mile **scenic drive** first takes you along the rim overlooking the Painted Desert, then crosses I-40 into the petrified wood areas (see Chapter XIII for activities). Stop at **Puerco Indian Ruin,** left behind by 12th-, and later, 14th-century inhabitants, and at **Newspaper Rock,** pecked with petroglyph messages from the past. See if the kids can find the hands, spirals and frogs that others say are here.

At **Blue Mesa,** take the short self-guided trail on a trip through an intricate maze of stark blue-gray clay. Have the kids look for pedestal logs ready to collapse and for petrified logs just emerging, and imagine what this bizarre landscape looked like covered with lush forest, when the trees last saw the light of day.

Continue on the scenic drive to the 111-foot **Agate Bridge,** spanning a 40-foot deep gully. Cowboy Tom Paine once won a $10 bet when he galloped his horse across the bridge in 1886. The bridge has since been reinforced with concrete to prevent it from falling into the gulch below.

A short self-guiding trail leads through the intensely colored

Long Logs, where many of the logs are 170 feet long. Among the fallen trees is **Agate House,** a partially restored pueblo built 900 years ago from the stone logs.

Other areas to see include the brilliantly colored logs on the valley floor jumbling together in **Jasper Forest,** and the kaleidoscope of wood in **Crystal Forest.**

The last stop is the **Rainbow Forest Museum.** Inside the museum are geological and historical exhibits, including a reconstructed pre-dinosaur reptile. Behind the museum is a path through a mosaic of colors and **Giant Logs.**

Although you can walk anywhere in the park, remember that taking petrified wood (even a very small sample) is illegal. If you want a souvenir, buy it from one of the numerous rock shops just outside the park and in Holbrook. It's cheaper than having the kind of guilty conscience that plagued one woman. She eventually returned the 47-pound boulder she took—by parcel post!

From Rainbow Forest Museum, continue out of the park and turn right on US Highway 180 to **Holbrook.** The town has numerous shops for rockhounds to explore, a museum in the Old County Courthouse, and several motels to spend the night.

Superintendent, Petrified Forest National Park, AZ 86028, 602/524-6228. Hours: daily, 6:00 am to 7:00 pm June through August, 7:00 am to 6:00 pm September and May, and 8:00 am–5:00 pm October through April, but some of the side roads close earlier. The park is locked at night. Admission is $5 per vehicle.

DID YOU KNOW?

—The silt, mud and volcanic ash covering the Petrified Forest was once as deep as 3,000 feet.

—Some of the petroglyphs at Newspaper Rock were apparently used as solar calendars.

—In the late 1800's the Petrified Forest was rapidly disappearing as pioneers carted off logs to build door frames and

Rock-layered mesa in Utah

Arches National Park *(Photo by Jim Ingwerson)*

Pahreah, Utah

Pahreah, Utah

"ET," Goblin Valley, Utah

Goblin Valley, "goblins" ,Utah

Mormon Temple, St. George, Utah

Looking up at Dead Horse Point, Cannyonlands, Utah *(Photo by Jim Ingwerson)*

The Great White Throne, Zion National Park *(Photo by George A. Grant, courtesy National Park Service)*

Kolob Arch, Zion National Park *(Photo by Allen Hagwood, courtesy Na-tional Park Service)*

Suspension bridge, Lake Powell

Chacoan masonry, Aztec National Monument, New Mexico

Pottery shards

Aztec National Monument,
New Mexico

Hornos near Taos, New Mexico

St. Francis of Assisi Church, Ranchos de Taos, New Mexico

High Prairie, New Mexico

Puye ruins, New Mexico

Puye ruins, New Mexico

Governor's Palace, Santa Fe, New Mexico

Square Tower House, Mesa Verde (*Photo by Jack Boucher, courtesy National Park Service*)

Pipe Spring, Arizona

Blue Mesa Trail, Petrified Forest, Arizona

Pipe Spring, Arizona

Jerome, Arizona

Arizona Sunset

Sedona, Arizona

table-tops and blasted them open for semi-precious jasper, agate and amethyst. In 1906 President Roosevelt declared the area a national monument, and the taking of petrified wood has been illegal ever since.

—According to early reports, before it was ransacked in the early 1900's, Crystal Forest was carpeted with sparkling chips that made the place look like a giant kaleidoscope.

—Numerous unusual fossils have been found in the park, including one nicknamed Gertie that paleontologists still don't know how to classify.

—The sheriff of Holbrook was once reprimanded by the U.S. President for sending out invitations to a hanging, promising cheerful surroundings and the use of the latest scientific methods.

—An estimated 25,000 pounds of petrified wood are stolen from the park every year.

Winslow, Arizona
Zip Code 86047   Area Code 602

The Mormons tried to call this place home, but they had the bad luck to settle Brigham City in a spot that was prone to annual flooding. That town was abandoned like an earlier nearby settlement, the ancient Hopi village of Homol'ovi.

It took the railroad in the late 1800's to bring life to the place, but most people today get here by car. Now on I-40, it used to be on Route 66 (Did Bobby Short have this town in mind when he sang about getting his kicks on Route 66?).

In the 1920's this paved road brought motor courts and short order restaurants out West. In the 1930's impoverished farmers fleeing memories of the midwestern Dust Bowl drifted through, followed in the 1940's by victorious World War II servicemen and their brides. Large numbers of tourists made their appearance in the 1950's, and they've been passing through ever since, even though Route 66 has passed into history.

THINGS TO DO

The **train depot** has an antique handcar and other railroad memorabilia. The rock group the Eagles took it easy on a corner in Winslow, and you can, too. Or you can try relaxing at **Clear Creek Reservoir,** a city park five miles southeast of town, which has boating, fishing, picnicking and swimming.

Just east of town is the newly established **Homol'ovi Ruins State Park.** Homol'ovi (Place of the Mounds) is thought to have been a major trade area for the Hopi between 1250 and AD 1500. When it was abandoned, ruins were left behind at four different sites. The place is still important to the Hopi today, and they return periodically with prayer feathers for the spirit of the clan elder whom they believe still lives here.

To visit Homol'ovi I and II, take 2nd Street east of town to State Road 87, then turn north for about ¼ mile, then left at the first dirt road. State Road 87 continues to the Hopi Reservation through the surrealistic Little Painted Desert.

Homol'ovi I, the ruins of a three-story pueblo, is about 2½ miles. About ½ mile further is the cemetery left from the first white settlement in the area.

A new visitor center and road improvements are scheduled to be completed by March of 1991.

Homol'ovi II, which includes an 800-room pueblo with three plazas, is about 2½ miles north of Homol'ovi I. The ¾ mile walk to the ruins is steep at the beginning, but then levels off. It has been left unexcavated and is a rare opportunity for the kids to see what a site looks like before archaeologists reconstruct it.

Homol'ovi Ruins State Park, 523 West 2nd Street, Winslow, 289-4106 or TDO for the hearing impaired, 289-4421.

The **Winslow Visitor Center** adjacent to I-40 has maps and information about the area. Behind the center to the east is what's left of the Mormon town of Brigham City, built in 1876 and occupied for only four short years.

From Winslow, continue west on I-40 about 18 miles to the paved road that leads six miles south to **Meteor Crater.** Although the meteor was only about 800 feet in diameter, it left a big hole—around three miles in circumference and 570 feet deep. The meteor was buried a quarter of a mile in the ground and only pieces of it have ever been found.

When it landed over 20,000 years ago, it was traveling around 33,000 mph and probably killed everything within a hundred miles. The crater is still so desolate that the Apollo astronauts trained for their mission on the moon here.

The astrogeological museum has exhibits, continuous films, a recorded lecture, and an Astronaut Hall of Fame. You can also view the crater from the rim.

Meteor Crater, telephone 602/526-5259, is a privately owned National Natural Landmark. Hours: daily 6:00 am–6:00 pm mid-May to mid-September, and 7:00 am–5:00 pm the rest of the year. Admission is $6.00 for adults, $5.00 for seniors, $2 for ages 12-17, and $1 ages 5-11.

Walnut Canyon National Monument

Continue west of Winslow on I-40 to the spur road to the cliff dwellings of Walnut Canyon.

The Sinagua Indians flourished in Walnut Canyon between about AD 1125 and 1250. The Sinagua (Spanish for "without water") migrated here from other parts of Arizona, and lived much the same as they had in the high desert region their ancestors once called home. By 1250 they had returned in the direction from which they came. Cleverly hidden among the limestone overhangs and outcroppings, their cliff homes lay camouflaged by nature for over 600 years after they were abandoned.

The **Visitor Center** has a small museum with an interesting exhibit of area plants and one depicting the three stages of excavation. The center also has information on ranger-conducted programs.

Ask for a map of the ¾ mile **Island Trail**, a self-guiding walk through the U-shaped gorge to some of the dwellings. The steep trail descends 185 feet with steps and paved paths to the canyon below. For an easier walk, follow the **rim trail** to the canyon overlook or the picnic area in the pines.

You can also arrange for a **horseback ride** through the canyon by contacting Fairfield Stables, Fairfield Flagstaff Resort, Walnut Canyon Road, Flagstaff, 602/526-3232 ext. 5205.

Superintendent, Walnut Canyon National Monument, Walnut Canyon Road, Flagstaff, AZ 86004, 602/526-3367. Hours: daily, 7:00 am to 7:00 pm in summer, 8:00 am to 5:00 pm in winter. The self-guided trail closes at 5:00 pm. Admission is $3 per vehicle.

DID YOU KNOW?

—The Sinagua used the rock overhangs as roofs for their dwellings.

—The Sinagua were farmers. Farming was done primarily on the canyon rims, and the main crops were corn, beans, pumpkins and sunflowers.

—The Sinagua were active traders, and items from as far away as the Gulf of Mexico have been found in Walnut Canyon.

3. FLAGSTAFF, ARIZONA
Zip Code 86001/86002   Area Code 602

Flagstaff is the largest city in northern Arizona. It is set amidst ponderosa pine, rolling meadows and the towering San

Ponderosa pine

Francisco Peaks, legendary home of the Indian gods. Over 200 extinct volcanoes dot a landscape that has been peopled by cliff dwellers, historical Indians, cowboys and lumberjacks.

The earliest prehistoric residents came here partly because of the fresh springwater. That same good water later attracted the white man, who brought along the railroad and logging ventures in the surrounding pine forests.

Reports about how the town got its name don't agree on the details, but they all trace its origin back to a tall, thin pine tree that was stripped of branches to support a United States flag. This flagstaff then became a guidepost for wagon trains traveling west.

THINGS TO DO

Two miles northwest of town on US 180 (toward the Grand Canyon) is the **Pioneer Historical Museum.** The museum is housed in what was once City Hospital and depicts the history of the area from the Conquistadors in 1540 to the 20th century. On the grounds are frontier displays, buildings and machinery, and the **Art Barn,** which has continuous art shows.

Pioneer Historical Museum, 774-6272, is open 9:00 am–5:00 pm, Monday through Saturday, 1:30 pm–5:00 pm on Sunday during the summer, and until 4:00 pm during the winter. Admission is free.

A mile beyond on US 180 is one of the best museums around, the **Museum of Northern Arizona,** dedicated to the anthropology, biology, geology, history and fine arts of the Colorado Plateau. The museum has an international reputation for its excellent exhibits on the history and religion of Native Americans and a large collection of native plants and animals.

Stop at the Study Center, with its pull-out drawers. Children will also enjoy exploring the hands-on room with the accompanying question guide. If you are in the market for Indian crafts, the Museum Shop has a good selection, as well as summer arts and crafts exhibitions and demonstrations.

Museum of Northern Arizona, Route 4, Box 720, Flagstaff

86001, 774-5211. Hours: daily, 9:00 am–5:00 pm. Admission is $3 for adults, $1.50 for ages 5-12.

For maps and information about the area and the numerous festivals and special events, visit the **Chamber of Commerce,** downtown by the railroad depot. One of the special events for which you can order tickets is the **All-Indian PowWow.** This four day celebration at the beginning of July has ceremonial and competitive Indian dancing, rodeos, parades, food booths and stalls selling Indian-made arts and crafts. Thousands come to enjoy, so be sure to make your lodging reservations early.

From the center of town, take Santa Fe Avenue west about one mile to Mars Hill and the world famous **Lowell Observatory.** It was tucked in the pines in 1894 by Percival Lowell, who advanced the theory that there are canals on Mars built by intelligent life. He also predicted the position of Pluto years before it was first seen from here by another astronomer in 1930.

Today the observatory is a private research center and a leader in analyzing data collected from the moon and Mars. Lecture tours are offered at the Visitor Center Tuesday through Saturday, 10:00 am and 1:30 pm, June-August, and at 1:30 pm only during the rest of the year. Evening telescope viewing is on the first day of each month and on every Friday, June through August, weather permitting, 8:00 pm–10:00 pm.

There are no public rest room facilities, and the telescope domes are not heated, so dress for outdoor weather.

Lowell Observatory, 1400 W. Mars Hill Road, Flagstaff, AZ 86001, 774-2096. Admission is by donation, suggested $1 per adult, $3 per family, children under 6 free.

On West Riordan Road, near the junction of US Highway 89A and US 66 and the Arizona State College campus at the west end of town, is **Riordan State Historic Park,** with the two Edwardian mansions of the Riordan brothers. These turn-of-the-century lumber barons built their look-alike homes side by side with elegant stained glass windows, foundations of native volcanic rock and exteriors of rough pine and stone, then connected them with a recreation room.

Older children might enjoy the guided tour of Timothy Riordan's mansion, complete with memorabilia of the Riordan family and many of the original furnishings. The homes are surrounded by a small park with a picnic area and large shade trees. Look for the logging wagon, a large, two-wheeled cart used to drag logs from the forest.

Riordan State Historic Park, PO Box 217, Flagstaff, AZ 86002, 779-4395. Hours: daily 8:00 am–5:00 pm, May through September, and Thursday through Monday the rest of the year. Tours are offered several times during the day. Cost is $2 per adult, under 18 free.

Budding gardeners might enjoy a visit to the **Arboretum,** with its 5,000-square-foot horticultural center and solar greenhouse. The Arboretum focuses on plants native to the area, including the mountains and desert. It is also involved in the conservation of rare and endangered species, so your visit will include a walk among not only the native, but also the exotic and experimental.

Take I-40 west of town to Woody Mountain Road, then turn south approximately 4 miles.

The Arboretum, PO Box 670, Flagstaff 86002, 774-1441, is open Monday through Saturday, 10:00 am–3:00 pm. Guided tours are available at 11:00 am and 1:00 pm. Admission is free.

DID YOU KNOW?

—The wagon trail that went through Flagstaff eventually became US Route 66.

—Both of the Riordan mansions are two-storied and both have 5000 square feet.

—Lowell Observatory has one of the largest collections of planetary photos in the world—around 2,000,000.

4. CIRCLE SOUTH FROM FLAGSTAFF—STORIES FROM THE PAST

Take I-17 south of Flagstaff to US 89A for a scenic drive through **Oak Creek Canyon,** one of Arizona's most beautiful. Gorges and forests fill the canyon and paint it with multi-colored grandeur. Scores of tiny waterfalls plunge from the canyon walls, and sycamores line the washes.

Stop at **Lookout Point,** where you can gaze at the canyon 2000 feet below. Have the kids look along the rim for the black basalt that indicates past volcanic activity.

If it's a hot day, don't miss **Slide Rock State Park** for a swim and a wet ride down a natural rock channel in Oak Creek. Make sure the kids wear their jeans—these are rocks they are sliding on! Current expansion plans for this popular park include a visitor center, refreshments, interpretive trails, and enhancement of the existing orchards.

Slide Rock is open 8:00 am to 7:00 pm during the summer, but it does close when full. Day use fees are $2 per vehicle for resident, $3 for non-resident and $1 for pedestrians.

If Slide Rock is full, the kids can swim at **Grasshopper Point** at the lower end of the canyon 1.6 miles north of the town of Sedona.

Before you reach Grasshopper Point, stop at **Indian Gardens,** the first settlement in the canyon. Here you can see the creations of Ted Conibear, said to be the world's only sand sculptor. Using red creek sand and white cliff sand, a spoon, paring knife and two brushes, he has fashioned a life-size replica of the Last Supper.

You can picnic in the canyon or stay at one of the rustic resorts or the National Forest campgrounds, open May through August.

For more information on the campgrounds, contact the Ranger Station, PO Box 300, Sedona 86336, telephone 602/282-4119.

Gateway to the Unusual 265

Sedona is at the edge of the Verde Valley, where juniper fires once burned to heat the branding irons for one of the most active cattle ranges in northern Arizona.

Sedona
Zip Code 86336   Area Code 602

Sedona's setting is a gorgeous one of towering, vibrant red buttes. Hollywood has used it for numerous television and motion pictures, including the 1988 opening segment of Sesame Street and a chase scene in "Midnight Run" with Robert De Niro.

The town is also a southwestern art center for contemporary, western and Native American art, and some say it rivals Santa Fe. It is loaded with art galleries—around 50 in a town with only 9500 residents.

THINGS TO DO
A favorite pastime of old-timers was naming the numerous red rock formations. Tell the kids to look for "Coffee Pot Rock," "Snoopy," and "Sleeping Camel," then to find their own rocks to name.

The main tourist attraction in town is shopping. **Tlaquepaque** (Spanish for "the best of everything") is an arts and crafts shopping center named after a village near Guadalajara, Mexico. Built to resemble an Old Mexico market square, it is a pleasant place to browse, with fountains, gardens, and courtyards. (See Chapter XIII, Discoveries for "A Three-Culture Salad," for shopping activities.)

To get there, take State Road 179 south of US 89A about ¼ mile and turn right at the cobblestone driveway. Special trolleys run between here and the motels in summer.

The kids can also take a **fire engine tour,** which operates daily from uptown Sedona.

Red Rock Crossing has one of the best views in the state. It is a day-use recreation area, great for picnics and scenery. Take US 89A west of town a little over four miles, then turn left at

Red Rock Loop Road. Around two miles, turn left at Chavez Ranch Road, travel about ½ mile to Route 216 and turn right for another ½ mile. The recreation area is open daily 9:00 am–8:00 pm in the summer. The road has no trailer turn-around.

For another great view, take **Schnebly Hill Road,** just past the bridge on State Road 179, then turn left on the gravel road.

Some people come to Sedona to experience the **vortexes,** energy centers that the Indians consider sacred. You can visit the main vortex areas and test the energy fields yourself. Or you can just visit them for the beautiful scenery.

Bell Rock is located on State Road 179 toward Oak Creek. Stop at the National Forest Vista Point for a view of the rock on the other side of the road. Have the kids test the energy by turning toward it and holding out the palms of their hands. Can they feel anything? Walk across the highway to the base of the rock. Can they feel anything now? If they can, what do they think it is?

Cathedral Rock, at Red Rock Crossing along the banks of Oak Creek, is another spot easily accessible, and so is **Airport Mesa.** Each vortex is said to have a different kind of energy and a different effect. For more information on the vortexes, stop at the New Age Information Center on Highway 179 or at the Chamber of Commerce.

The **Chapel of the Holy Cross,** considered an architec-turally important modern church, is a magnificent building that juts heavenward from the surrounding rugged red rock. It is about three miles south of US 89A just off State Road 179.

Several tour operators offer jeep tours of Sedona, the vor-texes, the Hopi Mesas, and ancient ruins. They often include information on Indian lore, wildlife, archaeology and geology. Airplane and helicopter rides, horseback rides and chuck-wagon suppers are also available.

The **Chamber of Commerce,** on the corner of US 89A and Forest Road, has a list of tour operators and lodging, including the several posh resorts in town.

DID YOU KNOW?

—According to old-timers, Cathedral Rock was originally named Courthouse Butte. But now Courthouse Butte is east of Bell Rock, even though this formation was originally called Church Rock. And if you have that straight, don't forget the other Cathedral Rock in Red Canyon.

—The Indians say the vortexes are energy points where man can realize his true dreams. According to legend, one of them, Boynton Canyon, is home of the Great Earth Mother.

—Many believe the medicine wheels you find at the vortexes help heal the damage done to Earth by modern civilization.

—Sedona was named in 1902 by fruit farmer T. C. Schnebly after his wife, Sedona.

—Oak Creek Canyon was the setting for Zane Grey's novel *Call of the Canyon.*

Sedona to Cottonwood

Take US 89A toward the town of Cottonwood. Midway there is a side road to **Page Springs Fish Hatchery.** Here, in the stocked Bubbling Pond, you can watch several species of fish, including trout, bass, and the endangered Colorado River squawfish and razorback sucker.

Kids can walk the graduated size raceways to see growth progress and feed the fish from the nearby vending machine. It's also a great place for bird watching and picnicking. Future plans call for a visitor center and expansion to a capacity of 1,000,000 rainbow trout a year.

Page Springs Fish Hatchery is open to visitors 8:00 am to 4:00 pm daily. For more information, call 602/634-4805.

DID YOU KNOW?

—It takes eight months for trout like those at Page Springs Fish

Hatchery to grow to nine inches.
—If it weren't for Page Springs and the other two fish hatcheries in the state, there would be no trout to catch in Arizona.

Dead Horse Ranch State Park

In Cottonwood, take the business route through town (Main Street) and turn right on North 5th Street to Dead Horse Ranch State Park. Be sure to negotiate the low-water crossing across the Verde River slowly. During flood times, access is via the Tuzigoot National Monument route, a rough dirt road not recommended for RV's.

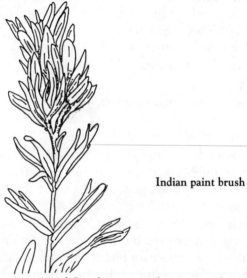

Indian paint brush

Dead Horse was named by the original owner. The story goes that he and his children were shopping for a place to live one day. When they came here, the children saw a bleached skeleton lying on the ground. Their father bought the land when they said they liked the ranch with the dead horse. This 320-acre, outdoor park is a pleasant place for camping, bird watching, hiking, or just relaxing.

The park has hiking trails, camp sites with hot showers and

RV hook-ups, and evening nature programs on spring and fall weekends. You can fish in the stocked lagoon or the Verde River. Buy your state fishing license at the park if you don't already have one.

Pick up a list at the park entrance station of the 350 native species of plants and the almost 150 species of birds you can see here, including the great blue heron, snowy egret, and bald and golden eagle.

When the Verde River floods briefly in spring and fall, the park can be temporarily isolated. If you plan to camp, arrive early, because spaces are on a first-come, first-served basis, and they are often full.

Dead Horse Ranch State Park, PO Box 144, Cottonwood, AZ, 86326, 602/634-5283, is open year-round, 8:00 am to 7:00 pm Monday through Thursday, 8:00 am to 10:00 pm Friday and Saturday, and 8:00 am to 8:00 pm Sunday. Cost for day use is $3 per vehicle, with Christmas and holidays free. Campsites range from $6 to $8.

Tuzigoot National Monument

A few miles northwest of Cottonwood is the turnoff to the Indian ruins of Tuzigoot.

Perched above the Verde Valley, Tuzigoot began around AD 1000 as a small village of about 50 people. It eventually grew into a prehistorical refugee camp as farmers from the north fled the surrounding drought. During the 13th century, around 400 Sinagua Indians lived here, using the natural springs for irrigation to farm the Verde Valley. The site is on a hillside, unlike many southwestern ruins, and affords an expansive view of the Verde Valley.

The **museum** displays many artifacts excavated from the site, and a ¼ mile, **self-guiding trail** leads you through the restored, walk-in ruins, where you can trace 300 years of Sinagua development. Its restoration and manageable size make it a good place for kids to explore.

Tuzigoot National Monument, Box 68, Clarkdale, AZ

86324, 602/634-5564. *Hours: daily, 8:00 am–5:00 pm during
the winter, 7:00 am–7:00 pm during the summer. Cost is $3 per
car.*

DID YOU KNOW?

—Tuzigoot is Apache for "crooked water."
—Entrance to the ground-floor rooms was not usually through
a doorway but via a ladder in the roof.
—The Sinagua mined salt from a deposit near the present
town of Camp Verde.
—The Sinagua buried some children beneath floors in the
pueblo, but adult dead have been found on the garbage pile.

Jerome
Zip Code 86331   Area Code 602

From Tuzigoot continue through the town of Clarkdale and
rejoin US 89A to the town of Jerome.

It doesn't seem possible for Jerome to hang like it does on
the steep slope of Cleopatra Hill. With a 1500-foot difference
between the highest and lowest part of town, it is not a place
for those afraid of heights. It is a place for those with a
hankering for the past of wild mining camps and for spectacular views that extend from the lush Verde Valley to the red
rocks of Sedona and the faraway San Francisco Peaks.

Only a ramshackle copper mining camp in the 1880's, by
1929 the town had become Arizona's fourth largest city, with a
population of 15,000. One of its mines, the Little Daisy, was
reported to be the richest vein of copper in the world. It
returned $125,000,000 in 22 years.

But the effect of the mines wasn't all good. The hundreds of
tunnels deep into the interior of Mingus Mountain resulted in
instability. In 1925 the United Verde Mining company set off
a dynamite blast in their Black Pit, causing an unprecedented
surface shifting with subsequent blasting. The town jail even-

tually ended up across the street, 225 feet away and 50 feet lower from where it was built.

The mayor once quipped about how progressive Jerome was—always on the move. Even today, the town is settling, and many buildings stand askew, propped up with concrete and wooden stilts.

As happened in so many western mining camps, the mines became losing propositions financially. The companies closed their doors and left town, along with most of the residents. A few hardy souls remained to keep the town alive. About 400 people now call the place home, and the "ghost town" is enjoying a resurgence as a mecca for artists and tourists.

THINGS TO DO

The town is a National Historic Monument, and it seems to operate tongue-in-cheek. Narrow streets snake through town, and steep trails and stairs are the only other way to get around.

The restored mansion of James S. Douglas, copper mining king, is set aside in **Jerome State Historic Park.** The turnoff is near the Old Mingus Union High School at the edge of town.

The white-plastered adobe house includes an early built-in vacuum cleaning system, marble bathrooms, steam heat, and a billiard room. There is also a fine collection of mining equipment, a three-dimensional scale model of the mines and underground workings, a slide show, and Douglas' memorabilia. The mansion overlooks the multi-million dollar Little Daisy Mine, where Douglas struck it rich in 1926.

Douglas Mining Museum, Box 156, 634-7349. Hours: daily, 8:00 am–5:00 pm. Admission is $1 for over 17.

In downtown Jerome, you can browse in the shops filled with antiques, rocks and minerals, copper, pottery and more, and visit Jerome Historical Society's Mine Museum on Main Street for $.50.

The **Chamber of Commerce,** 317 Main Street, can tell you about local guided tours of nearby historic spots.

One mile from the end of Main Street, across the bridge on a dirt road, is the **Gold King Mine and Ghost Town,** built with leftover buildings from the early 1900's. The kids can pan for gold, visit the walk-in mine, and see an historic working sawmill, old mining machinery, a 1900's blacksmith shop, and antique gas engines. There is also a gift shop, petting farm, and picnic area. This is a hands-on place.

Gold King Mine is open 9:00 am to 6:00 pm daily. Admission is $2.

DID YOU KNOW?

—The adjacent valley was named Verde (Spanish for "green") by explorers in 1582 because of the bright green copper ore. The Indians used the same ore as face paint.

—The road to the hospital was too steep for wagons, so the miners had to carry patients up the hill.

—Water was scarce in Jerome, and at three different times the people had to camp out after fire destroyed most of the wooden houses. The residents even hired Pancho Villa and his band of men to haul in water for them.

—The mining companies had little sympathy for the striking miners in the early 1900's. At one point, they loaded them into boxcars and dumped them off in the southeastern Arizona desert.

—The mines of Jerome produced $800,000,000.

—The town site is so steep roofs sometimes face streets that are above them.

—One of the churches in town was built out of powder kegs covered with stucco.

Clarkdale to Montezuma Castle

From Clarkdale, take US 89A southeast to State Road 279. At the junction of I-17 and Middle Verde Road (exit for Camp Verde) is the **Yavapai-Apache Visitor Center.** The center, open daily, has exhibits, slide programs, and tourist information on the Verde Valley. The museum is small now, but plans are to build it into an Indian cultural center with a museum,

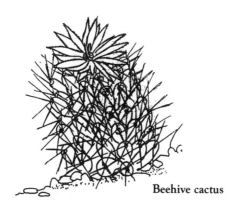

Beehive cactus

Indian art gallery, art educational center and library.

Continue to the town of Camp Verde and **Fort Verde State Historic Park.** A military post near here was called Camp Lincoln when it was established in 1866 to protect the settlers from the Tonto Apache and Yavapai Indians, but the United States Army changed its name when it moved the post to the present site a few years later.

Today you can see a museum with old military uniforms and equipment, original officer's quarters, and part of the parade ground and flagpole.

Ft. Verde State Historic Park, Box 397, Camp Verde, 86322, 602/567-3275. Hours are daily in summer, 8:00 am–5:00 pm, and closed Tuesday and Wednesday in winter. Admission is $1 for adults, children under 18 are free.

Montezuma Castle National Monument

Continue north a few miles from Camp Verde to Montezuma Castle National Monument.

It isn't a castle and Montezuma probably never heard of it, but this five-story, 20-room cliff dwelling is pocketed in the mouth of a cave halfway up a sheer cliff. It was a formidable fortress, with almost windowless 12″ thick walls of limestone and mud and limited accessibility by ladders which could easily be pulled up to thwart attacking enemies. The Sinagua Indians lived here from around AD 1100 to AD 1450, and the dwelling is one of the best preserved in the Southwest.

You can view Montezuma Castle from the shady, self-guiding **Sycamore Trail** that leads to the lower ruins along Beaver Creek.

The **Visitor Center** is small but has a good museum showing the history of the area. There is also a picnic area.

To reach the other portion of the monument, **Montezuma Well,** take I-17 north four miles to the McGuirreville exit, then follow the signs east and north a few miles, partially on a dirt road.

Montezuma Well is a 55-foot deep limestone sink filled with green water. Overlooking the pond are small cliff home ruins, and nearby are the remains of a prehistoric irrigation system showing how essential this reliable source of water was to the surrounding area—to the amount of 1,900,000 gallons a day. The water enters the pond from the underground caverns, then exits through the side cave to irrigation ditches.

Montezuma Trail is a self-guiding nature trail ⅓ mile past the pond and ruins to a lovely spot by the river.

Montezuma Castle, Box 219, Camp Verde, AZ 86322, 602/567-3322. Summer hours are 7:00 am to 7:00 pm daily; winter hours are 8:00 am to 5:00 pm daily. Admission is $3 for Montezuma Castle, free for Montezuma Well.

DID YOU KNOW?

—The water from Montezuma Well deposited a hard substance in the ditches which preserved them.

—The Sinagua Indians learned irrigation methods from the Hohokam sometime after AD 1225.

—The water of Montezuma Well, a constant temperature of 76 degrees Fahrenheit, is high in carbon dioxide. You won't find any fish there, but air breathing animals such as turtles thrive.

—Montezuma Castle was abandoned 100 years before Cortez conquered the Aztecs.

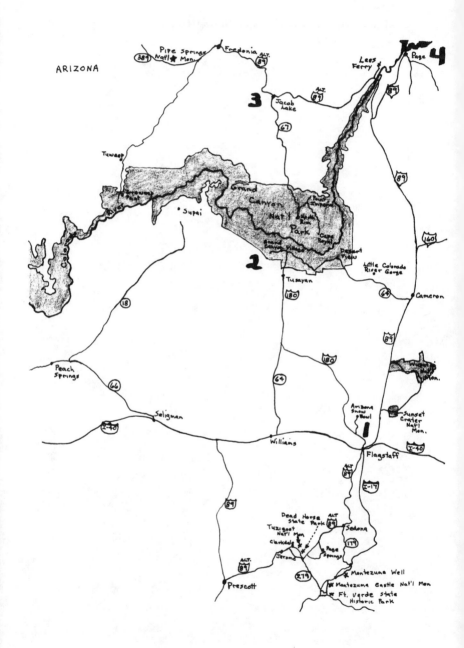

11

WET AND WILD:
Grand Canyon and Lake Powell

Northwestern Arizona is dominated by the handiwork of the Colorado River. For millions of years, this mighty torrent has been carving into the body of Mother Earth, revealing older and older pages of her past and leaving her cracked and wrinkled.

Dominguez and Escalante, those intrepid explorers of 1776 who left their names from one end of the Southwest to the other, were two of the first Europeans to see the river. They spent close to two weeks just looking for a way from one side to the other. The problem wasn't only the river, it was also her workmanship, the steep, confining walls of slick rock.

A wagon train of Mormon pioneers had a similar problem in 1879. The journey started as a "shortcut," but when the group reached the Colorado, they could go no farther. By blasting into the rock wall of Glen Canyon, they were able to cut an opening to lower their wagons to the river below. Instead of six weeks, the shortcut took six months. Three and a half miles below the confluence of the Colorado and Escalante Rivers, you can still see part of this Hole-in-the-Rock high on the canyon wall.

Of all the canyons of the Colorado, the Grand is perhaps the most awesome. There have been many explanations about how the canyon became so grand.

When the first tourists came in 1883, John Hance, their guide, told them he had shoveled it out and used the dirt to build the San Francisco Peaks near Flagstaff. Early theories claimed it was a cataclysm that opened a giant cleft in the earth. Others maintained the Colorado was once an underground river, and the canyon was formed when the roof collapsed. A more modern theory is less spectacular.

Millions of years ago, the Colorado River snaked through here on flat ground. Then, slowly, the ground began to rise—never fast enough to dump the river out of its original meanderings, just fast enough for the river to stay level by carving the stream bed deeper.

At the same time, the river was growing as melting glacial ice slid down from the rising Rocky Mountains. Mixed with cutting pebbles and stones, the water carved a path through the land.

However, just as new information disproved earlier theories, modern data is being used to formulate up-to-date, and more complicated, hypotheses. The experts still don't agree on the "how," but even if you believe Hance created it with a shovel, you can still enjoy the magnificent scenery.

Today, the canyon continues to grow in size, not so much in depth as in width. The canyon walls are eroding away, and eventually, hundreds of years from now, the lodges on the rims will crash to the floor below. Even now, major rockfalls are a common occurrence. If the earth holds still for long enough, with no more earthquakes or uplifts, the Grand Canyon may eventually become a wide valley, and then a flat plain with a meandering river like it once was.

Americans discovered the Grand Canyon in the early 1800's, but they weren't nearly as enamored with it as they are today. First reactions were summed up by James O. Pattie in

1825. "Horrid," he said. As far as he and the rest of America were concerned, this hugh gash in the ground was an obstacle to exploring, not to mention the fact that the farming was lousy, gold and beaver were nowhere to be found, and there was nobody to convert.

Somewhere along the line, though, the majesty of the Canyon lured the white man into testing his mettle on its stage of eons. Since then, he's tried to bridge it with everything from motorcycles to bicycles, glider-kites to twelve-year-old's spit.

He's also tried to run through it on the river—in hand-hewn plank boats, motorboats, inner tubes, rafts, kayaks, with a life jacket and no boat, and traveling upstream in jet boats. Hundreds of people each year travel down the river through the Grand Canyon, even grandmothers and tykes. That's not to say it can't be dangerous. There are still those who lose their lives in the attempt.

DID YOU KNOW?

—The Hopi believe the Grand Canyon is where man emerged into this world from the underworld.

—The Colorado River moves approximately 27,000,000 tons of silt and sand a day—about as much dirt every 2½ years as was removed to build the Panama Canal. And it has been doing this for several million years!

—When Dominguez and Escalante reached the site now called Lee's Ferry, they tried to cross the Colorado River, only to find the water was too deep and too swift. They nicknamed the place Salsipuedes, meaning "get out if you can."

The Grand Canyon and Lake Powell

1. To the South Rim of the Grand Canyon

2. Grand Canyon National Park
3. Jacob Lake to Pipe Spring National Monument
4. Glen Canyon National Recreation Area (Lake Powell)

1. TO THE SOUTH RIM OF THE GRAND CANYON

You can reach the south rim of the Grand Canyon by taking US Highway 89 north of Flagstaff (Tour 1); I-40 west to State 64, then north to where it joins US 180 through the San Francisco Peaks northwest (Tour 3).

Tour 1—US Highway 89 North

On US 89 15 miles north of Flagstaff is the turnoff to **Sunset Crater and Wupatki National Monuments.**

Sunset Crater was born around 900 years ago amid violent earthquakes and roaring eruptions that spewed chunks of fire and ash into the air. Today it looks like a giant anthill, its desolate gray-black slopes skirted at the bottom by trees, the rim stained the fiery red of eternal sunset by chemicals from deep within the earth.

When the volcano erupted, the surrounding land was inhabited by prehistoric man. The burned remains of his houses have since been found. The cataclysm drove him away, but it also brought a blessing. For 800 miles in all directions, a fine layer of ash blanketed the land, and when it had cooled, it acted as a garden mulch, trapping precious moisture and adding nutrients to the arid ground. Miraculously, corn grew where once it had shriveled and died.

The Sinagua Indians lived here after the eruption, and Wupatki, one of their most important villages, became a center of trade. More people lived here after the eruption than before. For 200 years several different groups of prehistoric Indians prospered, until the west wind piled the ash into erratic drifts, exposing the land once again to the moisture-robbing sun. By 1300, the people had disappeared.

The **Visitor Center** for Sunset Crater is about two miles from the entrance. Stop for information and for the kids to watch the film on volcanoes. The center is open daily, 7:00 am–7:00 pm in summer, with shorter hours in winter.

You can no longer walk to the top of Sunset Crater because an overabundance of hikers on the soft slopes was rapidly deteriorating the cone, but at the base is a self-guiding, easy nature trail (one mile loop) that leads you across Bonito lava flow with intriguing formations and an ice cave. Ask at the visitor center about other hikes and programs.

Bonito Campground, just west of the park boundary, is managed by the National Park Service. It is open April through mid-November. Nightly campfire programs are held in the amphitheater June through August.

The narrow, winding road in Sunset Crater loops north and west to **Wupatki National Monument,** which has some 800 ruins, dating mostly from the 12th century. Wupatki can also be reached by returning to the Interstate and continuing north.

The **Visitor Center,** open 8:00 am–5:00 pm daily, has exhibits on the 12th- and 13th-century inhabitants and features cultural demonstrations such as pottery making, stick figure making, and weaving. It also has information on ranger-led programs and hiking trails.

Behind the center is a short, self-guiding trail to **Wupatki ruins,** rising impressively from the black lava. Look for the rare ball court and the blow-hole that circulates air to underground caves.

Ask at the center about other interesting trails to ruins.

Sunset Crater National Monument, Rt. 3, Box 149, Flagstaff, AZ 86001, 602/527-7042.

Superintendent, Wupatki National Monument, Tuba Star Rt., Flagstaff, AZ 86001, 602/527-7040.

Admission to both monuments is free.

DID YOU KNOW?

—Mullein is a common plant growing on lava flows. It can grow up to seven feet high. Mullein tea is said to be good for respiratory problems.
—Sunset Crater is 1,000 feet high.
—Sunset Crater first erupted AD 1064–65, with periodic eruptions for 200 years after that.

Tour 2—I-40 West

I-40 west of Flagstaff will take you past the **Grand Canyon Deer Farm,** 25 miles west at Exit 171. Children can feed the fawns here in June and July. They may also walk among and pet some of the other animals—llamas, monkeys, miniature donkeys, and peacocks.

Summer hours are 8:00 am to dusk. Call 602/635-2357 for visitor hours during the rest of the year. The deer farm is closed January through March. Admission is $3.50 for adults, $2 for ages 3-13.

Five miles past the Deer Farm on I-40 is the turnoff to the Grand Canyon, State 64. Near the town of Williams, White Horse Lake offers camping and water sports.

If you have older children interested in backpacking, visit the **Havasupai Indian Reservation.** Since AD 1300 the peaceful Havasupai have lived in the oasis of Havasu Canyon, replete with dramatic waterfalls, lush fields, and streams. It's obvious they have spent that time contentedly living with nature rather than trying to conquer it.

When a Franciscan padre became the first white man to visit them in 1776, he was greeted with six days of celebration. Your reception may not be as elaborate, but the pristine land and way of life you will see is very much like it was 200 years ago.

The center of the reservation is the village of Supai at the bottom of Havasu Canyon, a side gorge of the Grand Canyon.

The only way to get there is by hiking or riding a horse down a seven mile trail. The trail begins at Hualapai Hilltop, a remote access point at the end of a 70 mile, partly gravel road that leaves from State 66 about seven miles east of Peach Springs.

Visitors must first obtain a tribal permit, available by writing Havasupai Tourist Enterprise, Supai, AZ 86435, 602/448-2141. Advance reservations are also required for an overnight stay at either the lodge (448-2111) or campground (448-2121). Make them around six months in advance to stay during March through October. If you or the kids aren't up to the steep, dusty hike, consider renting a horse and Havasupai guide when you make your reservations.

State Highway 64 continues to Tusayan and the Grand Canyon.

Tour 3—US Highway 180 Through the San Francisco Peaks

US 180 (Humphreys Street) north of Flagstaff travels through the **San Francisco Peaks,** the state's tallest mountains. You will pass through mountain forests and meadows of dazzling aspen that have invaded areas where fire has burned off the pine.

Pika

The peaks are volcanic in origin, and the tops are arctic tundra dotted with ancient bristlecone pines, some of the oldest living things on earth. Humphreys Peak, the highest point in Arizona (12,670 feet), was perhaps once 3000 feet higher before it blew its top.

San Francisco Peaks are the legendary home of the Hopi gods and possibly the home of their ancestors. They still make pilgrimages here.

A Hopi legend does tell of a fire that destroyed the wicked. According to legend, a light came from the mountain, growing brighter every day. The chief, disturbed by the moral degeneracy of the tribe, warned them the fire was a sign for them to mend their ways. Most ridiculed him, but some listened and fled the village. After four nights the light reached the village and burned or suffocated all who had remained. Some think the fire was the eruption of nearby Sunset Crater.

About seven miles outside of Flagstaff, turn right on Snow Bowl Road for another seven miles to the **Arizona Snow Bowl ski area.** On summer weekends and holidays, the scenic Skyride will take you to the top of Mt. Agassiz, 11,200 feet high, and a sweeping view of the Grand Canyon and northern Arizona. Cost is $6 for adults, $3 for ages 6-12. There are also picnic facilities and a snack shop.

US 180 continues through rolling hills of desert scrub 78 miles from Flagstaff to the Grand Canyon.

A few miles south of the Park is the town of Tusayan. Take the kids to the state-of-the-art **IMAX Theater** showing of "Grand Canyon: The Hidden Secrets."

Grand Canyon Theater, PO Box 1397, Grand Canyon 86023. Showings are between 8:30 am and 8:30 pm in the summer. Call 602/638-2203 for a winter schedule.

Tusayan also has several motels if the lodging in the park is full.

DID YOU KNOW?

—If conditions are favorable, bristlecone pines like those on the San Francisco Peaks can grow up to 50 feet, but if conditions are hostile (such as at tree line), they will survive thousands of years in a dwarfed condition. In fact, the oldest living trees are those that have grown the most slowly.

—San Francisco Peaks were named by 17th-century Franciscan priests in honor of St. Francis.

2. Grand Canyon National Park

For many, a visit to the Grand Canyon is an inspiring trip into nature's grandeur. Ferde Grofe wrote the "Grand Canyon Suite" expressing his awe.

For others, it's just another big hole in the ground, and they would agree with Marshal Foch of France, who exclaimed when seeing it, "What a marvelous place to throw your mother-in-law."

Very young children may lean toward the "hole-in-the-ground" sentiment. Older children will no doubt find it as spectacular as you do.

THINGS TO DO

There are two major parts of Grand Canyon National Park—the North Rim and the South Rim. Both give a completely different experience of the canyon. (See Chapter XIII for activities at the Grand Canyon.)

Without a doubt, the best time to visit the South Rim is in autumn, when the heat and crowds have dissipated and the snows have not yet arrived. The North Rim is over 1000 feet higher, with the resulting climate changes. It is cooler in the summer and colder in the winter. Over 12½ feet of snow fall then, and the North Rim road is closed from mid-October to mid-May, whereas roads and most facilities on the South Rim are open year round.

Because annual moisture on the North Rim is almost 10″ more than on the South, it looks lush in comparison, with a great forest of fir, spruce, ponderosa pine and aspen that opens into a vast land called the Arizona Strip. It also attracts fewer visitors, so if you're looking for a break from the crowds, try it. Some say the views are better there, anyway.

Park officials on both rims offer extensive daily programs on the anthropology, geology and natural history of the canyon. Look for a listing in "The Guide," a local newspaper with up-to-date park information. You can also call 602/638-9304 for a recorded message on park programs.

For more information on the Grand Canyon, contact Superintendent, Grand Canyon National Park, Box 129, Grand Canyon, Arizona 86023. Admission is $5 per car.

The South Rim

There is a series of viewpoints along the rim where you can take breathtaking looks into the canyon. Visit as many of them as you can. Each will give you a different, superlative view. Both Grandview and Lipan points have fans who call it "the most beautiful."

Pick an overlook where you can watch a sunrise or sunset. It will be an unforgettable experience. Yikes! Hang on to the tykes!

Grand Canyon Village, about three miles north of the south entrance, is the hub of the park. From here are two scenic drives—West Rim Drive and East Rim Drive, which leads 25 miles to the east entrance.

The Village has complete visitor services, including lodging, food, a pet kennel, medical clinic, taxi, service station, bank, dry cleaners and post office. You can visit the community theater for a half hour, multi-image slide presentation on the canyon (call 638-2224 for showtimes), or go to Lookout Studio to see the canyon through a powerful telescope.

Stop at the **Visitor Center,** one mile east of the village. The museum here covers the human and natural history of the area with dioramas and exhibits, including the discovery of the canyon by John Wesley Powell. There are also a slide program that overviews the Park, listings of lodgings and rates, and a schedule of the numerous ranger programs and tours, some especially for children.

The Center is open 8:00 am to 7:00 pm daily in summer,
until 5:00 pm the rest of the year.

Yavapai Point and Museum, ¾ mile east of the Visitor
Center, has spectacular views of the canyon and a series of
mounted binoculars directed at various parts of the canyon.
The small museum has exhibits on the geology and flora/
fauna of the area.

Yavapai Museum is open 8:00 am–6:00 pm daily in sum-
mer, 9:00 am to 5:00 pm in winter.

East Rim Drive is the main scenic drive and includes some
of the better known viewpoints. **Tusayan Ruin and Museum**
has anthropological exhibits on Indian tribes that inhabited
the canyon and a self-guided walk past pueblo ruins.

Skunk

The small museum is open daily, 8:00 am to 5:00 pm.

Desert View, the highest point on the South Rim, is near
the Park's eastern entrance. Take the kids to the Watchtower, a
recreation of an Indian watchtower, which affords a tremendous view of the Canyon and western portions of the Painted
Desert. There are also a curio shop, food, general store, and
service station.

West Rim Drive travels eight miles from the Village to

Hermits Rest, with several great viewpoints along the way. This road is closed to cars from Memorial Day to Labor Day, and the only access is by walking or riding the free shuttle bus. Free shuttle service is also available from the Village area to Yavapai Point from mid-May to September.

The Park has a **Junior Ranger** program for kids ages 12 and younger. It is outlined in "Kid's Guide," a newspaper for children available at the Visitor Center, Yavapai Museum or Tusayan Museum.

You can arrange for guided bus tours of the park from the Village. For times and rates, check at the Transportation Desks in Bright Angel, Maswik or Yavapai lodges.

The Grand Canyon is over 200 miles long. You and the kids can explore it further by horse, helicopter, airplane, mule, river raft, kayak or foot.

For an up-to-date list of concessionaires, call or write The Grand Canyon National Park Lodges, Box 699, Grand Canyon 86023, 602/638-2401. Reservations need to be made well in advance.

A good hike for kids is the relatively level **Rim Nature Trail,** a self-guided paved trail that you can begin at Yavapai Point Museum, the Visitor Center, or Verkamp's Curio Shop in the Village. You can take all or part of it, depending on your children's energy level.

There is also the short **Desert View Nature Trail** beginning from the campground or the Watchtower at Desert View.

Many trails in the park are strenuous. You should undertake an extended hike below the rim only with older kids, and only if both of you are in excellent physical condition. The high altitude (7000 feet), extreme changes in elevation, and summer heat make physical exertion more difficult than usual. Remember, it will take you about twice as long to climb back out as it did to go down.

An alternative to a death-defying hike to the bottom is to take the **Bright Angel Trail** or the **South Kaibab Trail** part way. Both can be less than grueling. The South Kaibab has probably the best views for a short hike, but it is steep and there is no shade. The Bright Angel is a moderate hike of three miles to Mile-and-a-Half Resthouse, where water is available in summer. After this, the path becomes very strenuous, and takes you to the Colorado River, eight miles farther down the trail.

The Bright Angel follows the trail used by the Havasupai Indians. One mule wide, with a precipitous drop, it is most easily taken on muleback.

Older children might enjoy one of these never-to-be-forgotten mule rides to the bottom. Minimum height is four feet seven inches, maximum weight is 200 pounds. Don't attempt this if you or the kids are afraid of heights!

Traveling from rim to river, you will descend through several life zones and strata of the earth. Like a cake, eon layered upon eon, the walls of the Grand Canyon are a picture of the past that stretches backward almost to the Beginning.

You'll pass layers of limestone littered with the fossil imprints of billions of ancient marine creatures; yellow sandstone etched with the bumpy lines of hardened sand dunes and the footprints of small animals; red shale abundant with plant fossils, imprints of dragonflies and footprints of amphibians and reptiles; dark, grim rocks that were the foundations of mighty mountains; and brittle rocks starred with mica and vertical seams of rose quartz that are among the oldest exposed rock known on earth, 2 billion years old.

At the bottom is the grand architect of it all, the Colorado River. A suspension bridge spans the river to Phantom Ranch, where you can spend the night in dormitory lodging. You can also camp. The bridge is the only crossing of the river for the 200 miles between Navajo Bridge and Lake Mead. You can also enjoy hiking, photography, swimming, wading, and ranger-led programs.

Nature at the bottom of the canyon is unexpectedly kind, and the feeling of isolation from the rest of the world (you can see the rim only from a few places) makes it seem like an oasis. The climate at the bottom is, however, similar to that in central Mexico. Summer days can be intolerably hot, with an average high temperature that exceeds 100 degrees. Early October is the best time to make the trek.

For information on a mule trip to the bottom or a shorter (and less expensive) day trip to Plateau Point, call or write the Reservations Department, Grand Canyon National Park Lodges, PO Box 699, Grand Canyon, AZ 86023, 602/638-2401.

Another great way to see the bottom of the Canyon is by raft. Trips of 2 to 22 days are available through Marble and Grand canyons. Most leave from Lee's Ferry, a few shorter ones from Phantom Ranch, with the peak season from April to October. Although there are numerous companies operating tours, it is wise to make reservations a year in advance.

For a list of companies, write River Unit, Grand Canyon National Park, Box 129, Grand Canyon, AZ 86023.

If you plan to do any overnight camping in the backcountry, you must have a permit. Contact Backcountry Reservations Office, Grand Canyon National Park, Box 129, Grand Canyon, AZ 86023, 602/638-2474 for advance reservations. Requests are taken beginning October 1 for the following year and are limited.

You can also arrange for guided half or full day hikes. Contact Grand Canyon Trail Guides, Box 2997, Flagstaff, AZ 86003.

For lodging, the South Rim has two national park campgrounds: Desert View, open mid-May to October, and Mather Campground at Grand Canyon Village, open April to December. Mather is one of the few national park campgrounds where you can make advance reservations (up to eight weeks ahead, May through September), and it is strongly advised. The park also has several lodges in the moderate to expensive price range.

You can make reservations through Grand Canyon National Park Lodges, Box 600, Grand Canyon AZ 86023, 602/638-2631 (same-day reservations), 638-2401 (advance reservations), or through Ticketron outlets for a $3.50 fee.

DID YOU KNOW?

—Temperatures at the bottom of the Grand Canyon are often 30 degrees hotter than at the top.

—A mule like those used for trail rides is a cross between a female horse and a male donkey.

—In 1971 a cook at Phantom Ranch quit his job, but he was too heavy to ride a mule to the rim. He rented a helicopter to get out.

—Somebody got out a calculator and figured that everybody on earth could be hidden away in one of the many side canyons.

—In 1944 three airmen parachuted out of their distressed B-24 airplane, 18,000 feet above the Village lights. As they reached ground level, they were surprised to watch the lights disappear above them. They finally landed safely in the canyon and were spotted three days later.

—The pinkish Grand Canyon rattlesnake is found nowhere else in the world.

Between the Rims

The gap between the North and South rims is only a few miles, but to get from one to the other requires a 240 mile drive.

From the south rim, take State 64 east. Stop at the **Little Colorado River Canyon** overlook for a staggering view. You can also browse with the Indian craft vendors, who will obligingly take plastic money (credit cards), as well as cash.

Turn left at US Route 89 to Cameron. **Cameron Trading Post,** founded in 1916, is one of the few remaining original trading posts on the Navajo reservation. Here you may find authentic Indian arts and crafts, tourists in polyester shorts, and Navajo women in long velveteen skirts.

The barter system is still active at Cameron, as Navajos swap crafts, wool and pinyon nuts for merchandise and groceries. The Trading Post is open from 6:00 am to 9:00 or 10:00 pm.

There is also the Collector's Gallery, with museum-quality crafts from most of the major North American Indian tribes, a motel, an Italian garden flourishing since 1916, and a restaurant serving Navajo tacos and fried bread. A campground is nearby.

Continue north on US 89 through a portion of the Painted Desert. If you are planning to visit the Navajo and Hopi reservations, turn northeast on US 160 (see Chapter XII).

US 89 continues north. Just beyond The Gap (a trading post) you will see your first view of the spectacular Vermillion Cliffs, bright red Navajo sandstone laid down during the Age of Dinosaurs, 2000 feet thick in some places.

At the junction in Bitter Springs, US 89 turns right to Lake Powell. US 89A continues to the North Rim, crossing the Colorado River on the narrow Navajo Bridge, over 600 feet long and 467 feet high. From its completion in 1929 to the building of Glen Canyon Dam in 1959, it was the only Colorado River crossing for 600 miles around.

At the settlement of Marble Canyon is a paved road to **Lee's Ferry,** historic crossing place on the Colorado River. A permanent ferry was begun here in 1871 by John D. Lee, a Mormon who originally operated it using a boat abandoned by Powell. Lee was hiding from the law for his role in the massacre of a wagon train of Missouri immigrants, an incident called the Mountain Meadows Massacre.

Although Lee spent many years as a fugitive, he was finally captured and executed. One of his widows then owned and operated the ferry until 1879, when it was sold to the Mormon church.

You can still see the house where Lee lived with two of his wives and their families, other historical buildings and a cemetery in the vicinity. There are boating facilities, a ranger station, public campground, store and restaurant nearby.

It is also a popular fishing spot and point of embarkation for boating expeditions through the rugged Marble and Grand

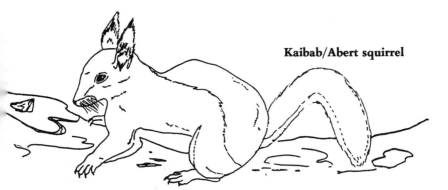

Kaibab/Abert squirrel

canyons. The kids can watch boatmen preparing for their trips most any day in summer and anglers pulling out trout 18 pounds and bigger!

US 89A continues along the foot of the Vermillion Cliffs, where, if the sun is right, you can see just about every color of red ever imagined, from crimson and scarlet to blood-red. You are now entering a remote section of the country called the Arizona Strip. So few people live here, if they claimed an equal portion of land, they would each have about two miles to themselves.

Just as the Colorado River gorges have acted as barriers to man, cutting the Strip from the rest of Arizona, they have also been barricades for animals, isolating relatives and leaving them to evolve in their own unique ways. The Kaibab and Abert squirrels are good examples.

The Kaibab, found only on an island plateau in the northern half of the Grand Canyon, 20 miles by 40 miles wide, is closely related to the Abert squirrel, common in the mountains south of the Canyon and scattered throughout the Southwest. The tassel-eared squirrels are almost identical in habits and looks, except the Kaibab has a black belly and white tail, and the Abert has a white belly and gray tail.

Jacob Lake is a popular wayside stop on the way to the North Rim. The village has a national forest service campground with ranger programs, picnic facilities, and a nature trail. The campground is open mid-May to the end of October, depending on snowfall.

The other places to stay in town are the inexpensive, rustic Jacob Lake Inn, open all year (602/643-7232) or the RV campground.

There is an extensive **hiking** trail system around Jacob Lake, including a trailhead to the Arizona Trail, which runs over 700 miles from the Mexican border to Utah. The trailhead is around two miles northeast of Jacob Lake off US 89A.

Jacob Lake Visitor Center has information on guided hikes and horseback riding in the summer, and cross-country ski and snowmobile tours in the winter, as well as a detailed forest map of the Kaibab Plateau. Ask for their children's packet of activities.

Ranger-led tours of the national forest are offered by the National Forest Service in conjunction with Kaibab Forest Products Company and the Fredonia Chamber of Commerce.

Call or write to make arrangements with the North Kaibab Ranger District, Box 248, Fredonia, AZ 86022, 602/643-7385.

North Rim Parkway (State Highway 67) travels south of Jacob Lake 30 miles to the park entrance, then 13 miles to the canyon rim through the dense forestland and flower-drenched meadows of the Kaibab Plateau. This road was Arizona's first designated Scenic Parkway, and some claim it is the most beautiful in the country. Have the kids look for the white-tailed Kaibab squirrel and for mule deer.

The road is usually closed by snow November through mid-May. If in doubt, call 602/638-2245 for road and weather information.

You'll pass the rustic Kaibab Lodge before you reach the entrance station to the park. For lodging reservations at an inexpensive to moderate price, call 602/638-2389. Also, you can camp at the nearby De Motte National Forest Service campground.

DID YOU KNOW?

—Large birds such as ravens sail across the Grand Canyon

from rim to rim, but small song birds go down the sides and across the bottom.

—Lees Ferry was part of the Honeymoon Trail followed by young Mormon couples to St. George, Utah, to have their marriages sanctified in the temple.

The North Rim of the Grand Canyon

The 1000-foot higher elevation here will give you a different perspective of the canyon than at the South Rim. Many think the views are more spectacular, and everyone agrees it's less crowded. Savor it slowly, and let the kids explore.

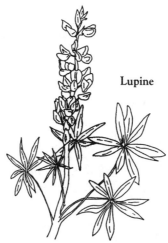

Lupine

THINGS TO DO

North Rim Drive will take you to Grand Canyon Lodge. Before you reach the lodge, a 17 mile paved side road leads to **Cape Royal,** where an easy self-guided nature trail takes you to a gorgeous view of the Colorado River. From Cape Royal you can see for miles into the canyon and often as far away as Flagstaff, 70 miles south. A branch from this road leads to **Point Imperial,** the highest point in the park (8,803 feet).

Good hiking trails for kids include **Bright Angel Point,** a ½ mile round-trip, paved self-guiding trail that leaves from the parking area of the Grand Canyon Lodge and is popular at sunrise or sunset; **Transept Trail,** which follows the rim for 1½ miles from the Lodge to the campground; **Cliff Spring Trail,** a one mile round trip down a ravine to the spring.

The only maintained trail into the canyon is the **North Kaibab Trail.** Although it is long and strenuous, you and the kids can hike a small portion of it for great views.

Ask the rangers about other roads and trails that will take you to little-visited places.

North Rim Drive ends at the Grand Canyon Lodge and Bright Angel Campground.

For reservations at the lodge, contact TW Recreational Services, PO Box 400, Cedar City, UT 84720, 801/586-7686. No reservations are taken for the campground.

The Park Service **Information Desk** *is in the lodge, and is open daily in the summer, 8:00 am–7:00 pm, and in October 8:00 am–6:00 pm. It has information on ranger programs and backcountry permits. You can make advance reservations for permits through the Backcountry Reservation Office, PO Box 129, Grand Canyon, AZ 86023, 602/638-2474.*

Gasoline, laundry, showers and supplies are also available. Both the lodge and campground are open mid-May to mid-October.

You can arrange for half-day (minimum age 8) and full-day (minimum age 12) mule trips into the Canyon between June and mid-October, or short horseback rides along the rim (minimum age 6, maximum weight 200 pounds). Contact Grand Canyon Trail Rides in the lodge, 602/638-2292. Horseback rides are normally available on a daily basis.

You can also arrange for guided full- and half-day hikes or guided bus tours.

DID YOU KNOW?

—An early tourist forgot to set his parking brake and lost his car over the edge of the canyon.

—Indians knew about the Grand Canyon at least 4000 years ago; perhaps as long as 12,000 years.

—In 1937, the mile-high Shiva Temple inside the Canyon was believed to be so separated from the rest of the world that evolution had passed it by. A large expedition from the American Museum of Natural History was sent to explore, with expectations of finding strange creatures dating back to the Pleistocene era. All they found were Indian artifacts, plants and animals common to the area—and an empty carton of Kodak film.

—Fossils of trilobites, some as small as pinheads and some as big as two feet long, are found in the Grand Canyon. This primitive crustacean ruled the world for millions of years. Why this species became extinct while his contemporary, the scorpion, survived, may never be known.

3. JACOB LAKE TO PIPE SPRING NATIONAL MONUMENT

From Jacob Lake, take US 89A about 30 miles northwest to the town of Fredonia. Mormons settled here in 1885. They claimed it was to escape religious persecution; others said it was to hide their extra wives from the law.

For moderately-priced Mexican food with unusual sauces, visit **Nedra's Cafe.** Movie stars and other notables such as Barry Goldwater, former United States senator, have enjoyed the good food, including the deep fried ice cream.

Turn west on State 389 to Pipe Spring National Monument. For those looking for a backcountry experience, and a remarkable view of the Grand Canyon, take the graded road, nine miles west of Fredonia, south to **Toroweap Overlook.** This road, generally in good condition, but impassable when wet, travels 65 miles to Tuweap Ranger Station, then another five miles to Toroweap. Be sure you have a full gas tank and drinking water. A limited number of primitive campsites are available.

Continue on State 389 to Pipe Spring National Monument, a Mormon fort and ranch house built in the 1870's for protection from Indians.

Pipe Spring National Monument

Pipe Spring is an oasis, known to Indians, Spanish explorers, and early settlers as the only reliable source of water for miles.

Story has it the name came when a group of Mormon missionaries camped here beside the natural spring. The others challenged one of their members, William "Gunlock" Hamblin, an expert rifleman, to shoot a hole in a silk handkerchief from 50 paces. Since the challengers hung the handkerchief by its upper edge, the bullets merely pushed it aside when they passed.

Hamblin, his pride wounded, then bragged he could shoot out the bowl of a clay pipe placed on a rock some distance away. He made good his claim this time, and the place where it happened has been called Pipe Spring ever since.

The Mormons saw potential in Pipe Spring, and in 1863 Dr. James Whitmore began a cattle ranching operation here. Hostile Navajos drove them away in the late 1860's, but when a treaty was signed several years later at Ft. Defiance, Arizona, the Mormons returned with more ambitious plans.

Construction was begun on a fort to protect the water supply and what was to be a cattle tithing center for animals donated to the church. Under the direction of Anson Perry Winsor, the tithing herd grew. A fort (Winsor Castle) was begun as protection from the Indians, but was only partially completed.

Children will enjoy visiting this memorial to the early Mormon ranchers and cowboys. (See Chapter XIII for an activity.)

Stop at the Visitor Center for information. Arrangements can be made for a demonstration on the loom, and Paiute Indian women can often be seen doing beadwork. During the summer there are living history demonstrations, such as candle dipping and baking in the wood stove.

You and the children can tour the monument either with a

guide or on your own with a self-guiding brochure. Be sure to watch the little ones around the duck pond and livestock.

Superintendent, Pipe Spring National Monument, Moccasin, AZ 86022, 602/643-7105. Hours: 8:00 am–4:30 pm daily. Admission is $1 for ages 17-61.

DID YOU KNOW?

—The President of the Mormon church bought Pipe Spring and 160 acres of the surrounding land for $1000.
—The cold temperature of the spring water (56 degrees) was helpful in making cheese.
—At one time, the fort had 80 head of cattle, which produced 60-80 pounds of cheese daily and 40 pounds of butter. Much of this was insulated in flour and sent by wagon to the temple workers in St. George, Utah.
—Pipe Spring had the first telegraph in Arizona Territory, called the Deseret Telegraph.

4. GLEN CANYON NATIONAL RECREATION AREA (LAKE POWELL)

Lake Powell, the heart of Glen Canyon National Recreation Area, holds 27 million acre feet (multiply that by 326,000 to find the very large number of gallons) and is 186 miles long at capacity. It backs up behind Glen Canyon Dam in a maze of sandstone gorges, a swatch of vivid blue surrounded by desert red, an anomaly in a place that gets less than 8″ of precipitation a year.

As you approach the lake overland, you will see the same country that greeted early explorers, but the past soon disappears in an exclamation of modern technology. Lake Powell has buried Glen Canyon, most of its sheerest cliffs, vegetation, Indian ruins, natural arches and grottoes under tons of water.

Lake Powell

The Anasazi lived here the same time Genghis Khan was intimidating Europeans. They were followed by Paiutes, Utes and Navajos. Major John Wesley Powell, after shooting down from Green River, Wyoming atop the raging Colorado River in 1869, found the tranquil waters of the canyon a welcome relief from the hair-raising rapids of Cataract Canyon behind and the dangers of the Grand Canyon ahead.

THINGS TO DO

If you want a quiet, pristine, backcountry visit, you should have come before water behind Glen Canyon Dam began flooding the gentle Glen Canyon in 1963. But if you want water fun—fishing, water skiing, swimming, boating, scuba diving, sailing—you've come to the right place.

Fishing in the lake is great, particularly for bass, catfish, and pike. Angling for brown and rainbow trout is popular on the Colorado River between the dam and Lees Ferry.

You can still find a spot to drop anchor and spend a day, or two, or three, in relative seclusion exploring the miles of convoluted shoreline.

The marinas sell supplies and rent houseboats, power boats

and water skis. Houseboats, complete with kitchen, bathroom and sleeping facilities for six to eight people, are a comfortable, relaxing way to explore the lake, especially with children. You can also rent a motel/hotel room, house trailer or campsite at the marinas, and free camping from your boat is allowed for up to 14 days any place on shore except in developed areas.

Just over the top of the canyon walls, unpaved roads and trails lead into a country that is still largely unexplored. This is a great place for hiking, backpacking, camping, photography, and nature study. Especially good for wilderness hiking is the Escalante River canyon system, an area similar to the original Glen Canyon with deep narrow gorges of tranquility, natural arches, and Indian antiquities.

The average annual temperature at Lake Powell is a mild 68 degrees. Since midsummer temperatures may reach 100 degrees, many prefer the spring and fall, with cooler temperatures and smaller crowds. Even winter can be pleasant. Lodging and boating facilities are open all year, but backcountry roads may be snowpacked or muddy at times.

Do be aware of the potential tourist hazards at Lake Powell. Make lodging and equipment rental reservations well in advance. Houseboats are often booked a year ahead.

For maps and information on lodging, marina services, tours, rentals, and food, contact the private concessionaire, Del E. Webb Recreational Properties, 2916 N. 35th Ave., Suite 8, Phoenix, AZ 85017-5261, telephone 800/528-6154, 602/278-8888 in the greater Phoenix area. They also have a list of special events, which often includes programs for children.

There are three marinas on the north end of the lake—Bullfrog, Hite, and Hall's Crossing. On the southern end is Wahweap Marina, Lee's Ferry (on the Colorado River below the dam) and the town of Page, Arizona. The southern end is larger and has more visitors. In addition to boat rentals and supplies, the marinas have camp stores, guided tours, housekeeping trailer units complete with kitchens, camping facilities, and access to swimming beaches.

Wahweap Marina, the principal marina and recreation facility for the southern half of the lake, is accessible by US 89. It has a variety of lodging, an RV park, restaurants, and stores. The large National Park Service campground has evening ranger talks and a swimming beach is nearby.

Stop at the **Carl Hayden Visitor Center and Glen Canyon Dam** for information on the campfire programs, as well as exhibits and a slide show on the dam. You can also visit the observation deck. Be sure to take the kids on a free self-guided or guided tour of the dam to marvel at this feat of engineering.

The dam, rising over 700 feet above bedrock, cost almost $1,500,000 to build. The power plant has eight generating units that put out enough energy to provide electricity for a city of a million people.

The Carl Hayden Visitor Center, telephone 602/645-2511, is open daily, 7:00 am–7:00 pm in summer, 8:30 am–4:00 pm in winter.

Fifteen miles from Wahweap on a mesa overlooking the lake is the town of **Page, Arizona,** built in 1957 by the government as a construction camp. The small **John Wesley Powell Memorial Museum** on Lake Powell Boulevard has Indian, pioneer and river running artifacts. You can also get information here for boat trips from Glen Canyon Dam to Lee's Ferry 15 miles away, scenic flights, raft trips and other recreation in the area.

The museum, 602/645-9496, is open daily May–August, Tuesday through Saturday during February–April and September–November.

Hite Marina, on the east side of the lake, is several miles south of State 95, and is one of the less developed marinas. It sits opposite the site of old Hite and the first ferry. Cass Hite lived here in a rock hovel in the early 1880's as a renegade. He survived by washing out "flour" gold from the sandbars of the Colorado River. His tales began a gold rush, but nothing of significance was ever found.

Bullfrog Marina and Resort, on the west side of the lake, is the second largest marina, with an extensive beach area, lodging and food. A National Park campground has showers available and evening ranger talks, and there is also an RV/camper park.

Across the bay is **Hall's Crossing Marina,** which also has a public campground, lodging and restaurant. Although it is only two miles from Bullfrog by water, it is 160 miles by land. The John Atlantic Burr Ferry, which operates daily, connects the two marinas on State Highway 276.

Midway between Bullfrog and Wahweap is **Rainbow Bridge National Monument,** one of the seven natural wonders of the world. It is the largest natural bridge ever discovered, large enough for the Statue of Liberty or the U.S. Capitol Building to fit underneath.

The bridge, formed by stream undercutting, has been sacred to many. Rocks blackened by what may have been ceremonial fires indicate prehistoric people used it as a shrine. Navajo legend says the bridge was created by a spirit who, upon hearing the prayer of another supernatural being trapped in the canyon by a flash flood, threw down a rainbow for him to tread to safety. Beneath the spirit's feet, the rainbow turned to stone.

The first white man to see Rainbow Bridge was John Wetherill, led here by a Paiute Indian named Nahja-begay. It was a difficult trail, through 20 miles of some of the wildest country in the United States. The only other access was by 100 miles of hazardous white water rapids, followed by a seven mile hike through debris-strewn narrows. Few were willing to make the effort to get there, and even by 1960, less than 10,000 people had visited.

Lake Powell changed all that, and now more than 100,000 come each year. The spirit of Rainbow Bridge has been harder to feel since then. The crowds can be pressing, and as the lake waters have risen, so have concerns that future stability of the bridge may be affected by the water saturating its abutments.

Still, it's a beautiful place. The Navajo recite a special prayer to pass safely underneath, and they feel there is a strong connection with sacred Navajo Mountain looming to the southeast. If you walk underneath, try to imagine the Indian's prayer. And caution the children to be careful climbing on the nearby rocks. It was named "slickrock" for a very good reason.

Superintendent, Glen Canyon National Recreation Area, Box 1507, Page, AZ 86040, 602/645-2471.

DID YOU KNOW?

—Glen Canyon Dam has enough concrete to construct a paved, four-lane highway from Phoenix, Arizona to Chicago, Illinois.

—The shoreline of Lake Powell is nearly 2,000 miles, longer than the U.S. Pacific coastline.

—Lake Powell is the second largest man-made lake in the United States. Lake Mead, 200 miles downstream, is the largest.

—Most of Lake Powell's shoreline is Navajo sandstone, which began as dune sand in long-ago deserts. It is very porous and is estimated to hold about as much water as the lake.

—Lake Powell has 96 major canyons, most accessible only by water.

—The suspension bridge near Glen Canyon Dam was assembled in San Francisco, sent here in pieces, then put together again like a giant erector set. It is the world's second highest steel-arch bridge, spanning 1,028 feet.

—A few of the plants in the hanging gardens of Glen Canyon are so specialized they live nowhere else in the world.

—Conservationists were outraged with the building of Glen Canyon Dam. Many of those who saw Glen Canyon before it was flooded by Lake Powell claimed it was the most beautiful spot on earth. Even today, controversy is generated by those for and those against the dam.

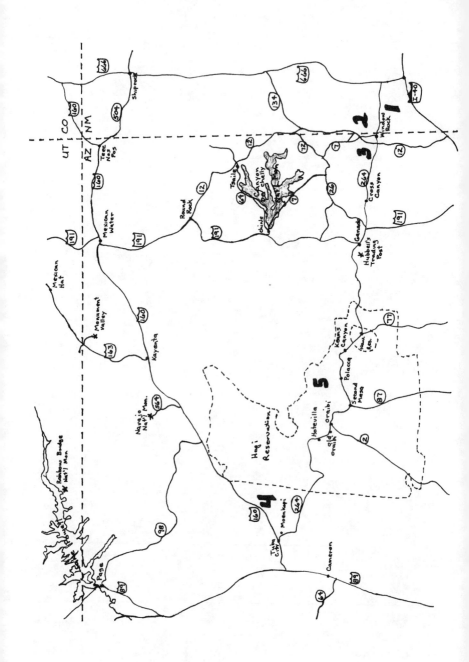

12

THE HOPI AND NAVAJO INDIAN RESERVATIONS

Reservation Policies

A sunset over the valley ignites the sky and paints the rocks an even more startling red. A dramatic monsoon rain sweeps across the mesa, disappearing as quickly as it came and leaving behind air bathed in the pungent smells of sagebrush and juniper. Hypnotic chanting, colorful costumes, and the hush of reverence vibrate in a dance passed down for generations. The unexpected green of corn punctures the drab, sandy hillsides with tiny, isolated oases of life. These are part of the magic of the reservation.

Although the Indian reservations chronicle a past of conflict and broken promises to Native Americans by the white culture, in the Southwest they have helped preserve the rich, and often mysterious, heritage of the Indians. Visiting is a rare opportunity for you and your children to experience these unique cultures, much like a trip to a foreign country with its own exotic customs and language. Talk to the kids beforehand about some of the differences, especially the local rules.

Each reservation has its own policy concerning photography and sketching. In the national parks located on the Navajo

Reservation, you may take photographs for noncommercial use. However, you will need permission to photograph or sketch privately owned land, residences or individuals. If you want to photograph an individual, ask his/her permission first, especially those in traditional dress or craftspeople. If the individual agrees, you are expected to pay a small gratuity. On the Hopi Reservation, all photography, sketching and recording is strictly forbidden without the approval of the village leader.

The reservations also prohibit littering and alcoholic beverages.

Dress modestly—no bikinis or short-shorts—especially to ceremonies. Would you wear a halter top to church?

An open range policy means encountering livestock on the road is likely. Be aware of this and drive cautiously. Any off-road or off-trail travel is prohibited.

Remember that you are a visitor on private property. Respecting the privacy of the residents should be an obvious given. To spend an extended amount of time in the Hopi villages, it is courteous to ask permission of the village leader.

The center of activity is the Tribal Headquarters. You can inquire here about local customs and regulations and obtain the necessary licenses and permits for such things as photography, fishing, camping and hunting.

Many people visit Indian reservations to buy their hand-crafted items, and the demand for these works of art continues to increase as more people recognize their timeless beauty. The best way to insure quality and authenticity is to buy on the reservation or from an established, reputable dealer off-reservation. It is not unheard of for an unscrupulous merchant to buy an item in Taiwan, remove the sticker, and resell it as authentic Indian ware for a huge profit. A reputable dealer will be glad to provide you with a certificate of authenticity if you ask. If you are considering a major purchase, such as a Navajo rug, learn the signs of authenticity (*Southwest Indian Arts And Crafts* by Mark Bahti, as mentioned in the Reading List, or the booklet *Genuine Navajo Rug—How To Tell* by Noel

Bennett are good places to start). Most quality crafts are expensive, but for kids on a budget, a cedar bead necklace (between $3 and $5) makes a charming souvenir. According to Navajo tradition, they are said to ward off nightmares.

Another point of interest are the Hopi Dances, ceremonies performed to assure physical and mental health by maintaining harmony with the spirit world. Although some are not open to the public, others are. Attending one will give you and your children a chance to observe the heart of Indian culture.

Don't ask questions, just watch and follow the Hopi's lead. Don't wear hats or shorts if they aren't wearing them. And the chairs around the plaza are for the Hopi and their invited guests.

The reservations are in a state of flux today. In many places, the ancient ways continue as they did before white man's civilization invaded the Southwest. Only recently have paved roads, lodging and restaurants made them accessible to the average tourist. But modern times have brought challenges to tradition. As you travel through the reservation, look for the old and the new. Discovering how to live within the United States while maintaining their cultural integrity is perhaps the biggest challenge facing Native Americans today.

Take the time to visit with a few of the residents if they are willing. You may be surprised by their underlying friendliness and at the wealth of native lore they are willing to share with you. You and your children just might come away with a deeper understanding of this land and the people who are so much a part of it.

DID YOU KNOW?

—Many Indian tribes have a custom during ceremonies called a "give away." It is a thank-you for the bounty of the universe and a prayer that what has been asked for will be granted. Free food and gifts are distributed among those present.

—Arizona officially recognizes Navajo medicine men and women as healers.

—Indians were given citizenship in 1924 for their role during World War I, but they were not allowed to vote until 1948.

Visiting the Reservations

1. Window Rock, Arizona
2. From Window Rock to Canyon de Chelly National Monument
3. From Window Rock to Hubbell Trading Post National Historic Site
4. Tuba City, Arizona to Monument Valley Navajo Tribal Park
5. The Hopi Mesas

THE NAVAJO RESERVATION

The Navajo Reservation is over 24,300 square miles, approximately the size of West Virginia. It is the largest Indian reservation in the country, blanketing most of northeast Arizona and edging into New Mexico and Utah.

Although the Navajos are relative latecomers to the area (probably in the last 600 years), they regard it as their homeland. Here, between their four sacred mountains, they settled down after wandering for thousands of years.

They call themselves the Dine (meaning "The People"), and when they arrived in the Southwest, they had few possessions and followed the simple life of the nomadic hunter. Imagine their wonder when they were greeted by the complex pueblo civilizations.

But one of the Navajo's greatest strengths is his ability to adapt. It was this adaptability that enabled him to change with the land as he migrated southward with the great bison herds. It was this same trait that helped him settle among the Pueblo

Indian girl

Indians, borrowing the crafts, ceremonies, lifestyle, and skills needed to survive in his adopted homeland. As he raided and traded with his new neighbors, he learned—how to farm, how to weave, how to make pottery, and how to worship new gods.

By the early 1700's, many of the Navajo had clustered in small extended families at the bottom of Canyon de Chelly. When the Spanish and Mexicans came, he continued to borrow, learning the skill of silversmithing and acquiring sheep and horses (an animal which was immediately put to use raiding Spanish settlements).

Spanish, and later Mexican, military presence in the area was almost nonexistent, but when the United States gained possession of the land in 1846, settlers were drawn to the area. Hostilities escalated until, finally, in 1863, the United States government launched a full-scale campaign.

Under troops led by Colonel Kit Carson, Navajo homes, fields and livestock were systematically destroyed. Carson's orders were to starve The People into submission. By 1864, he had succeeded, and 8000 men, women and children were herded together and forced to walk over 300 miles to Fort Sumner in eastern New Mexico. Food was scarce, clothing and shelter even scarcer.

Many died on the "Long Walk," but for those who survived, life became no easier. In captivity, thousands fell to white man's diseases and to shortages of food, fuel and water. Finally, after four long years of banishment, those few still alive signed a treaty allowing them to return to their cherished homeland around Canyon de Chelly as the Navajo nation.

The same adaptability and durability that served the Navajo people so well in the past enabled them to recover from their exile. They have been more successful than most in adjusting to the white man's world, and approximately 170,000 Navajo now make up the largest group of Native Americans in the United States.

Their society is traditionally matrilineal, that is, women own all property and pass it on to their daughters. Although a married man oversees the family goods, he is never the owner.

As a Navajo journeys through life, he is surrounded by the Holy People, powerful supernatural beings who travel on the sun, wind and lightning. Of these spirits, the only one always benevolent is Changing Woman, who built the first hogan, gave man the gift of corn, and taught him to live in harmony with nature.

The others are harmful or helpful, depending on their mood. There is Spider Woman, who taught man how to weave; Spider Man, who warns of imminent danger; and the Twin War Gods, who slew the monsters. All these, and more, must be continually mollified with rituals and offerings.

In addition to vindictive spirits, a Navajo must protect himself from the chinde, fearsome ghosts of the dead, and the witches, greedy men and women who have taken up the evil craft for their own personal gain or for revenge. Although witches eat human flesh and rob graves, perhaps the most frightening thing about them is that during the day, they are indistinguishable from ordinary people.

When a Navajo is around seven years old, he is conducted into adulthood on the eighth night of the Yeibichai ceremony. At that time, masked representations of the Holy People bless the initiates with sacred cornmeal, lightly whip them with

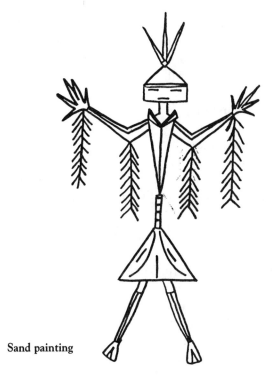

Sand painting

yucca leaves, and reveal to them that the identities behind the ritual masks are mere mortals. They are sworn to protect this startling secret, and are promised that some day, they, too, may have the honor of representing one of the spirits.

As a Navajo follows his perilous path through life, he chants prayers—to ward off danger, to cure illness, to restore harmony with the universe, to mark the important milestones of his life, and to ease his way. Some of these chants are the basis for elaborate ceremonies, "sings," that can last as long as nine days.

Of all the Navajo, the shaman, or medicine man, most excels in the knowledge of complex ceremonies. Part of his knowledge includes the technique of sandpainting, making intricate designs with colored sand as integral parts of many curing ceremonies. Some of these are so elaborate, it takes 15 men a full day to make just one.

But the Navajo takes the time to maintain his harmony with life. And as he tends his sheep or drives his pickup truck to the trading post, he may feel the beauty of this traditional chant: "I will be happy forever, nothing will hinder me.
I walk with beauty before me;
I walk with beauty behind me;
I walk with beauty above me;
I walk with beauty below me;
I walk with beauty around me . . ."

In the Navajo's land of majestic peaks, jagged rock and grassland, the Dine still devote their lives to walking in beauty.

DID YOU KNOW?

—The Navajo call the land "Earth My Mother."
—The Navajo shaman uses minerals such as charcoal, gypsum and ocher to make the colors in sand paintings.
—Traditionally, when a Navajo man married, he moved into a new hogan near his mother-in-law's house, but not too near. He was never to gaze at or speak directly to her at the risk of going blind.
—The Navajo language group is Athabascan, closely related to the language spoken by natives in Canada and around the Arctic Circle. This complex language was used as a code by Navajo radio operators in World War II. It was a code the Japanese were never able to break.
—Eye contact is considered impolite by the Navajo, and a light touch in handshaking is preferred to a firm one.
—When weaving a blanket, a Navajo woman will never complete the border design. She leaves a spirit path to the edge so her soul will not be entrapped.
—When a blanket is taken off the loom, it is curled. To flatten it, Navajo women bury it in damp sand for a few days.
—Although the Navajo are the richest tribe in the United States because of mineral, agricultural and timber resources, there is a 40% unemployment rate on the reservation.

THINGS TO DO

As you drive through the reservation, look for hogans, their doors facing east to the rising sun. To the Navajo, these round little dimples on the land symbolize the cycles of nature, and in addition to being a dwelling, they are often used for ceremonies. Older hogans are made of logs, mud and earth; more modern ones of boards. Out back may be a sweat lodge, used for spiritual and physical purification.

Also remember that, although the rest of Arizona elected to stay on Mountain Standard Time year-round, the Navajo Reservation is on Mountain Daylight Time.

If you are traveling at night, you may notice a large bonfire which indicates the place of a **Navajo ceremonial,** or "sing." If you stop, you are often permitted to watch.

For weather in English and an experience of the Navajo language, listen to the Navajo Radio Station KTNN, 660 AM.

Outdoor activities abound on the reservation. Lakes, reservoirs and mountain streams in the Chuska Mountains offer excellent fishing. Permits are available at several stores throughout the reservation and at tribal headquarters. Camping is permitted in the campgrounds for a small fee.

For information on fishing and hunting, contact Navajo Fish and Wildlife, PO Box 1480, Window Rock, AZ 86515, 602/871-5388. For information on hiking, camping and back-country use, contact Navajo Parks System, PO Box 308, Window Rock, AZ 86515, 602/871-4941, ext. 1645 or 1646.

For more information on points of interest, motels, maps and a calendar of events, write Navajoland Tourism Office, PO Box 308, Window Rock, 86515, 602/871-4941, ext. 1436 or 1659.

For information on reservation stores and trading posts where you can purchase crafts, contact Navajo Arts and Crafts, PO Drawer A, Window Rock, AZ 86515, 602/871-4095.

1. WINDOW ROCK, ARIZONA

Window Rock has been an important Indian community

since AD 1300, and the Navajo capital since 1935. The **Tribal Headquarters** in the northeast part of town is where the Tribal Council meets and enacts legislation in a huge hogan-shaped Council Chambers. The building is open 8:00 am to 5:00 pm most weekdays.

The Council Chambers looks out on the graceful sandstone window in the rock that has named the town. This same wind-scoured arch, located in **Navajo Tribal Park,** plays a role in the Navajo Water-Way Ceremony.

On State 264 is the **Navajo Arts and Crafts Enterprise,** the largest Navajo owned and operated craft shop on the reservation. Crafts from other Indian tribes are also for sale here.

In the same building is the **Navajo Tribal Museum,** with exhibits on Anasazi archaeology and Navajo tribal history and culture. The adjoining art gallery has extensive displays of jewelry, textiles, pottery, historical trade items, and exhibits by contemporary Navajo artists, and the bookstore carries numerous texts about Navajo history and culture.

Navajo Tribal Museum, PO Box 308, Window Rock, AZ 86515, 602/871-6673, is open year round, Monday through Friday, 9:00 am–4:45 pm. Admission is free, donations are welcome.

If you need a place to stay, one of your only choices on this side of the reservation is the tribally owned **Navajo Nation Inn.** It has a heated swimming pool and a cafe, as well as evening programs and information on guided tours.

For reservations, write PO Box 1687, Window Rock, 86515, 602/871-4108. Moderate.

Tse Bonito Park is just east on State 264. This was a stopping place when Kit Carson marched the Navajo from Ft. Defiance to New Mexico on the Long Walk in 1864. The large sandstone monoliths in the park are called "The Haystacks." In the park is also the **Navajo Nation Zoological and Botanical Park,** which has native plants and animals, as well as domestic animals important to the Navajo.

The zoo is open 8:00 am–5:00 pm daily. Admission is free; donations are welcome. You can stay at the primitive camp-

ground for $2 a night.

If you plan to visit Window Rock in early September, don't miss the **Navajo Tribal Fair,** the largest Indian fair in the world. This celebration is the most important event on the Reservation, and includes a rodeo, ceremonial singing and dancing, powwow, carnival, arts and crafts exhibits, food concessions, agricultural and livestock exhibits, contests, and the crowning of Miss Navajo.

For more information, contact Navajo Nation Fair Office, PO Drawer U, Window Rock, AZ 86515, 602/871-4417 or 6702.

2. FROM WINDOW ROCK TO CANYON DE CHELLY NATIONAL MONUMENT

North of Window Rock on Navajo Route 12 is the **Navajo Veterans Cemetery,** a poignant tribute of pride to the tribe's veterans.

If you continue on Navajo Route 12, you travel towards the Chuska Mountains, known as the Navajo alps. The scenery is stunning, especially at sunset.

In the town of Tsaile is **Navajo Community College,** the nation's first Indian college. Visit the **Ned A. Hatathli Museum** in the Navajo Culture Building. Plans for the museum include dioramas of Navajo legends, huge 8-foot by 8-foot sand paintings, reproductions of Navajo rock art, and Navajo arts and crafts for sale. Harry Walters, curator, will present a one hour slide show on Navajo history by request. If you have time, take one of the college's seminars for non-Indians on Navajo culture.

Ned A. Hatathli Museum, 602/724-3311, ext. 206. Hours: 1:00 pm–5:00 pm Sundays, 8:00 am–5:00 pm other days. Admission is free.

From Tsaile, Navajo Route 64 travels along the north rim drive of Canyon de Chelly to the visitor center.

Canyon de Chelly National Monument

Deep red canyon walls, sculpted sandstone, a canyon stream edged with stately cottonwoods, hundreds of Anasazi ruins, red-roofed hogans, and tidy Navajo farms combine to make Canyon de Chelly (d'shay) a unique and stunning place to visit.

The canyons have been inhabited for over 2000 years, first by the Anasazi, then by the Navajo. Today the land belongs to the Navajo nation, while the National Park Service administers the prehistoric sites.

The National Monument consists of a trio of giant gorges sliced into the red sandstone plateau by the Rio de Chelly River and its tributaries. In places, the walls are so close together it seems you can reach out and touch both sides.

THINGS TO DO

The **Visitor Center,** three miles east of Chinle on Navajo Route 7, has a craft shop and a museum with informative exhibits, a touch table, and a traditional hogan out front. In summer, rangers demonstrate Anasazi skills such as flintknapping and toolmaking, and Navajos demonstrate craft skills such as weaving and silversmithing. The rangers also conduct daily cultural programs, lectures and hikes during the summer. In addition, the center has hand-outs for the Junior Ranger program. Ask at the desk.

Nearby Cottonwood Campground is operated by the National Park Service. Refreshingly situated in a grove of cottonwood trees, it has picnic tables, fireplaces, toilets with running water, and evening ranger programs May through September. The free campground is open all year, but no water is available from November to March. No reservations are taken.

To really experience Canyon de Chelly, take a guided tour, but if time or money don't allow, you can view the canyons from **two rim drives** that are open year round. Allow 1½ to 2 hours for each of these approximately 35 mile round trips. The Visitor Center has a guide book. Dig out the binoculars for the best views. Caution: Heed the warnings to watch your children at the steep drop-offs!

North Rim Drive (Navajo Route 64) follows Canyon del Muerto (Canyon of the Dead). Antelope House cliff dwelling, Massacre Cave, and Mummy Cave can be seen from overlooks. In an alcove across from Antelope House is the Tomb of the Weaver, where the well-preserved mummy of an old man was discovered wrapped in a blanket of golden eagle feathers and accompanied by a thick bow, baskets of food, and over two miles of cotton yarn to weave in the next world. At Mummy Cave many perfectly preserved early burials and artifacts have been found. In the cliff nearby are the eroded hand- and toeholds the ancient ones used to climb to and from their fields.

Canyon del Muerto also contains the best rock art in the area, and many think it is the more impressive canyon of the two.

South Rim Drive (Navajo Route 7), following the old Fort Defiance Trail for 22 miles, has overlooks to the floor of Canyon de Chelly, White House Ruins and Spider Rock, among others. Spider Rock is home of the legendary Spider Woman.

If the kids want a closer look at the ruins, take the self-guided trail 1¼ mile to the canyon floor and the 900-year-old **White House Ruins,** named for the white plaster on the cliffs above. The dwelling was easily defended from enemies by drawing up the ladders. The trail is a moderate two hour hike. Be prepared for a wade across Chinle Wash on the canyon bottom.

Quicksand is prevalent in parts of the canyon, and any other entry is prohibited without a **guide.** You can make advance arrangements through the monument office for either hiking ($7.50 per hour) or driving with your own 4-wheel drive vehicle ($7.00 per hour) accompanied by a Navajo guide who will give you an intimate glimpse of his homeland.

If you don't have your own 4-wheeler, **Thunderbird Tours** offers tours in clattering, pea-green Korean War trucks, also with Navajo guides. Included are discussions on native plants and their uses. Taking a pillow to sit on will soften the bumps.

Contact Thunderbird Tours, Box 548, Chinle, AZ 86503, 602/674-5443.

Horseback tours *of one day to a week are offered by Twin Trails Tours, PO Box 1706, Window Rock, AZ, 86515, 602/871-4663 or 602/729-5954; and Justin's Horse Rental, PO Box 881, Chinle, AZ 86503, 602/674-5678.*

The closest place to stay is **Thunderbird Lodge,** ½ mile southwest of the Visitor Center. This historic motel was begun as a trading post in 1902 and eventually became a place for early tourists to get a hot meal, spend the night, and take an organized tour of the canyon. In addition to lodging, the Thunderbird has a gift shop and a restaurant where meals are prepared by an all-Navajo staff.

For reservations, contact Thunderbird Lodge, Box 548, Chinle, AZ 86503, 602/674-5841 or 5842. Moderate.

The other place to stay in the area is the **Canyon de Chelly Motel,** one block east of US 191 in downtown Chinle.

For reservations, write PO Box 295, Chinle, AZ 86503, 602/674-5875. Moderate.

For more information on the monument, contact the Superintendent, Canyon de Chelly National Monument, Box 588, Chinle, AZ 86503, 602/674-5436. Hours: 8:00 am to 5:00 pm, October through April, until 6:00 pm May through September. Admission is free.

DID YOU KNOW?

—Beans, corn and squash once grown by the Anasazi are still the main crops grown in Canyon de Chelly.

—Except during severe winters, 40 or 50 Navajo families live on the canyon floor.

—The first guided tours into the canyon were in horse-drawn wagons, and later, in Model T Fords.

—The oldest layer of rock in Canyon de Chelly was deposited approximately 280 million years ago, before the Age of Dinosaurs.

—Although the canyons were usually impenetrable, (even referred to as the "Gibraltar of Navajodom"), Kit Carson starved the Navajo out of Canyon de Chelly in the 1860's by destroying their cornfields and orchards.

From Chinle, continue on US 191 to the town of Mexican Water, and on US Highways 160 and 163 to Monument Valley (see page 326); or return to State 264, which continues northwest through the Hopi Reservation to the Navajo town of Tuba City.

3. FROM WINDOW ROCK TO HUBBELL TRADING POST NATIONAL HISTORIC SITE

Twenty-two miles west of Window Rock on State 264 is Cross Canyon Trading Post. Just before the trading post, turn north via a 2½ mile dirt road to **Kinlichee Ruins Navajo Tribal Park,** which includes Anasazi ruins, a self-guiding trail, and picnic grounds. Keep to the right when the road forks.

Continue six miles west on State 264 to the town of **Ganado,** named after Ganado Mucho, leader of the western Navajo until his death in 1892.

Children will enjoy a stop at Hubbell Trading Post, one of the most authentic in the West. It is one mile west of town.

Hubbell Trading Post National Historic Site

Customers have been coming to Hubbell Trading Post since 1878. It is stuffed with merchandise, old and new, as well as with priceless paintings and Indian artifacts accumulated by the Hubbell family. It is one of the few trading posts that continues much as it did in the days of the cavalry when the Navajo families rode to trade in covered wagons. Now, they come in pickup trucks, but you can still witness the inter-cultural blending with a dose of the past.

Trading posts have played a crucial role on reservations ever since the Civil War, as centers for buying, selling, socializing and catching up on the latest gossip, as well as serving as one of the few points of direct contact between the worlds of the red man and white.

Hard cash was scarce, so the medium of exchange was often tokens that belonged to each individual post. The Indians also traded crafts and raw goods such as wool. Anything left to spend could be kept in the form of a credit with the post. The system depended on the honesty of the trader, for when language was a barrier, the Native Americans simply pointed to what they wanted until the change on the counter was gone.

Many traders were friends to the Indian, helping not only with food and supplies, but also with legal and medical advice, emergency help and credit. In addition, it was through the traders the American public gained its initial awareness of the richness of native cultures.

John Lorenzo Hubbell was a trader who believed his first duty was the welfare of his Indian clients. Throughout his life, he helped the Navajo learn to deal with the white man's world. He was one of the first to recognize the value of their silverwork and weaving, and he advised and encouraged design changes he believed would sell. It's no wonder he was respected by the Indians for his honesty, hospitality and wisdom.

Stop in the **Visitor Center** to browse through the small museum or watch Navajos demonstrating traditional crafts such as weaving and silversmithing. You can also arrange for a National Park Ranger to guide you through the **Hubbell home.** Daily tours are free.

While inside the post, have the kids watch for the business of trading and listen for different languages. German and Japanese are sometimes as prevalent as Navajo. (See Chapter XIII for trading post activities.) If it's lunchtime, enjoy the picnic area. If you forgot the food, buy it at the post.

Superintendent, Hubbell Trading Post National Historic Site, Box 150, Ganado, AZ 86505, 602/755-3475. Hours: daily, 8:00 am–5:00 pm in the winter, until 6:00 pm in the summer. Admission is free.

DID YOU KNOW?

—Hubbell's is the oldest active trading post on the Navajo Reservation.
—Hubbell and his two sons owned 24 trading posts.
—Hubbell was sheriff of Apache County in the 1880's. He was also an Arizona state senator.
—When a smallpox epidemic broke out on the reservation in 1886, Hubbell turned his house into a hospital.

Continue west of Hubbell Trading Post on State Highway 264 to the junction of US 191. Turn north to the town of Chinle, an Indian crossroads and settlement that serves as headquarters for Canyon de Chelly. Or continue on State 264 to the Hopi Reservation.

4. TUBA CITY, ARIZONA TO MONUMENT VALLEY NAVAJO TRIBAL PARK

Tuba City is the largest community in western Navajoland. Although named after a famous Hopi leader, Chief T Ivi (pronounced Tuba), and once their domain, the town was actually settled in 1877 by Mormon pioneers. That explains the cottonwood-lined main street and the early 1900's sandstone homes.

Stop at the hogan-shaped **Tuba Trading Post,** built in the 1880's. Many famous people, including Zane Grey and former President Theodore Roosevelt, have enjoyed a visit here. Next door is Pancho's Restaurant and the only place to stay in town, the comfortable **Tuba City Motel.**

For reservations, contact PO Box 237, Tuba City, AZ 86045, 602/283-4545. Moderate.

Young coyote

The kids may get a kick out of seeing the **dinosaur tracks,** just off US 160 around five miles west of town. Take the unpaved road north (right) at the sign to Moenave. A three-toed dinosaur left his prints here in a mud flat over 180 million years ago. If you pour water in the tracks, they will be more vivid. Navajo craft vendors announce the location a short distance from the road.

US 160 travels northeast from Tuba City toward Navajo National Monument. Near Tonalea, look for the **Elephant Feet,** two huge, solitary rocks that resemble elephant's feet.

Navajo National Monument

Fifty-four miles northeast of Tuba City on US 160 is the turnoff to State 564. Follow this paved highway nine miles west through stands of centuries-old pinyon and juniper trees to Navajo National Monument.

Navajo National Monument contains three of the largest and best preserved cliff dwellings in the Southwest. These intricate homes were built by the Kayenta Anasazi around AD 1250, then abandoned just 50 years later.

The **Visitor Center** has exhibits, a slide slow, arts and crafts for sale, and a touch table. Have the kids look for the objects that are a puzzle to archaeologists, and see if they can figure out what they were used for.

Behind the center is a traditional hogan and sweat lodge, and the trailhead for Sandal Trail. This is a one mile, easy round trip to **Betatakin Overlook.** Actually visiting the ruins calls for a more demanding guided tour.

Betatakin (Navajo for "ledge house") is in a huge alcove in Tsegi Canyon. The Hopi believe this 135-room ruin was ancestral home to their Fire Clan. The ruins, in an excellent state of preservation, are really only two stories high, but because they are built on different levels, they appear taller.

To visit the ruin, you must be accompanied by a guide. The 5½ hour tour leaves daily at 8:00 am, noon and 4:00 pm during summer months, and the climb back out is taxing for young children, especially since bus service to the trailhead has been discontinued, adding 1½ miles to the hike. Register at the desk that day for this free hike, but arrive early. Space is available on a first-come, first-served basis.

The remote **Keet Seel** is the largest cliff dwelling in Arizona, and its 160 rooms and five kivas are some of the best preserved. An aura of peace pervades this magnificent setting, where you can almost feel the spirit of the ancient ones. Unfortunately, the strenuous, 16 mile round trip hike puts it out of reach for most kids. If the older children (and you) are in good shape, a free guided hike leaves at 9:00 am in the summer. Most hikers spend the night at the ruins.

A slightly easier way to visit is by horseback. A commercial tour for ages 12 and over leaves the Visitor Center every morning at 8:30 am between Memorial Day and Labor Day, returning the same day. Since only 20 people a day are permitted to visit Keet Seel, make reservations as early as possible, up to two months ahead.

Inscription House Ruins is 30 miles from headquarters and not open to the public.

There is no charge for camping in the campground near the Visitor Center, open mid-May to mid-October. Campfire talks on the history, archaeology and natural history of the area are offered Wednesday through Sunday.

For information and tour arrangements, contact Superintendent, Navajo National Monument, HC 63, Box 3, Tonalea, AZ 86044-9704, 602/672-2366/2367. Hours: daily, 8:00 am–6:00 pm. The Visitor Center and overlook trail are open year-round, but trails to the ruins close in winter. Admission is free.

DID YOU KNOW?

—When the people abandoned Keet Seel, they sealed many of the doorways, as if to protect their homes until they could someday return.

—The fields where the inhabitants of Betatakin raised their crops are a mile away.

US 160 continues from the junction with State 564 to the town of **Kayenta,** where large pools of water have made it an Indian oasis for centuries. The **Black Mesa Indian Arts and Crafts** is a good place to buy crafts.

Monument Valley Navajo Tribal Park

From Kayenta turn north on US 163 and travel 23 miles to Monument Valley Navajo Tribal Park. The formations of the park will be visible long before you get there. Turn right to the Visitor Center one mile before you reach the Utah state line.

Imagine towering monoliths, stately mesas, fragile arches, delicate spires, and fanciful figures in stone, all cast in hues of red, pink and purple. Then come to Monument Valley and see beyond your imaginings.

Did a giant sculptress skillfully carve out these works of art?

Her handiwork is majestic, awe-inspiring. Spend some time here, especially at dusk, watching as the colors and shapes of the land mystically change with the deepening shadows.

The small **Visitor Center,** east of US 163, has a few displays, a gift shop, a picnic area and Mitten View Campground, with showers and an RV dump station. No reservations are accepted, and only primitive camping sites are available in winter.

To take the 17 mile loop **Valley Drive** through the heart of the Valley, pick up a self-guided brochure from the Visitor Center. You will be greeted with numerous landmarks: The Mittens, disembodied hands pointing skyward; the amazingly thin, 470-foot high Totem Pole; the Three Sisters, with Faith praying, Hope gazing up at her, and Charity looking like Mother Superior with her arms folded across her chest. Have the kids play a game and guess which is the Camel, Dragon, Submarine, Rabbit, Elephant, and Bear.

Valley Drive, open between 8:00 am and 7:00 pm only, is a rough dirt road, especially at the beginning. It is the only access without a guide, but if you want to save the wear and tear on your car, take a **tour.** Tours not only visit areas closed to the general public, but often include a visit to a currently occupied hogan, native lore and a Navajo cookout. Contact the Tribal Park for an up-to-date listing of tour operators.

The best place to stay (and the only one nearby) is the historic **Goulding's Lodge,** six miles west of the Visitor Center. Goulding's also offers guided tours and has a fine gift shop.

For reservations, write PO Box 1, Monument Valley, UT 84536, or call 801/727-3231 or 3232. Moderate.

If Goulding's is full, try the two moderately-priced motels in Kayenta, the **Holiday Inn-Monument Valley,** *PO Box 307, Kayenta, AZ 86033, 602/697-3221 or the* **Wetherill Inn Motel,** *Box 175, Kayenta, AZ 86033, 602/697-3231 or 3232; or the two inexpensive motels in Mexican Hat, Utah, the* **San Juan Motel,** *PO Box 535, Mexican Hat 84531, 801/683-2220 or* **Canyonlands Motel,** *PO Box 11, 683-2230. There is also a KOA campground near Goulding's.*

*For more information on Monument Valley, contact the
Superintendent, P.O. Box 93, Monument Valley, Utah 84536,
801/727-3287. The Visitor Center is open 8:00 am–5:00 pm
October through April, 7:00 am to 7:00 pm in summer. Admission is $1 per adult, free for children under 13.*

DID YOU KNOW?

—Around 100 Navajo live in Monument Valley.

—Monument Valley is the geographic center of the Colorado
  Plateau.

—Hoskinini Mesa was named after Chief Hoskinini who,
  during the Long Walk, managed to hide his followers from
  Carson among the intricacies of stone.

—The two square Mitchell and Merrick Buttes are named
  after a pair of prospectors who discovered silver in the area
  and were killed by Indians when they returned to claim
  their fortune. The lost mine has never been found.

—John Ford filmed many of his classic westerns here, including "Stagecoach."

—Monument Valley has been called the "Eighth Wonder of
  the World."

THE HOPI RESERVATION

The Hopi are believed to be descendants of the Anasazi.
They arrived at these three treeless mesas around AD 1100
and have lived here ever since, surrounded by their sacred
landmarks.

According to their legends, three worlds existed before this
one, but the God of the Sky destroyed them because of man's
evil. Each time, a new world was furnished for the faithful.
When the Fourth World was formed (the one we are inhabiting today), the Hopi entered it from a spot near the confluence
of the Colorado and Little Colorado rivers, then scattered to
the Four Winds. Eventually, they were allowed to settle where
they are now, to prepare for entry into the Fifth, and final,
World.

The Hopi are a gentle people (even their name means "Peaceful Ones") and believe they have evolved through greed, war and hatred. They vow never to pass that way again. This dedication to nonviolence has produced unique solutions to problems.

In the early 1900's the people of Oraibi were divided over how much interaction to have with the white man. The "Hostiles" opposed all U.S. government reforms. The "Friendlies" did not. The controversy deepened, until the problem was resolved with a forceful pushing match to see who would stay. The "Friendlies" literally pushed the "Hostiles" out, who moved to the mesa below and established the town of Hotevilla, probably still the most traditional of all the villages.

The Hopi are still closely linked to their past, and despite all efforts by the white man to change them, have remained staunchly loyal to their traditions, although their agricultural economy is falling to modern times.

The Hopi farmer raises corn, beans, squash, melons and other crops by a method called dry farming. In a land with only 10″ of rain a year, it is a system uniquely suitable. Every morning the farmer leaves his village on the high mesas and scrambles down the steep cliffs to fields in the desert below. Often, he walks as far as ten miles to tend his crops on land assigned by the village chief.

With a stick, he digs a hole 8″ or more deep in the sand, drops in a few corn seeds, covers them, walks four feet away and repeats the process throughout his small field. When the corn germinates, it grows in green clusters surrounded by barren sand. The corn is a hardy variety, for it must survive with only the rain and groundwater for moisture.

When the corn is harvested and dried, women pound it between stone manos and rough metates. One of the delicacies made from this cornmeal is piki. The cornmeal is mixed with water and wood ash to make a thin batter. Then, it is baked on a hot, greased duma (a slab of sandstone). The skillful cook dips her hand in the batter and *quickly* spreads it

over the duma. Almost immediately, the piki is done, lifted off
the polished stone and rolled into a crackling, cylindrical
treat. It takes a proper duma to make good piki, and these
special stones have been passed down from mother to daughter
with great pride.

The Hopi tribe is divided into a complex matriarchal system
of clans. Women own all property, and it is through them that
families are related. When a couple marries, the man comes
to live with his wife's family and work her fields.

To the Hopi, every action is considered sacred. In underground ceremonial chambers (kivas), the people maintain a
complex system of beauty. Each clan is responsible for one or
more of the numerous rituals. Ceremonies to ask for rain, to
promote health and to produce well-being are held throughout
the year. Kachinas, representing the spirits in all things, take
part in some of these.

For half of the year, the 250 or so kachinas stay with the
people. After six months they return to their homeland, the
sacred San Francisco Peaks. From there, they ascend to the
stars, carrying the prayers of the people with them.

Hopi men spend hours carving and painting representations
of kachinas out of wood. Even the very young are given these
kachina dolls, not so much to play with as to help them learn
their intricacies.

When a child reaches the age of eight or nine, he may be
initiated into one of the kachina societies. At that time, it is
revealed that mortal men are allowed to portray these spirits. It
is a revelation the child swears to keep a secret from the
uninitiated.

The Hopi perform their elaborate ceremonies, not only for
themselves, but for the entire world. They believe their purpose in the universe is keeper of the sacred way, and that their
traditions must be honored to maintain the vital balance that
supports all life on earth.

They also believe that, just as the three previous worlds were
destroyed by man's erring ways, this world, too, will end. Only
the faithful, living and dead, will survive to enter the Fifth

World, a purified land where love will prevail. The destruction will come in a time when people have again abandoned truth and allowed evil to rule. On that day, the great dances will be forgotten and the rituals no longer understood.

Already, this prophecy seems to be coming true. As the modern world encroaches ever more persistently, many of the young turn away from the past. No longer do they have the dedication or time to learn and perform the complicated rituals. Slowly, the elders are dying with their secrets, having found no one to pass them to, and the great dances are slipping away with them.

But, today, there is still time to experience one of these majestic ceremonies: the kachinas resplendent in their costumes, the chanting dancers swaying in unison, and the rhythm of the drums pulsing with the heartbeat at the center of the universe.

And although some Hopis have adopted western jobs, clothing, and language, many still come home to their beloved mesas and the ancestral villages of their foremothers, where their belief system and the Hopi place in it has changed very little.

DID YOU KNOW?

—Hopi parents often leave the disciplining of children to aunts and uncles.

—When a Hopi baby is named, he is bathed in yucca soap and cedar water. Each of the mother's womenfolk give the child the gift of a different name.

—The Hopi Reservation is surrounded by the Navajo Reservation. Today, these two tribes are embroiled in a bitter land dispute (caused in large part by the United States government) which has forced many members of both to relocate.

—The kiva symbolizes the World Below, where the spirits of all things live. It is used as a place of worship, as well as a men's clubhouse, and women are rarely permitted inside.

—The rites performed by the kachinas are very ancient. One

sings a song so old the language is no longer understood by
the modern Hopi.

—The Hopi believe even the smallest mistake in a ceremony
may void it, bringing misfortune.

—The Hopi deity, Masauu, told the people that even though
the land here is harsh, beneath it are riches, and he warned
them to never give it up. In addition to the underground
reservoirs of water that bubble up when digging a few inches
under the ground, vast deposits of coal and uranium have
since been discovered.

—Ancient Hopi predictions state that they will one day address
the leaders of the world in a "house of mica" to explain how
man is destroying the earth, and that a white brother will
one day bring back the other half of a sacred tablet.

5. THE HOPI MESAS

Modern civilization is intruding on the Hopi's traditional
way of life at a confusing pace, and the people's generosity has
been taken advantage of in the past. Because of this, some
Hopi are wary of visitors, and the tribe has implemented strict
rules to remind you that visitors are welcome only as long as
they show respect.

Photographs, recording and sketching of villages, ceremonies, or people is strictly prohibited. In addition, molesting
shrines or removing religious articles such as prayer sticks or
sacred stones is forbidden.

No regular public medical services are available on the
Hopi reservation. The nearest are in Ganado on the Navajo
Reservation, and in Holbrook, Winslow and Flagstaff, Ari-
zona. Emergencies are treated at the United States Public
Health Service Indian Hospital in Keams Canyon.

If you visit the reservation on a summer weekend, you will
have a good chance of finding a **public ceremony**. Although
the most sacred portion may be held in private in the kivas,
public dances are open to all. Most of these begin at sunrise on
Saturday or Sunday in the village plaza, and continue inter-

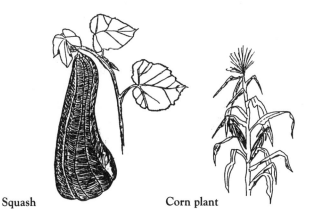

Squash   Corn plant

mittently throughout the day.

Although there is usually at least one Kachina Dance every weekend, May through mid-July, and "women's dances" on weekends in late September and early October, finding dates that coincide with places can be a bit difficult. Try asking at the Hopi Cultural Center on Second Mesa, the Tuba City Motel, or the Museum of Northern Arizona in Flagstaff, but don't be surprised if the information doesn't agree.

Sometimes the easiest way to find a ceremony is to drive through the mesas and look for a crowd of people standing on the housetops. If you join them, just remember, you are going to church, so act and dress with the same degree of respect. Bring a folding chair to sit on, and remember than on hot, summer days, children may not last long under the glare of the sun.

A Kachina Dance is an event of great beauty and emotion. The kachinas, resplendent in their colorful costumes and masks, emerge from the kivas and enact the movements of their spirit selves. The rhythmic chanting, drumming and shaking of rattles adds majesty and pageantry, and in some dances, the clowns play tricks and elicit bursts of laughter from the audience.

In addition to the Kachina Dances, others are performed during other parts of the years. The most famous of these is the Snake Dance, where Hopi men dance with poisonous sidewinders in their mouths. It is performed in late August to bring rain to ensure a good harvest.

The Hopi are famous for the artistry of their crafts, especially kachina dolls and silver crafts. You can buy them from the tribal store or directly from workers in their homes. Look for signs in the windows that advertise crafts for sale.

Most Hopi live in their ancestral homes on First, Second and Third mesas, which splay like fingers from the giant hand of the sacred Black Mesa. State 264 travels through the middle of the Reservation.

Keams Canyon

Keams Canyon is not a village but the Indian Agency headquarters, on the eastern edge of the reservation. A few miles up the canyon is a picnic area and Inscription Rock, where Kit Carson carved his name.

Keams Canyon Motel has inexpensive, modest accommodations (a series of trailer modules) and a popular cafe (closed Sundays and after lunch on Saturdays). The gift shop is a good place to buy Hopi and Navajo crafts. Because this motel and the one at the Hopi Cultural Center are the only two motels on the Reservation, it is advisable to make reservations early, especially on weekends of public ceremonies.

Call 602/738-2296 or write PO Box 188, Keams Canyon, AZ 86034.

Ask at the motel about conditions at the free campground across the road.

First Mesa

First Mesa is 15 miles west of Keams Canyon. At the base of the mesa is the town of Polacca ("butterfly"), founded by a man from Hano in the early 1900's. As more and more Hopi move down from the mesa for convenience, they settle here.

There is a dirt road to the villages of **Hano/Tewa** and **Sichomovi** on top of the mesa. From there you can park your car and walk to the village of **Walpi**. Be aware that the road leading to these villages is narrow, and vans, trailers and RV's are restricted.

Hano is sometimes called Tewa, because the people who settled it were Tewa-speaking Indians from the Rio Grande Pueblo. They came here to help the Hopi during the 1680 revolt against the Spaniards and brought with them their excellent pottery making skills.

The town of Sichomovi was established as late as the 1700's as a suburb of Walpi. Park your car here to walk the short distance to Walpi. It's a must-see. Perched 600 feet above the desert floor, it has hugged the edge of these sheer cliffs for 300 years in terraces reminiscent of a mystic village in the Near East.

The path around the village is often close to the precipice, with ceremonial kivas only a stone's throw away from the edge. Look for the covered passage ("kiska") which has connected the plaza to other parts of town since ancient times.

Second Mesa

Second Mesa is eight miles west of First Mesa. The villages of Shungopovi, Sipaulovi and Mishongnovi are here. If you have been camping, you can take a shower for a small fee at the community center in **Mishongnovi** as long as you bring your own soap and towels.

The tiny Toreva at the base of the mesa is home to Christianized Hopis and is not recognized as a Hopi village by the tribe.

Shungopovi is considered the mother village. Although it was established in the 1100's (before Old Oraibi), it hasn't always been in the same place. It was moved here after the 1680 revolt from its original site below the rim, where it was called Maseeba. Hopis consider it the center of their Sacred Circle.

Also on Second Mesa is the **Hopi Cultural Center,** with a museum that includes exhibits on Hopi history, information on handicrafts, and approximate dates of ceremonies. You can also make arrangements for a Hopi guide to take you through parts of the Reservation.

The museum is open daily, 9:00 am–5:00 pm. Admission is $3 for adults, $2 for students, $1 for children.

The **Hopi Cultural Center Motel** is the first choice for lodging on the Reservation. It's a modern, comfortable place to stay, and inexpensive. Reservations are important. Near the Cultural Center is a small campground with space available on a first-come, first-served basis.

The motel restaurant offers good, inexpensive Indian and American fare, including piki bread. Let the kids try the blue cornflakes. In addition, the Hopi Craftsmen Guild operates several shops that sell and demonstrate crafts. A proposed highway, called the Turquoise Trail, will one day travel northeast from Second Mesa to the Navajo Reservation.

To contact the Cultural Center and motel, write Box 67, Second Mesa, AZ 86043, telephone 602/734-2401.

Third Mesa

Third Mesa, five miles west of Second Mesa, has the villages of Bacavi, Hotevilla, Old Oraibi, and New Oraibi (or Kykotsmovi) at the base of the mesa, where you will find the Hopi tribal office and a trading post and small cafe.

Old Oraibi is a village of terraced pueblos and ancient kivas. Founded between AD 1125 and 1150, it has the distinction of being the oldest continuously inhabited settlement in the United States. The village is wary of visitors and is often closed to the public. Stop at the village leader's home on the left outside the main village for permission if you want to visit.

Near Old Oraibi is **Monongya Gallery.** The owner has won many prizes for the kachinas he carves, and you can often watch him working.

The village of **Moenkopi,** near Tuba City, is the most modern of Hopi villages, and includes orchards, cornfields and small stone pueblos. The town was founded by residents from Old Oraibi and is the only Hopi village not on or at the base of the three mesas. Even before it was settled in the late 1800's, farmers from the mesas ran the 45 miles between here and Third Mesa to tend their fields.

13

DISCOVERIES FOR CHILDREN

CHAPTER 1. PREPARATION AND PACKING

1. Recipes

Get a real taste of the Southwest by cooking and sampling the traditional food. You can find more recipes in any Southwestern cookbook.

ATOLE (Pueblo Indian)
Atole *(ah-TOE-lay)* is cornmeal mush. Combine 1 cup of cornmeal, 3 cups water and salt to taste. Add a pinch of sage and chopped green chilies if you like. Cook slowly until thick and smooth. You can also chill it in a bread pan, then cut it in slices, dredge in flour and fry in oil.

NAVAJO FRY BREAD *(da'di'nii'li'gazh)*
Mix 2 cups flour, 2 teaspoons baking powder, and 3/4 teaspoon salt. Add 1 tablespoon shortening and rub it into the mixture with your fingers. With a fork stir in enough warm water or

milk (about 3/4 to 1 cup) to form a soft dough. Mix well and shape into thin pancake-sized patties. Fry in hot oil until golden brown, turning once. Drain on a paper towel and serve with syrup, honey or chili beans (see below).

CHILI BEANS (Indian/Spanish)
Rinse 1 cup dried pinto beans, then soak them overnight in a pan with enough water to cover. Saute a chopped onion and minced garlic clove in a small amount of oil and add to the beans, along with 1 tablespoon chili powder, salt to taste, and 2 teaspoons each of ground cumin, oregano and basil. Bring to a boil and simmer covered until the beans are tender, 1½ to 2 hrs. If you want, brown 1 pound of ground beef or bulk pork sausage, drain and add to the beans.

NAVAJO TACO (Indian)
Top hot fry bread with chili beans (see above), shredded cheese, shredded lettuce, sliced green onions, chopped tomatoes, salsa, and/or sour cream.

BURRITO (Spanish)
Cook pinto beans as above, except drain and mash the beans before adding the meat and spices. Also add 1 can of roasted, peeled green chilies if desired. Cook the bean mixture for 10 minutes over low heat, then melt in 1 cup shredded cheese. Spread mixture on tortillas, roll them up, and serve.

MEXICAN CHOCOLATE (Spanish)
Chocolate was a royal beverage of the Aztecs. When the Spanish came, they added sugar and spices to it. Make your own hot chocolate by mixing 1 ounce of unsweetened chocolate, 1 tablespoon sugar, ½ teaspoon cinnamon, and a dash of salt with 2 cups of hot milk. Stir over low heat until the chocolate melts. Blend slowly in a blender a few seconds at a time until foamy, and reheat the milk to a boil. Add more sugar if you want and drink.

SNOW ICE CREAM (Pioneer)
Fill a pan with snow and add milk, sugar and a little flavoring.
Try vanilla, almond, or lemon. Food coloring can be added
for fun.

COWBOY COFFEE (For the brave)
Grab a a handful of coffee beans, tie them in a bandanna or
old dirty sock and throw them in a pot of boiling water.

2. General Science

The Southwest is a great place for scientists. Many branches
of science are named with a word ending in -logy, meaning
"the science or study of." See how many of these "-logies" you
know.

Use these words to fill in the blanks: geology, paleontology,
archaeology, meteorology, ecology, zoology, biology, herpetology, anthropology, lithology. The prefix of each word is
hidden in the sentence. Add it to "logy" or "ology" for the
answer. Each sentence will give you a clue to the answer.
We've done the first one for you.

a. She visited the **zoo** to see her favorite animals. Answer:
zoology, the study of animals.
b. She took her pet snake for a walk.
c. They teased her, saying her age on her birthday was older
than the hills.
d. The moon shone pale on the bleached bones.
e. The rock monolith towered majestically in the canyon.
f. He could feel the wind as the meteorite rushed by.
g. The arch, aesthetically pleasing, framed the ruin.
h. When he visited the Gobi on his field trip, he found only a
few living things.
i. Plants and animals have adapted to the environment on the
Colorado Plateau.
j. Man through the ages has developed many cultures.

Answers: a. zoology (animals) b. herpetology (reptiles and amphibians) c. geology (history of the earth & its life) d. paleontology (fossil remains of life) e. lithology (rocks) f. meteorology (weather) g. archaeology (material remains of man) h. biology (all living organisms) i. ecology (interrelationship of organisms and their environment) j. anthropology (man)

3. Archaeology

a. Ask your parents to prepare an archaeological dig for you by burying "artifacts" in the backyard or in a box of dirt. They may want to relate them to an imaginary culture. You can mark the "dig" off in squares with string. Remove the dirt carefully with soft brushes, and make drawings on graph paper as you find things. Then hypothesize about the culture.

b. Break a flower pot in a plastic bag with a hammer and see if you can glue it back together again.

c. "Excavate" a wastebasket. What is the oldest and youngest trash? What does it say about the people who used the wastebasket?

4. Biology

a. Take a chili pepper or dried corncob and predict the number of seeds you'll find. Count them to see how close you were. Make something out of the dried seeds—a collage or mosaic, necklace or picture.

b. Make a Southwest plant and animal scrapbook. List one plant or animal for each page. Cut out pictures from magazines or draw your own. Write down interesting information for each and keep track of how many of them you see on your trip.

c. Sit outside in your backyard or in the park. Make a list of all the birds, animals, and insects which can be found there. Keep your list and compare it to different spots on the trip. You can also do this with plants.

5. Ecology

a. Check for air pollution. Take white index cards and smear a spot with vaseline. Put them in different places in your yard and house and leave them for a few days. Predict which one will be the dirtiest and why, then see if you are right. You can also take four cards and put them in the same spot, removing one card each day to measure the daily buildup of pollution. Try this in different places on the trip.

b. Prove that oil and water don't mix (as on lakes frequented by motorized boats). Fill a jar halfway with water and add a few drops of food coloring. Then fill it to the top with mineral or vegetable oil. Screw the lid on tightly and gently rock it back and forth to see the patterns in the water.

6. Geology

a. Many rocks contain crystals. You can grow your own from sugar. Heat 1 cup of water with 2 cups of sugar over medium heat. Stir until all the sugar melts, then add more sugar until no more will dissolve. Cool the liquid to warm and pour it into a glass jar. Tie a heavy string to the middle of a pencil and let the string hang into the liquid. Crystals will form in a few hours. The next day, remove the string, reheat the sugar, then cool and reinsert the string. Do this until the crystals are as big as you want. Eat them.

Here's a recipe you **can't** eat. Mix together 6 tablespoons of each: ammonia, water, salt, and bluing. Add food coloring if you like. Pour part of the mixture over several pieces of charcoal briquettes in a glass bowl. Try adding branching sticks for the crystals to form on. Spray some of the rest of the mixture on the briquettes every day.

b. Test the power of freezing water. Fill a plastic container to the top with water and cover it tightly. Put it in the freezer overnight and see what happens.

c. Watch the effects of erosion by dripping water on sugar cubes.

d. Show one way caves are made. Wrap two sugar cubes in a ball of clay, leaving an opening for the cave entrance. Put your cave in a jar of water until the cubes are dissolved. This is similar to what happens when salt or limestone deposits in the earth dissolve.

e. Test sand for limestone. Pour vinegar over it. If it fizzes, you have calcium carbonate and probably limestone.

Pass a magnet covered with a light colored cloth over the sand to see if any of the particles are magnetic.

f. Make your own quicksand. Cut a hole in the bottom of a plastic bucket and stick in the end of the garden hose. Make a watertight seal around the hose (try using chewed gum or caulking). Fill about ⅔ of the bucket with sand and put a heavy rock on top. Trickle water into the bucket from the hose. When quicksand forms, the rock will begin to sink. Experiment with different objects and see which sinks the fastest.

7. Paleontology

a. Make your own fossils. Spread thick mud or clay on a piece of cardboard and press in a leaf or shell to make an impression. Or stir plaster of paris into water until thick, then spread on a paper plate or wax paper. Press in a leaf or shell coated with vaseline. When the plaster is dry, remove the leaf.

You can also pour plaster of paris around the shell in a small milk carton, and when it dries, break it apart to see the "fossilized" shell.

b. Be a paleontologist and put a skeleton back together. Buy a chicken and boil or eat off the cooked meat. Notice how the joints fit together when you're eating. Scrape and dry the bones and try to put them back together with white glue and wire.

8. Meteorology

People have been predicting the weather by looking at the sky for hundreds of years. Modern science has discovered that much of the local folklore surrounding weather was surprisingly accurate in the short run.

For example, rising atmospheric pressure usually means fair weather, while falling pressure foretells a storm. Smoke tends to rise farther under high pressure, thus the adage, "If smoke goes high, no rain comes by. If smoke hangs low, watch out for a blow."

The clouds can also help you predict the weather. Those that form a thin veil of a halo around the sun or moon mean rain is possible within 15 to 20 hours. Thick fluffy clouds that look like cotton balls (cumulus) mean fair summer weather, but watch out if they start to build vertically, for they can soon become the ominous looking thunderheads that bring violent storms.

Clouds that resemble long rolls of cotton with splotches of blue sky in between foretell the possibility of precipitation. The small cloudlets and wisps seen on windy days (cirrus or mackerel clouds) often warn of a change in the weather, since wind usually accompanies such a change. Morning ground fog often means no rain that day, particularly if the previous night was clear.

a. Observe the sky for a week and see if you can predict the weather. As a last resort, you know it's going to rain when you feel the raindrops falling on your head.

b. Test for wind direction by holding up a wet finger and feeling which side is colder as the breeze evaporates the moisture. You can also toss leaves in the air and watch which way they blow.

Follow these basic rules for your predictions. A change in wind direction often foretells a major change in the weather. Wind blowing in a clockwise direction (e.g. west to north) means fair weather. Unsettled weather follows wind blowing in a counterclockwise direction (e.g. east to south).

c. Make a calendar to track the weather on your trip. Then, each morning, predict the daily weather based on the clouds and weather lore. At the end of the day put down what actually happened.

d. Keep track of the daily temperatures for a few days. Be sure to take it at the same time each day. Find the mean (the average found by adding all the temperatures and dividing by the number of days), the median (the middle temperature), the mode (the temperature that occurs most often), and the range between the lowest and highest temperature. Chart the temperature on a graph. Do the same thing on the trip and compare the two.

9. Astronomy

a. The Indians used the seasonal movements of the sun to plant their fields and conduct their ceremonies. Find a point on the horizon where the sun comes up around your home. Over time, watch to see if it changes. Predict where it will be in a week, a month, a year, when you come back from your trip. See if the position of the sun is the same in the Southwest as at your house.

b. Learn to find constellations, then look for them in the Southwest.

c. Make up your own constellations by looking at the stars and forming pictures by imagining lines connecting them.

10. Geography

a. Start a booklet for information about the states you will visit. Make a page in your book for each state and add other information to it on the trip. Possibilities include state flowers, songs, population, places visited, capitals, major source of income, and weather. Almanacs and encyclopedias are good sources of information.

b. Learn how to use a compass. Locate due north, south, east and west. Map out a course in your backyard. How would you give directions from the back door to the apple tree? For example, walk due N for 15 spaces, then turn E for 2.

c. Many of the early Spanish explorers followed maps compiled from hearsay and speculation. Needless to say, most were highly inaccurate. You and your family will be better off if you use an accurate one.

Get out an atlas, chart your course, then draw a map for your family to follow, including just the roads you plan to take and the towns and attractions you want to visit along the way. When you get there, you can add the animals and birds you see, other attractions, natural features, etc.

You can draw your map on the back of a paper bag so it will look like an old Spanish map. Cut out the bottom of a grocery bag, slit it down the side, crumple it up a few times, then open it flat to make a large map.

11. Arts and Crafts

a. Make a friendly puppet out of a clothespin to take on the trip. Paint it, then hang it to dry. Your puppet can double as a clip to keep papers on your lap board. Make the lap board out of wood or cardboard.

b. Make a scrapbook to fill with items from the trip. Have pages for photographs (polaroids work great if you have them), information, things you collect (restaurant napkins, matchbook covers, etc.), pictures you draw, poems you write, and comments.

c. Decorate a shoe box. Put a rubber band around it and use it to collect treasures on the trip. A coffee can and lid will also work.

12. Native Americans

a. Make your own pottery using the same coil method the Anasazi Indians used. To form the pot, flatten (a rolling pin works well) a piece of clay for the base, then cut it to the shape you want the bottom to be. Roll more clay into a finger-width coil and attach it to the base by pinching the clay together. Build the pot by circling the coils and adding more as needed. To smooth it, wet your fingers and run them along the sides, or scrape with a butter knife. If you want the pot to harden when it dries, you can buy special clay at an art shop.

b. Make a sand painting. Put sand in a container and wash it in water to clean it. Color the damp sand by putting it in small covered jars with food coloring and shaking. Spread it out to dry on newspapers before using it.

Use glue to paint a design on a piece of thick paper or cardboard, then sprinkle the sand on the glue to make a picture. You can also layer the colored sand in a jar and use a pencil to push down through the layers near the outside of the jar so the colors form a design.

c. Build irrigation canals in the sandbox and channel water from one place to another.

d. Build a pueblo using sugar cubes as building blocks. Make ladders using sticks and string. Add clay figures and pottery if you want.

e. Indians created special individual designs to paint on their faces. Buy face paint and create your own designs.

13. Mountain Men

The trappers carried with them a "possibles bag," which was a bag filled with their necessities. Make a cloth bag with a drawstring to carry things you may want on the trip. Or use a shoe box, metal cake pan with lid (magnetic letters can be used on it, and it can also be used for a writing surface) or backpack (very roomy). Put in fun things to do in the car and on the trip.

Here are possible things to put in your "possibles bag": pipe cleaners, washable markers (crayons will melt in the desert sun), glue, scissors, string, white paper, colored construction paper, clipboard, decorated clothespins, small chalkboard and chalk, magnifying glass, compass, small butterfly net, twine or string, graph paper, bubbles, tape, sketch pad, scrapbook, play clay, journal, plastic puzzles, puppets, magnetic letters and games, notebook, audio tapes, books. You may have to negotiate with your parents on space available.

14. Pioneers

a. Dip your own candles. With your parents, melt paraffin in a double boiler. Add old crayons for color. Use heavy cotton twine with a washer tied on the end for a wick. Tie several wicks to a stick and dip them into the paraffin. Alternate dipping the wicks into the paraffin and into ice water until you have built the candles to the size you want.

b. Many pioneers kept a journal. Make your own trip journal by stapling paper between two covers (possibilities are wallpaper, poster board or construction paper). Decorate it, and take it along to keep a record of your trip. Include special events that happen on the trip (the day and time of departure, the day we got a flat tire, the day my brother got a terrible sunburn, etc.), as well as things you like and dislike and descriptions of places you visit.

15. Spanish

a. Learn Spanish words and phrases. See Appendix D for a few of them.

b. Make a piñata. Blow up a balloon. Cover it in a crisscross pattern of newspaper strips dipped in a paste made of flour and water. After the balloon is covered, attach a bent wire so you can hang it later. After the paste dries, cut the piñata in half and fill with candy and other goodies. Glue it back together with paper strips dipped in paste. You can decorate your piñata with bits of colored crepe paper or paint it. Have a party and break the piñata.

CHAPTER 2. THE GREAT OUTDOORS

1. Take a nature walk to look for animals, plants, nests, etc. Look for animal tracks near riverbanks and in sandy soil. Make

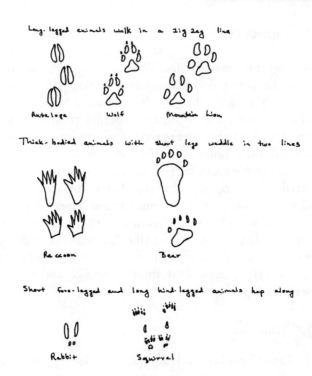

Long-legged animals walk in a zig zag line

Antelope   Wolf   Mountain Lion

Thick-bodied animals with short legs waddle in two lines

Raccoon   Bear

Short fore-legged and long hind-legged animals hop along

Rabbit   Squirrel

sure they are fresh, e.g. with sharp edges and no debris in them, and see if you can follow them to the animal. If you lose the path of the tracks, ask yourself which way you would go if you were the animal, then explore in that direction. Be careful that what you are following is friendly.

Look for other animal markings—v-shaped cut branches with beaver teeth marks; uneven cuts on small seedlings or aspen to indicate deer or elk; the small gnaw marks of mice; the complete girdling of the bark of a tree caused by a porcupine; a heap of nutshells on an old stump to indicate a squirrel.

Touch different rocks and trees to see how they feel. See if you can find four different kinds of soil to feel. Crush a leaf or pine needle between your fingers and smell it. Make sure what you touch is safe. Sit quietly and listen. How many different sounds can you hear? How many different smells can you detect? Can you identify the source?

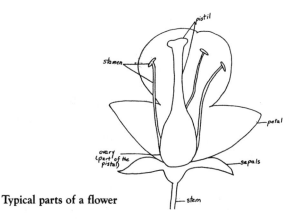

Typical parts of a flower

2. Find as many different kinds of wildflowers as possible. Compare their color, size, shape, petals, kinds of leaves and stems.

Use your magnifying glass to examine the different parts of a flower. See if you can find the stem, sepals, petals, pistil, and stamens.

Pick out a blossom to watch and count the number of visitors it has in 15 minutes.

3. Collect a few things from nature—pine cones, twigs, seeds, leaves, rocks. Take only as many samples as needed and only those things that are no longer alive. Make a nature collage using these things and other pictures or drawings.

4. Play a night game with flashlights. Have two people walk a hundred yards or so apart, then move towards each other quietly. Have a third person call "lights on." Turn on the flashlights, holding the beam steady, and try to find each other. Then turn off the lights and change positions.

Send signals in Morse Code with your flashlight. See Discoveries for Chapter 11 for the code.

5. Draw a picture of an animal or plant. First draw the basic

geometric shape of the body—an oval for a bird, a square or rectangle for mammals. Then add the head, tail, legs, etc. For mammals, practice first on side views.

Fish are easy to draw. Start at the front, add the arc of the back, then the belly, fins and tail. For insects, remember one side is usually a mirror image of the other, so draw half and copy it.

To draw flowers, start with the heads, then add the leaves and stem. Draw a tree the way it grows, that is from the ground, rising into the trunk, sweeping up into the major branches, then branching into the small twigs and leaves.

6. Take a scavenger hunt walk. Give yourself a point for each thing you find (possible 20): something beautiful, something ugly, something wrinkled, changing, useful, living, non-living, threatening, bumpy, shiny, increasing, decreasing, smooth, cool, soft, hard, hairy, wet, dry, and calming.

7. Take a "hands and knees" hike. Mark off an area with string about four feet by four feet. Explore the area carefully and keep track of what you see. Make a path to interesting things you find with the string, then find someone to show your discoveries to.

8. Draw a picture on a piece of paper, making the marks with natural things, such as a stick, a blade of grass, a yellow dandelion, or a red rock.

9. Make a trail for someone in your family to follow by using markings such as rock cairns (small piles of rocks) and broken twigs. A pile of two rocks with one rock on the right side means turn right, one rock on the left means turn left, and three rocks on top of each other means straight ahead. Twigs broken to the right mean turn right, and to the left, turn left. Bring along a parent if you are young enough to get lost.

10. Tell how much time is left until sundown. Hold your

arms out straight in front, palms facing you. How many fingers will fit between the horizon and the sun? Each finger width is equal to about 15 minutes.

11. Learn to tell the direction in the woods without a compass. Spring flowers and spider webs usually face south; moss and tree rings are thicker and bark furrows deeper on the north side of trees. What other things do you notice?

12. The Indians played a stalking game to sharpen their hearing and alertness. One player stands blindfolded in the center of a large circle. Other players try to sneak up, one at a time, and touch the player in the center without being detected.

13. Play an observation game. Stand quietly in one spot and count how many different sounds you can hear. Now open your eyes and count the different plants and animals. Can you find 20 different things?

14. Find a large branched stick to serve as a loom. Wrap yarn between the branches and weave in natural objects you collect. Or without a loom weave grass into a mat.

15. The desert comes alive at night. You can see many of the animals that hide from the heat of the day by taking a night hike. Evenings with a full moon are especially good times.

The secret to a successful hike is to be very quiet. If you aren't comfortable being alone in the dark, ask one of your parents to come along.

Pick a place you explored during the day, and look for landmarks that will help you in the dark. If you're going far, be sure to take a map, compass and an adult. Move slowly, watch your step, and by all means, avoid steep or rocky slopes, trails near cliffs, or unknown areas that may have hidden dangers such as fences or old mine shafts.

Wear dark pants, a dark shirt and high topped shoes, and

take along a flashlight. Cover it with red plastic and many nocturnal animals won't be able to see it. If you want to avoid any creepy crawlers while sitting, take along a folding chair.

As you walk, look, listen and smell. It will take up to 45 minutes for your eyes to fully adjust to the dark.

Look for animal eyes glowing in the dark—the bright yellow eyes of a raccoon, the fiery white eyes of a dog or coyote, the green eyes of a bullfrog, or the yellowish white of a bobcat. In the water, look for a flash of silver that indicates a fish, splashing from a raccoon or bear fishing, and a trail of bubbles from water mammals such as beaver and otter. In the air, zigzag movements may be bats or large hawkmoths. Watch the grass for the darting movements of mice and shrews or the leaping of rabbits and kangaroo rats. Get close to the ground and shine your flashlight to see insects.

Sit and listen for animal sounds. Are they afraid, angry, threatening, friendly? How are the sounds different in the grasslands, the forest, by a lake, or in canyon country? Is that a coyote or a mountain lion you hear?

Take a picture using the camera's flash equipment. Animals and flowers will show up particularly well against the dark background. Or take a picture of the stars.

Smell the night. Wet your finger and rub it over your nose to increase the smells. Put your nose close to the ground and sniff. Some smells will be pleasant, others won't!

Work on developing your sixth sense. Turn around and have a partner walk far enough away from you so you can't see each other. Turn back and see if you can tell where the other person is. Walk toward each other until you can sense each other's presence.

16. Set out water in a jar in the morning. Mark the water level on the outside of the jar with a pen so you can see how much is gone at the end of the day. Do you know what happened to the water? This is an example of why it is so important to drink water in the desert.

17. Make adobe by adding grass and sticks to mud. Try it in different kinds of soil to see which works best.

CHAPTER 5. SOUTHWEST LIFE ZONES

1. Plants and animals survive by adapting to their environment. A plant with thick, waxy leaves is well suited for the hot, arid desert. One that bursts into flower and turns to seed in a short time has adapted to the abbreviated growing season on top of a high mountain.

Fill in the following categories with the adaptations listed below. Would the plants and animals with these characteristics live in the hot desert or the cold alpine tundra (home)? What purpose(s) do you think the following adaptations serve (reason)? We've given examples of a plant or animal that uses each adaptation. For more of a challenge, try to find your own examples.

adaptation/home/reason/example

Adaptations: 1. hibernation in winter 2. thick fur 3. never needing to drink water 4. aestivation (state of inactivity in the summer) 5. hooves adapted for climbing rocks 6. flaps that can be closed over eyes and ears 7. eggs that can lie dormant for years 8. a cold-blooded animal with scaly skin 9. a plant that can store large amounts of water in its tissues 10. shrub whose roots extend over 40 feet under the ground 11. plants needing no soil to grow 12. growth inhibitors in the roots that prevent seeds from other plants from germinating 13. over-sized ears

(Answers: 1. alpine/escape harsh winter/marmot 2. alpine/warmth/mountain goat 3. desert/lack of water/kangaroo rat 4. desert/escape extreme heat/pocket gopher 5. alpine/escape predators on rocky slopes/mountain goat 6. desert/protection from sand/fringe-toed lizard 7. desert/waiting for enough moisture/tadpole shrimp 8. desert/reduces moisture evaporation/horned lizard 9. desert/low moisture/ cactus 10. desert/ tap underground water/mesquite 11. alpine/ adapted to rocky landscape and sterile, shallow soil/lichens 12. desert/reduces competition for limited water and nutrients/ creosote bush 13. desert/dissipate heat and locate prey in the dark/kit fox)

2. Pretend you're a lizard, cottontail rabbit, or any other animal in the Southwest. Where do you live? What do you eat? When are you active? What color are you? What does your skin feel like? Who are your friends? Enemies? Act like the animal does. What kind of movements and sounds do you make? See if your family can guess what animal you are.

3. Many movies were filmed in southwestern Utah. You can write, produce and direct your own movie. First write beginning, middle and ending scenes for your story. Then assign each person in the car to be a character. You can pretend they are famous movie stars if you want. What popular record album would you choose for the sound track? Have the characters act out your movie. Add costumes if you want. Old Pahreah is an ideal place to do this.

4. Put the words "bear," "bird," and "snake" at the top of a paper. List the following statements under the correct category. Some will go in more than one category.
a. Abandon their children before they are ever born
b. Usually have no more than one brother or sister
c. Appearance changes dramatically from young to adult (other than just size)
d. Father does not help raise the children
e. Mother is very protective
f. Bear their young alive
g. Babies are cute and cuddly
h. Stays with the mother two years

(Answers: a. some snakes and birds b. bear and some birds c.

bird d. bear, snake, some birds e. bear, some birds f. bear, some snakes g. bear, some birds (admittedly a value judgement—in our opinion snakes are not) h. bear)

Now answer the same questions for a human being.

5. Like animals, human beings have several unique physical characteristics that help them adapt to their environment. One is the opposable thumb. You can see what it would be like not to have one by taping your thumb to your palm and trying to do daily tasks, such as writing, eating, or tying your shoes. If that's how human beings really came, how would you redesign a zipper and other common items so they were easier to use?

6. Look for different patterns in nature:

spirals	circles/spheres
triangles	concentric circles
squares	branching lines
hexagons	

7. The Mormon pioneers walked hundreds of miles to get to Utah. Measure how far you can walk in five minutes. Multiply that by 96 to see how far you could travel each day if you walked for eight hours.

8. The Mormons can usually trace their family roots back for many generations. How far back can you trace yours? Ask your parents for information, or write to your grandparents or other relatives who might know. If you're living in a step-family, choose which parents you want to trace back. Or trace them all. Collect family photographs when you get home.

If you want to get more elaborate, order a booklet for tracing your family history from "Family Tree," Dept. PCMP, 50 E. North Temple Street, Salt Lake City, Utah 84150. Cost is $.75. Have the booklet sent to your home so you can use it after the trip.

Which hereditary features does your family have? Can you

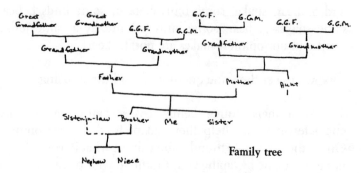

Family tree

roll your tongue, wiggle your ears, or touch below your wrist with your thumb? Do you have a second toe longer than your big toe? Whose nose or eyes do you have, Mom's or Dad's? How about the color of your hair or the dimple in your cheek?

9. How well do you know your parents? Try to answer these questions for each of them, then check to see if you are right.
a. Where and when were they born?
b. Favorite color
c. How many years of school did they complete?
d. What was their first job?
e. Favorite song
f. Favorite food
g. What do they like to do in their leisure time?
h. What was the best vacation they ever took?
i. Best friend
j. What are their hobbies?
k. Something they are good at, and something they don't do very well
l. When they were your age, what did they want to do when they were adults?
m. What was their favorite thing to do when they were your age?

CHAPTER 6. CANYON COUNTRY

1. You can demonstrate the layering of sedimentary rock with

a sandwich (this also works with layers of different colored construction paper). Gather your ingredients and let each one represent a type of rock—try lunch meat for conglomerate, mayonnaise for limestone, cheese for shale, and bread for sandstone. Make your rock sandwich. Which layer is youngest and which is oldest (which did you add first and last?).

Apply pressure to the sides and see what happens. When lateral pressure is applied to rock layers, they fold and sometimes break.

Cut the sandwich in half. Move one half up to simulate an earthquake. Where are the layers in relationship to each other now?

2. Wind is a force of erosion. Take a straw and blow on the sand to see its effects.

3. Canyon country is a great place to play with shadows. You can make shadow pictures using your hands or your whole body. How about an elephant, Indian, pig, or squirrel?

You can also make a group picture. Try a caterpillar, with one person standing up and two or three others kneeling down in a line behind. Sway back and forth. How about a strange bug, with everyone standing together with their arms flapping. What others can you think of?

Have someone measure your shadow at three different times of day—mid-morning, noon, and late afternoon. When is your shadow the longest? The shortest?

Play a game of shadow tag by touching each other's shadow.

4. Butch Cassidy hid out from the law in the canyons of Utah. Draw a wanted poster for an outlaw. Be sure to include the outlaw's name, what he's wanted for, and the reward being offered. Then pretend you're the sheriff (or the outlaw). Buy a water pistol and practice shooting at targets.

5. You can test the hardness of rocks you find. Moh's Scale is the standard used by geologists. Here are some examples from

the scale: 1-talc   2.5-fingernail   3-copper penny   5.5-knife blade, window glass   6.5-steel file   10-diamond

Scratch your rock sample with a penny. If it scratches the rock, you know the hardness of your sample is less than 3. If it doesn't, try scratching your sample with something harder until you find the approximate hardness.

6. A section of Canyonlands is called The Maze. Draw your own maze. Hold up a mirror and try to trace your way through it by looking only in the mirror. Hint: Keep the maze simple at first. After you practice, try it with more complicated mazes.

Petroglyphs

7. There are still many unanswered questions about the petroglyphs (scratched in the rock) and pictographs (painted on the rock) left by ancient man. Do handprints serve as trail markings for the early traveler, or are they just the signature of the artist? Are the images part of a story, a prayer to the gods, or just doodles?

Draw your own petroglyphs and pictographs on a piece of paper. Assign meanings to the different symbols you use. Write a message using your symbols and see if your parents can read it.

8. In places where it is allowed, collect samples of different kinds of rocks. Wrap each in a newspaper labeled with a number. For each number, record information about the rock, such as the date and place you found it and the rock formation

it came from. At home you can display your collection.

9. The Geologic Time Scale is a record of the history of the earth. It is divided into four major eras (Pre-Cambrian, Paleozoic, Mesozoic, and Cenozoic) that are in turn divided into 12 periods. Each division is based on a major change that happened in earth's past. For instance, the Mesozoic Era is called the "Age of Reptiles" because they were the most abundant form of life on earth. The next era, the Cenozoic, is characterized by the dominance of mammals and flowering plants.

Make a time scale for your own life. Divide it into several eras that begin with a major event, then divide those into periods. Name and date the eras and periods.

CHAPTER 7. LAND OF THE ANCIENT ONES

1. Much of the information archaeologists have about the Anasazi comes from items found in their abandoned homes and in their trash heaps. When you left for your trip, what was in your wastebasket? Was your room clean or messy? If you never went back and someone found it 500 years from now, what would they be able to tell about you? Would they know why you left or where you went? How about your likes and dislikes? Your daily life? What did you use those computer games in the corner for? Make up a story about yourself using only the clues that are in your room.

2. Life for the Anasazi was ruled by the seasons. Spring was the time of planting, housecleaning, and marriages, and summer was spent watering and guarding the crops. Autumn was for harvesting and storing, and winter was filled with ceremony and socializing in the warm kivas. What seasonal events do you follow in your life? (Examples: planting the garden, Thanksgiving, your birthday, beginning of school.) Mark a

calendar with some of them. How are they the same and how are they different from the Anasazi? Why?

3. The Anasazi used the plants growing in the area for a variety of things. Match some of the plants commonly found in the pinyon-juniper forest of the high mesas with their uses. Some uses will be found under more than one plant.

juniper (5 uses)   yucca (9)   Gambel oak (2)
serviceberry (2)   pinyon pine (5)

USES—food, construction, sandals, clothing, diapers, medicine, baskets, ropes, digging sticks, paintbrushes, firewood, soap, sewing needles, nets, waterproofing baskets

(Answers: Juniper—medicine, firewood, roofing material, the bark used for diapers, the berry used for food; yucca—sandals, clothing, baskets, ropes, nets, sewing needles, paintbrushes, soap, flower and fruit used for food; serviceberry—dry berries used for food, wood for construction; Gambel oak—digging sticks, acorns used for food; pinyon pine—medicine, firewood, roofing material, resin used for waterproofing baskets, pine nuts used for food)

4. Archaeologists hypothesize about the past based on physical evidence they find. For instance, parrot feathers in the Southwest probably mean the Anasazi maintained a trade network with Central America. Pretend that you are an archaeologist from the future. What could you conclude about the U.S. civilization if you found these things: portable radio, German automobile, women's high heels, computer, microwave oven, silk flower arrangements, fountain pen, paper clip, camera, toy gun, a prescription drug bottle, freeze dried tomatoes, can of green beans, television set. Now what if you were brought in a time machine from the past and had no idea what electricity was?
    Now describe some of these objects and see if your family

can guess what they are. Remember, you have no idea what they are used for.

Here's an example. Item: prescription drug bottle. Description: dark colored plastic cylinder-shaped container; lid opened only with definite sequence of movements; paper label on front with what looks like writing; affixed with clear adhesive strip; inside are small round white pills. Possible conclusions: dark-colored glass for decoration or for protection from light; nonbreakable container to be carried around, priceless, or rare; lid opened only by a select few who could break the code; label writing is instructions for the elite on opening the bottle or consuming the pills, or a description of the contents (Are the elite the only ones that can read them?); removable label for secrecy, or for trading or reusing the bottle; contents are medicine or ritual drugs; they took them for beauty, health, religion, recreation. This is either a privilege of the elite or they are diseased.

5. Mark off five columns on a piece of paper, and label them Hunters and Gatherers BC (H/G), Basketmakers AD 1-450 AD (B1), Basketmakers AD 450–750 (B2), Pueblo AD 750-1250 (P), Historic Pueblo AD 1500 to present (HP). Dates are approximate. See if you can put the first appearance of the following during the proper time.

1. irrigation systems, 2. turkey bone tools, 3. atl-atl, 4. bow and arrow, 5. silversmithing, 6. corn and squash, 7. finely crafted yucca baskets, 8. mano/metate, 9. pithouses, 10. mission churches, 11. early pottery of plain gray, 12. kivas, 13. cotton garments, 14. parrot feathers, 15. feather blankets, 16. beans, 17. decorated pottery, 18. metal tools, 19. multi-storied dwellings, 20. isolated small fire circles

(Answers: 1.P 2.B1 3. H/G 4. B2 5. HP 6. B1 7. B1 8. H/G 9. B2 10. HP 11. B2 12. P 13. P 14. P 15. B1 16. B2 17. P 18. HP 19. P 20. H/G)

6. You can play a version of a game the Anasazi may have

played called the Moccasin Game. Two rows of players sit across from each other a few feet apart on the ground. The side facing west represents the night animals, the side facing east the day animals. Put a pair of shoes in front of each group. Someone on one side holds up a blanket in front of the shoes while the captain hides a small ball, about the size of a marble, in one of them (the Indians used a ball of yucca fiber). The blanket is removed, and the other team guesses which shoe has the ball by hitting it with a stick. If that team is successful, it is their turn. If not, the first side continues.

Keep track of points for each team. The Indians used decorated or painted tally sticks to keep score. They also sang songs during their guessing games, which often lasted all night. You can make the game more difficult by including a pair of shoes for each player.

7. Try the Anasazi version of marbles. Find a large, flat piece of sandstone and dig between 2 and 6 holes in it. Then try to flip small rounded stones into the holes.

8. See if you can match what happened in the Southwest (the numbers) with what happened at the same time in Europe (the letters).

New World
   1. Pueblos built along the Rio Grande River
   2. People live in caves and dig storage pits; corn and squash first grown; fine baskets made
   3. Large cliff dwellings built; superb pottery, weaving and jewelry made
   4. Kivas built; cotton introduced; aboveground dwellings clustered in small villages
   5. Pit houses; bow and arrow; first pottery

Old World
   a. Decline of the Roman Empire and beginning of Middle Ages

b. Renaissance begins; first book printed, the Gutenberg Bible; Columbus discovers the New World

c. Continuation of Dark Ages; feudal wars in Europe

d. Leif Ericsson lands in America; reign of Charlemagne; trade guilds in Europe

e. Crusades

(Answers: 1b (AD 1250 to 1500), 2a (AD 10 to 450), 3e (AD 1100 to 1250), 4d (AD 750 to 1100), 5c (AD 450 to 750)

9. Collect three natural things and create your own game that an Anasazi child could play. Take the same three items and think of different ways the Indians could use them.

10. Tear open the leaf of a yucca plant and look at the fibers. Put the leaf in water and predict what will happen overnight. Check in the morning to see if you were right. Do the same thing with needles from a juniper tree and compare the two.

11. Use two stones like a mano and metate and try to grind things—rocks, sticks, seeds, etc.

12. After you've heard the theories, why do you think the Anasazi disappeared?

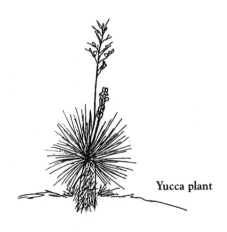

Yucca plant

CHAPTER 8: MOUNTAIN SPLENDOR

1. See if you know the meaning of the following mining terms:

a. drift   __1. lunchroom or break station

b. pie can   __2. horizontal passage following the vein and providing work access

c. lode

d. jackleg   __3. place where workers change into mining clothes from street clothes

e. muck

f. trammer   __4. miner's warning before setting off explosives

g. fire in the hole

h. doghouse   __5. ore with large amounts of gold or silver

i. highgrade   __6. vein of metal

j. dryroom   __7. mining drill

__8. broken rock caused by blasting

__9. lunch bucket

__10. mine car

(Answers: 1.h, 2.a, 3.j, 4.g, 5.i, 6.c, 7.d, 8.e, 9.b, 10.f)

2. See if you can fill in the blanks.

Beaver are nocturnal _____, the largest in the United States. The animal has been around a long time. Ancient corkscrew tunnels have been found dug by prehistoric beaver, some as old as _____ years.

The dams they build are often several feet high and up to _____ long. To take advantage of the beaver's dam construction skills, the government once released eight of them to control creek _____ at two places in Wyoming.

It takes a beaver only _____ minutes to chew through a 4" tree, and he can stay underwater the same amount of time.

Beaver mark their territory with a strongly scented substance called _____ that smells similar to creosote. When swimming, they use their _____ for a rudder.

(Answers: rodents; 25,000,000; ½ mile; erosion; 15; castor; tails)

3. You'll need three people for this. Fold a piece of paper from top to bottom in thirds. The first person draws the top third of a mountain man. Extend the lines slightly into the next section. Then, folding the paper so no one can see what has been drawn, pass the paper to Drawer #2. After #2 draws the middle third of the mountain man and extends the lines, he folds the paper and hands it to Drawer #3. When everyone is finished, look at the drawing, but don't peek before all three have had a turn.

4. Make the shirt and leggings of a mountain man. Cut fringe from newspaper and tape or safety pin it to the arms of your shirt and legs of your pants.

5. Make gravestone rubbings in old cemeteries. Use a white piece of paper and a crayon. Put a newspaper behind the white paper to protect the gravestone and rub hard. In addition to gravestones, you can make rubbings of tree bark, rocks, and almost any other hard surface. Experiment.

6. A pine tree is a bit like a city. It supports many living things. Draw a picture of a pine tree and around it draw pictures or use words to show how different animals and plants use it. Don't forget to include man. Give yourself one point for each use you think of.

(These are a few possible answers: birds for nesting and food of insects and pine cones; bears and deer for scratching post; squirrels for food and nesting; pine beetles and other insects for food and home: porcupines for food; mistletoe, fungus, and moss for home; caterpillars and spiders for homes. Man uses it for building; to make paper, food (pine nuts), firewood, shade, windbreaks, beauty, toothpicks, arts and crafts, erosion control.)

7. Play a version of a Spanish shell game. Find four paper cups, decorate each to tell them apart, and hide a small rock

under one while no one is looking. Slide the cups around with the rock underneath. The other player tries to guess which cup has the rock.

8. GREAT SAND DUNES NATIONAL MONUMENT

A. Which of these statements about sand are true and which are false?

__1.   Sand can move as much as 100 feet an hour.
__2.   Sand is used to make glass.
__3.   Sand can be many colors.
__4.   Most deserts have more sand than rock and dry soil.
__5.   Sand dunes move by many individual grains hopping a few feet at a time.
__6.   There is no life on sand.
__7.   Sand can cut through telephone poles.
__8.   The wind needs to be 11 mph to move sand.
__9.   Some plants in the Great Sand Dunes have roots 50 feet long to find water.
__10. Sand can be millions of years old.
__11. Sand is almost indestructible.
__12. Sand often comes from granite, and since there is quartz in granite, you can sometimes see glassy grains.

(Answers: Questions 4 and 6 are false. The rest are true.)

B. Check to see if you have sand, silt or gravel. Take a handful and lay the grains side by side. Measure the length and estimate the number of grains. Sand is between 10 grains and 1000 grains per inch. Silt grains are smaller and gravel larger.

C. How many uses for sand can you think of?

(Did you include all of these—sandblasting, sandpaper, concrete, mortar, plaster, casting molds, fun, glass making, traction on ice, minute timers, Navajo sand paintings, art, road surface?)

CHAPTER 9. A THREE-CULTURE SALAD

1. KIT CARSON HOME IN TAOS

Here are a few things to look for:

a. The death carts in the chapel.

b. In the Indian room, the hollow log storage box and the picture of the 1914 Taos pueblo. Has the pueblo changed since then?

c. The adobe brick mold in the walkway.

d. The dolls with marshmallow heads in the Spanish room.

e. In the Early American room, the wolf trap, cradle scythe and bullet molds

f. In the Carson room, foofuraw (traded by mountain men to Indian women), beaver hat, tent stove and rocking horse

g. The bird cage and wooden stocking dryer in the kitchen

h. The human hair wreath in the living room

2.

See if you can match these common architectural features and furnishings of New Mexico with their definitions. Martinez Hacienda and the plazas at Taos and Santa Fe are good places to look for many of them.

a. latillas	b. vigas	c. corbels
d. shepherd's bed	e. olla	f. banco
g. nichos	h. bulto	i. retablos
j. portales	k. luminarias or farolitos	

___1. wooden roof beams that hold up the adobe roof

___2. clay pot

___3. the logs laid across the vigas in a ceiling

___4. cubbyholes in the wall above the fireplace

___5. brackets or weight-bearing members which project from the face of a wall and support a cornice or arch

___6. fireplace with a long flat shelf on top, used for a bed

___7. adobe bench adjoining the walls, like built-in furniture

___8. statue of wood

__9.   painted figures on wood

__10. lights in paper bags, displayed around buildings at Chris:mas

__11. south or west facing low, broad porches with slightly raised wooden floors

(Answers: 1b, 2e, 3a, 4g, 5c, 6d, 7f, 8h, 9i, 10k, 11j)

3. THE ALBUQUERQUE MUSEUM—As you visit the central exhibit of Spanish colonial artifacts, look for the following:

a. In the armor room—leather map case, two-handled sword, horse armor, powder flasks, Spanish "hard-hats," and chanfron (horse hard-hats)

b. In the early settlers' home and church room—padlock and key, communion wafer press, chocolate mug, 1850 chapel in the corner

c. Vaquero suit and cigarettes, wooden water trough, lariats, repostero of the Duke of Alburquerque

d. Weaving room—cedar ceiling to keep the moths away, child's serape on the wall, Comanche woman's saddle, leather shield

e. Santa Fe Trail—baby stroller in the traders' warehouse, pouch with silver pesos, mourning jewelry

4. Taos and Santa Fe have been painted by many artists. Draw or paint your own picture of an early Spanish or Indian pueblo. Or pick a favorite painting or object and try to duplicate it. Imagine dividing it into quarters or eighths and draw it a section at a time. Start with the easiest part and work up to the hardest. Outline the basic shape and add details.

Turn a drawing you want to copy upside down and follow the lines. This will give you a different perspective on how to draw.

See "The Museum" in Chapter I for more art activities.

5. SHOPPING is a favorite pastime in Taos, Albuquerque,

and Santa Fe. Try the following activities while there.

A. Pretend you are shopping for the perfect gift. If you had $100 to spend for a present for your grandmother, friend, dad, etc., what would you buy? Make a list of people to buy for, and look for a gift for them. Be sure you don't go over your price limit. Now, if cost were no object, what would you buy?

B. Practice comparison shopping and find the best buy on toothpaste. To compare two brands, you'll have to find the cost per ounce. Divide the price by the number of ounces in the toothpaste tube to see which is cheaper. Other factors can enter your decision of which brand to buy. Do you have a favorite brand or flavor? If it's more expensive, is it worth the extra money? Is the size too big or too small for your needs? Are you particular about the ingredients?

You can also compare prices in two different stores. Try comparison shopping for other items, such as gasoline. For a real challenge, try to figure out what elements in one piece of art make it more expensive than another.

6. See if you know who first brought the following to the Southwest—the Spanish, Indians or Americans: peach trees, pottery, metal, sheep, atomic energy, automobiles, kachinas, pueblos, television, railroad, silversmithing, plazas, horses, trading posts, missions, amusement parks, kivas, Christianity, irrigation, frontier whiskey, military forts,

(Answers: Spanish—peach trees, metal, sheep, silversmithing, horses, missions, Christianity; Indians—pottery, kachinas, pueblos (although the name is Spanish), plazas (the Spanish named these, too), irrigation, kivas; Americans—atomic energy, automobiles, television, railroad, frontier whiskey, military forts, trading posts, amusement parks)

7. Take a "nature walk" through Taos or Santa Fe. List the different sounds, smells, textures, tastes and unique sights. How does this compare to the nature walk you took in the

country?

8. For a challenge, unscramble the names of these early
Spanish weapons.
a. srodwdoarb   b. cteemha   c. bsqeuurah
d. drbehla   e. ooonntps   f. slfui
g. oalrercet   h. entyaob   i. rrpaei
j. beirnac

(Answers: a. broadsword (sword with a broad blade), b. ma-
chete (large knife), c. harquebus (type of matchlock gun), d.
halberd (battle-axe and pike mounted on a long pole), e.
spontoon (a short pike), f. fusil (light flintlock musket), g.
tercerola (short carbine carried by the cavalry), h. bayonet
(blade for end of a musket), i. rapier (two-edged sword with
narrow blade), j. carbine (short-barreled firearm)

CHAPTER 10. GATEWAY TO THE
UNUSUAL

1. The pioneers used their five senses to give names to the
places and landmarks around them. Here are a few colorful
examples in Arizona using the five senses—Bitter Springs,
Sweetwater, Onion Creek, Mint Valley, Thunder River,
Growler Mountains, Painted Desert, Chocolate Mountain,
and Breezy Point.

They also used other descriptive terms: Twenty-four Draw,
Million Dollar Slope, Poker Mountain, Horse Thief Basin,
Where the Mexican Wept, Water Without Ambition, Grief
Hill, Doubtful Pass, Lousy Gulch, Paradise, Tom Mix Wash,
Jim Sam Butte, Cremation Creek and the town of Bumble
Bee.

Use your own senses and imagination, and make up stories
about what happened here. Then come up with original
names for the places and landmarks you experience (for example, Broken Plate to name the campground where your little

brother knocked the dish you were drying out of your hand).

2. Collect unusual names. Ask locally how to pronounce them, then write a rebus (a symbol and picture code) to show someone else how they sound. 2 + Z + goot for Tuzigoot. You'll find many others in the Southwest.

3. PETRIFIED FOREST NATIONAL MONUMENT

A. How many colors can you find in the Painted Desert? Besides the common ones like blue, pink, yellow, tan, and rust, there are more subtle and unusual ones. Here is a list of other colors. Match them with their definitions *(Webster's New Collegiate Dictionary)* and look for them in the Painted Desert. This won't be easy!

1. __Amethyst	a. sky blue
2. __Vermillion	b. clear purple or bluish violet
3. __Scarlet	c. vivid reddish orange
4. __Saffron	d. black
5. __Puce	e. bright red
6. __Ebony	f. orange yellow
7. __Azure	g. dark red
8. __Violet	h. reddish blue
9. __Jasmine	i. reddish brown
10. __Auburn	j. light yellow
11. __Chartreuse	k. bright yellow green
12. __Teal	l. dark greenish blue

(Answers: 1b, 2c, 3e, 4f, 5g, 6d, 7a, 8h, 9j, 10i, 11k, 12l. If you got all 12 right, you cheated; 10, you're an interior designer; 8, you're a genius; 4, very good; 2, normal; 0, don't tell your art teacher.)

B. The one mile *Blue Mesa Trail* in the Petrified Forest leads through a stark land of gullies, washes, layers, and naked conglomerates. Remember that each layer is from a different time period. As you take the trail, look for these things.

Find the first big piece of petrified wood by the trail (on the right past the conglomerate sign).

Find the petrified wood that litters the valley floor. Where do you think it came from?

Find the petrified wood that's still half buried where the trail starts to descend. Also look for the conglomerate rock along the side of the trail.

Try to trace a water trail all the way to the top. When the water starts at the top and disappears under the clay, where does it end up?

Find evidence that nature is slowly reclaiming the area.

Where the trail forks, see how many bands of color you can find.

As you continue on the trail, look for different stages of trees falling down. How long will it take for them to fall?

Create an animal that could live in this harsh environment. What would he look like? What would he eat? Where would he live? What would he need for protection from the weather? How about enemies? When you get back to the car, draw a picture of your animal.

C. Imagine you are a Tyrannosaurus Rex, or another kind of dinosaur. Write a story about your life. Where and when do you live? What do you eat? What plants and animals are around you? Do you have any friends and enemies? Draw a picture of what you look like.

Now what if dinosaurs were still alive today? How would your life as a person be different?

4. COLORS

A. The earth is painted many colors in Arizona. Each color is created by a different mineral or organic matter. See if you can match the color with the source.

1.	iron	a.	black
2.	cobalt	b.	red and yellow
3.	manganese	c.	grayish white
4.	carbon	d.	greenish blue
5.	gypsum	e.	white

6. copper   f. blue-green
7. sulphur   g. yellow

(Answers: 1b, 2d, 3c, 4a, 5e, 6f, 7g)

B. Write a poem about a color. Describe how it makes you feel, what it reminds you of, etc. You can also write a poem using a different color for each line, or write about one color and describe its various shades.

> Blue is robins' eggs, cool water,
> The summer sky behind puffy clouds.
> Blue can be Mondays,
> Or saying goodbye.

5. American Indians were enthusiastic players of games of chance and of dexterity. In the Southwest many of these were thought to be of divine origin, first played by legendary heroes or divinities competing against enemies of mankind.

Dice games were popular, but the dice the Indians used were far different from our cubical dice. The Indians fashioned two-sided dice from bone, bark, corn kernels, shells, or pottery discs, with one side carved or decorated with a geometric pattern. They also made stick dice from thin pieces of wood or reeds split down the middle.

Make your own dice, either from wood chips, pieces of bark or cardboard. Decide how many dice to make (the Indians used three for some of their games), and color the dice red on one side and white on the other. Or you can decorate each side differently so you can tell them apart.

Assign point values to each combination, throw the dice in the air and tally the score. For example, three white sides are worth ten points, two white and one red worth two points, two red and one white worth three points, and all red worth five points.

You can also use a basket or bowl to toss the dice on the ground or to toss them in the air and catch them in the basket.

6. The following is a true story. See if you can tell what the real words should be. Or have fun adding implausible ones. Just be sure to use the part of speech indicated (Hint: don't use forms of "to be" or -ing words for your verbs). Then try making up your own stories.

In 1889, four men stole a thousand *plural noun (1)* from the *singular noun (2)* station at Canyon Diablo, Arizona. A *singular noun (3)* chased them for two weeks and 300 miles to southeastern Utah. Meanwhile, the robbers had *past tense verb that goes with "had" (4)* the *adjective (5) plural noun (6)* of Cannonville, forcing them to *present tense verb (7)* their *plural noun (8)* and leave town. When the posse caught up, a *adjective (9)* battle ensued. However, none of the participants happened to be *adjective (10) plural noun (11)*. Although over 50 *plural noun (12)* were fired, the only thing hit was a *singular noun (13)*. The robbers eventually surrendered and the *singular noun (14)* was returned. One robber did *present tense verb (15)* from the train window on the way back, but he was soon recaptured.

(Use these words to see what really happened. 1. dollars 2. railroad 3. posse 4. terrorized 5. good 6. citizens 7. stack 8. guns 9. wild 10. sharp 11. shooters 12. shots 13. horse 14. money 15. escape)

7. The Spanish conquistador expeditions were fueled by half truths and unfounded rumors. To see how easily stories can be distorted, play a game of gossip. One person whispers a sentence to another. That person then whispers it to someone else. The last person to hear the sentence says it aloud. Remember, you can only whisper the sentence once.

8. The early explorers followed maps that were often inaccurate. Fortunately, most maps today will get you where you want to go. Practice your map reading skills and find the treasure city. The checked letter in each word will spell out the place.

a. Mountains west of Los Alamos, New Mexico

— —. — — —
X

b. National Monument on State Highway 53 southwest of Grants, New Mexico   — —   — — — — —
X

c. River that flows through New Mexico from Colorado to the Gulf of Mexico   — — —   — — — — — —
X

d. Arizona town at the junction of I-40 and State Highway 77 south   — — — — — — — —
X

e. National Monument in Arizona near the junction of I-17 and State 279 (exit 289)

— — — — — — — —   — — — — — —
X

f. State park near Cottonwood, AZ

— — — —   — — — — —
X

Answers: a. Jemez b. El Morro c. Rio Grande d. Holbrook e. Montezuma Castle f. Dead Horse (Treasure City: Jerome)

CHAPTER 11. WET AND WILD

1. GRAND CANYON
A. Can you predict from the name what you will see at Desert View? If you renamed it, what would it be? How about

other viewpoints?

B. See if you can unscramble the names of the rock layers
at the Grand Canyon. They read across from youngest to
oldest.

1. bbaaik   2. wpaeoort   3. noocconi
4. mireht leahs   5. aispu   6. laledrw emloitsne
7. meelpt teubt   8. vmua neotsemli   9. hgrbit glean lhase
10. ptaaest ndsasotne 11. hunioms   12. sabs
13. hnisuv

(Answers across: 1. Kaibab, 2. Toroweap, 3. Coconino,
4. Hermit Shale, 5. Supai, 6. Redwall Limestone, 7. Temple
Butte, 8. Muav Limestone, 9. Bright Angel Shale, 10. Tape-
ats Sandstone, 11. Shinumo, 12. Bass, 13. Vishnu)

C. Conduct a license plate survey in the parking lot at the
Grand Canyon or other national parks. Predict which state
will have the most plates, then find the actual numbers by
counting the ones from each. Take the total number of plates
and divide it by the total number for each state to find the
percentages. If you want, make a bar graph showing each
state. You can turn it into a line graph by connecting the top of
each bar with lines.

D. Count how many foreign accents you hear at the Grand
Canyon. You can make a graph of this, too.

2. PIPE SPRING NATIONAL MONUMENT
A. See if you can find these things and answer these questions as you tour the monument.
1) What do you see here that you don't see on the surrounding prairie?
(Trees. Pipe Spring was an oasis in the dry land because of
water from the spring.)
2) Find the home for the "traveling faithful."
(Covered wagons brought the Mormon settlers across the

many miles from Missouri to Salt Lake City and then here. Imagine putting everything your family owned inside the small wagon box. Which things would you choose to bring and which to leave behind?)

3) What did the Mormons grow in the garden?

(Black and yellow native currants, apples, plums, potatoes, onions, corn, peas, and cabbage were some of the crops. Can you tell which fruits and vegetables are ripe enough to eat? Which are your favorites?)

4) At the gate of the fort, find indications of the Deseret Telegraph.

(Look to the second story on the right to see the insulators and wires. The wire reaches to each corner of the balcony, and then east and west to connect the fort with San Francisco in one direction and New York in the other.)

5) As you climb the stairs to your left, find the holes in the wall. What were they used for?

(The holes were used for gunports in case of Indian attack, but they were never used. The Mormon women stuffed rags in them to keep out the cold and dust.)

6) In the middle bedroom upstairs, look for the bed.

(Underneath the coach is a hide-a-bed. Pull out the bottom to find it.)

7) Ask if you can play the organ.

8) Find the telegraph office.

(In the room to your right, on the table by the window are wires and a telegraph key. It was from here the first message was sent on December 15, 1871 by Ms. Louella Stewart, the 16-year-old operator.)

9) Find the bullet hole in the southeast bedroom (the room on your left).

(The hole is in the footboard of the bed. How do you suppose it got there?)

10) Find the tool marks in the sandstone.

(On the northwest balcony wall are markings left when the sandstone was quarried in the distant cliffs. The rock was then loaded on juniper sledges and pulled by oxen to build the 20″

thick walls. Look for the stone signed by Brown in 1888. Do
you think he was young or old?)

11) What holds up the mattresses in the bedroom?

(The beds were strung with wet rawhide that dried tight,
then covered with a mattress of straw ticking and goose feathers. The tighter the rawhide was, the more comfortable the
bed, hence the origin of "sleep tight.")

12) If you were a pioneer baby boy, what would you have
worn?

(The white baby gowns in the corner were worn by both
boys and girls until about the age of two.)

13) Find the trapdoor.

(The door in the ceiling led to the lookout tower and
flagpole.)

14) In the main kitchen, why are the plates face down on
the table and the chairs turned backward?

(The Mormons always set the table this way to remind
people to kneel for prayer before eating.)

15) Why would this room stay cool?

(In addition to the thick walls, the back wall is up against the
dirt. Even though the door in the meeting room above is on
the second story, it opens out on ground level.)

16) Find the toys in the parlor.

(Dancing Dan was a favorite of the time. Ask for a demonstration if someone is in the room. The children also played
with dolls, and in the evening, musical instruments were
played and scriptures read.)

17) Find the bathtub in the courtyard.

(The old #3 tin tub hanging on the wall was used for baths
in the summer. For pioneers in the Southwest, water was often
scarce, so everyone used the same bathing water, the adults
first and the children drawing straws to see who was next. With
a reliable source of water here, everyone may have used clean
water.)

18) Why are the corn and herbs hanging from the ceiling
in the working kitchen?

(This protected them from rodents and allowed them to dry.

Can you identify the different herbs? Dill, horehound that was used for medicinal purposes, and sage are some of them.)

19) On the table are several kitchen implements. Try to identify the bee smoker (used to calm bees), lye soap, two butter churns, butter mold, egg beater, grater, sausage maker, and keg faucets.

20) Visit the blacksmith shop and see the tools that were used to make part of the fort.

Morse Code

A .—	J .———	S ...
B —...	K —.—	T —
C —.—.	L .—..	U ..—
D —..	M ——	V ...—
E .	N —.	W .——
F ..—.	O ———	X —..—
G ——.	P .——.	Y —.——
H	Q ——.—	Z ——..
I ..	R .—.	

B. Telegraph messages from Pipe Spring were sent in Morse code. Here's the Morse Code alphabet. Make up your own messages and send them to your family.

3. The Grand Canyon and Glen Canyon have inspired many writers to wax eloquent. Be your own poet and compose a poem about one of them. Use descriptive words to tell how you feel. If you like, use one of the following forms for your poem.

A. A cinquain is a short poem with five lines. Compose your own using the following variation. The first line has one word, the title or the subject of the poem (noun). The second line has two words describing the title (adjectives). The third has three action words that tell about the title. The fourth has a short phrase expressing how you feel about the title. The last line has one word, either a repeat of the first line or a synonym.

Vacation
Happy, fun
Exploring, learning, playing
Let it never end
Vacation

or maybe:

Vacation
Hot, tired
Driving, sitting, fighting
Will it never end
Vacation

B. A haiku is a form of Japanese nature poetry. A haiku has 17 syllables, five in the first line, seven in the second, and five in the third. Try not to repeat any words, and remember to use figurative language. Here's an example by Noah Dowd about a sunset in the mountains.

Stony sentinels
Watch the distant horizon
As the sun god falls.

C. Cut a piece of paper in the shape of the subject and write the poem on it (a tree-shaped piece of paper for a poem about a tree).

4. John Wesley Powell, the first white man to explore the Colorado River, had only one arm. Imagine how difficult it was for him to be an explorer. Tie one arm behind your back and go through a part of your day. Try performing your everyday activities, such as dressing, eating, and taking down the tent.

5. Send a postcard of your favorite view of the Grand Canyon or Lake Powell to a friend. Write your message, cut the card into odd shaped pieces to make a puzzle, and mail it in an envelope.

6. LAKE POWELL

Have a family discussion about water.

Water is power in the Southwest. With an ample supply, life flourishes and develops; without it, life withers and dies. Of all the political and economic issues facing the Southwest, the issue of water rights is one of the most emotional and most vital to the future.

States and countries fight among themselves, because those downstream (Arizona, California, Mexico) know two things: if those upstream use all the water, none will reach them, and if the rivers are left to rage out of control, they will be visited by devastating floods. Neighbors in the same community also fight: conservationists want to leave the wilderness unspoiled, ranchers want to graze their stock, farmers to irrigate their fields, and developers to quench the thirst and energy needs of new communities.

Water reclamation and control projects such as Glen Canyon Dam have been part of the result of people's demand for water. What do you think? Would you rather have Lake Powell or the original Glen Canyon? How would you divide the water among the people who want it?

CHAPTER 12. THE HOPI AND NAVAJO INDIAN RESERVATIONS

1. HUBBELL TRADING POST HISTORIC SITE

Inside the trading post, see if you can find items that may have been for sale a hundred years ago and those that are more modern. Then answer these questions.

a. What things are in here that you didn't expect to see?

b. Where is the trader's office?

(the wood enclosure with the cash register, wooden files and wooden safe)

c. In the room with the trader's office, see if you can you find two baskets on the ceiling with the same pattern.

(We found many similar, but none the same. Which is your

favorite?)

d. In the rug room, what were the ends of the antlers hanging on the ceiling used for?

(powder horns)

e. What were the fuzzy leggings hanging on the ceiling used for?

(chaps)

f. On the wall are photographs of Navajo designs that have been hanging in Hubbell's since before 1904. Which are your favorites? Why do you like them? See if you can match the patterns and colors of the pictures to similar ones in the rugs.

g. Find the baby carrier.

(cradle board by window)

h. Find something used in World War I.

(helmets on the ceiling)

i. The kachinas offered for sale change frequently. Which ones are here now? Do any represent birds, animals, plants? If you want to buy one, ask about the $7 ones in the next room.

j. Find the rifle with the snake on it.

k. The rifles hold a clue as to one reason Custer was defeated at the Battle of the Little Big Horn. Do you know what it is?

(The bottom six rifles facing the door are repeating rifles, such as those owned by the Indians. The three above are Springfield rifles, single-shot guns such as the ones Custer had.)

l. Find the Apache "backpacks."

(Apache burden baskets on the ceiling were used for carrying. They hung down the back and were held by a strap around the head.)

m. Find something that looks like "King Kong's hands."

(gloves hanging from the ceiling)

n. What animals would you find in the corrals behind Hubbell's home?

(sheep, horses, cattle, mules)

2. The ancient skill of bartering was kept alive on the Indian reservations. Practice your bartering skills. First, decide what

you are willing to trade. You can barter with things you make, things you have, and services you can offer to others. What does someone in your family have that you would like to trade for? What would you trade for lunch?

3. Although Navajos do not believe you can own the land, they do believe you can own ceremonial songs. Make up your own song that you can own. Include what makes you happy. What do you do well? What do you care about? It doesn't have to rhyme or make sense to anybody else. It's your song about you.

4. Kachinas are thought to be the spirits in everything. Think of something you like—an animal, plant, mountain, etc.— and design a kachina for it. Draw a mask and costume that represents the important parts of that kachina. What colors will you use? What will your kachina carry? What will you use to make its costume?

Sun Kachina

For instance, Tawa, the Sun Kachina, is decorated with eagle feathers. The forehead is painted the warm sun colors of red and yellow, the lower portion of the face is the green of growing plants. This young, handsome kachina is considered kind and gentle.

5. Rituals, a series of actions that are periodically repeated, are important to individuals and to societies. They can be elaborate, or they can be simple. Even brushing your teeth and washing your face in the morning can take on the role of a ritual.

In many societies, especially those without writing, rituals are woven into elaborate ceremonies that serve not only as a means of communing with God, but also of remembering the history and culture of the people. In some societies, such as the Hopi, ceremony plays such a pivotal role that the rest of life revolves around it.

Each of the Hopi ceremonies has a specific purpose, and that purpose is often related to the season when it is performed. For instance, the women's dances in autumn celebrate the harvest, just as our Thanksgiving Day originally celebrated the harvest of the Pilgrims.

Can you think of any other such events in your life? Make a list of those you look forward to. Are they related to the seasons? Or are they based on something else, such as days when something special happened?

You can make up your own ceremony. It can be as simple or as elaborate as you want. How about one for the morning? Or maybe one for Monday, July, the first day of school, the day your baby brother was born, or the day you lost a tooth? Plan what you will do in your ceremony. If you want, ask your family to join in. Some of the things Hopis do in their ceremonies are singing, dancing, and sharing food.

6. The Navajo language was used as a secret code in World War II. You can make up your own secret code to use. One of the easiest is a space code. See if you can read this. "It-

şureishot." Here are two other ways to write it. "Its urei shot," or "I tsu reish ot." Make it harder by writing the message bakcward. "ti erus si toh."

Alphabet codes are others you can use. Give a number to each letter of the alphabet, such as a-1, b-2, 3-c, 4-d, etc. Then write your message with numbers. 9-20 19-21-18-5 9-19 8-15-20. You can also use other symbols for each of the letters. a*, b#, c+, d>, etc.

Make up your own messages and see if your family can decipher them.

(Did you figure out our message? It sure is hot.)

7. One of the favorite games of American Indians is cat's cradle, or web weaving, and they believe there is magic in the weavings. Navajo legend says the game was taught to them by Spider Woman, and they play it only in winter when the spiders are asleep.

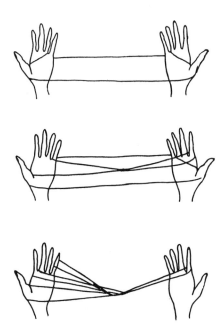

Fish spear (string game)

Take a piece of string five or six feet long (the more elaborate the design, the longer the string you'll need). Tie the ends together to make a loop and, palms facing with fingers up, hold the string behind the thumb of each hand, crossing the palm and passing behind the little finger. Using your fingers (the Indians even used their teeth and toes), make smaller loops until you form a design.

One of the easiest patterns is the fish spear. From above, insert the right index finger behind the string at the left palm. Pull and twist the loop twice to the right with the index finger. From below, insert the left index finger through the string on the right palm, being sure to pick it up through the right index finger loop. Draw your hands apart and release the loops from the right thumb and little finger. (See illustration.)

Experiment and see what other patterns you can make. You can also use a partner.

8. Indian children have traditionally enjoyed playing "Follow the Leader." Encourage the leader to imitate animal movements and perform Indian dance steps for others to copy.

APPENDIX A

VISITING PUBLIC LANDS

FEDERAL OFFICES

I. Bureau of Land Management

Arizona State Office—3707 N. 7th Street, PO Box 16563, Phoenix, AZ 85011, 602/241-5547

Colorado State Office—2850 Youngfield, Lakewood, CO 80215, 303/236-2100

New Mexico State Office—Joseph M. Montoya Federal Building, South Federal Place, PO Box 1449, Santa Fe, NM 87504-1449, 505/988-6000

Utah State Office—CFS Financial Center, 324 South State Street, Suite 301, Salt Lake City, UT 84111-2303, 801/539-4001

II. United States Fish and Wildlife Service

Southwest Region 2, Box 1306, 500 Gold Ave. S.W., Albuquerque, NM 87103, 505/766-3966 (Arizona and New
Mexico)

Rocky Mountain Region, Box 25486, Denver Federal Center,
Denver, CO 80225, 303/236-7920 (Colorado)

Utah State Office, Administration Building, 1745 W. 1700
South,. Room 2078, Salt Lake City, UT 84104, 801/524-5630
(Utah)

III. United States Forest Service

The Forest Service has information and maps of hiking
trails and campgrounds.in the national forests. Forest Service
topographical maps are $2; road and trail maps are $1, available for each of the National Forests and Grasslands. You can
also make reservations at some National Forest campgrounds,
800/283-2267.

A. Southwestern Region, Region III, Federal Building, 517
Gold Ave. S.W., Albuquerque, NM 87102, 505/842-3292—
information for Arizona and New Mexico

ARIZONA
Coconino National Forest, 2323 E. Greenlaw Lane, Flagstaff,
AZ 86001, 602/527-7400. Includes forestland in Oak Creek
Canyon and on the San Francisco Peaks.

Kaibab National Forest, 800 S. 6th Street, Williams, AZ
86046, 602/635-2681. Includes both sides of the Grand Canyon.

Prescott National Forest, 344 S. Cortez Street, Prescott, AZ
86301, 602/445-1762. Includes forestland around Jerome.

NEW MEXICO
Carson National Forest, Forest Service Building, PO Box 558, Taos, NM 87571, 505/758-6200. Includes Sangre de Cristo Mountains in the Upper Rio Grande Valley, Pecos Wilderness and around Taos.

Cibola National Forest, 10308 Candelaria Rd. N.E., Albuquerque, NM 87112, 505/766-2185. Includes Sandia Peak and Acoma.

Santa Fe National Forest, PO Box 1689, 1220 St. Francis Dr., Santa Fe, NM 87504, 505/988-6940. Includes forestland around Santa Fe and in the Sangre de Cristo and Jemez Mountains.

B. Rocky Mountain Region, Region II, PO Box 25127, Lakewood, CO 80225, 303/236-9431—information for Colorado.

Grand Mesa-Uncompahgre National Forest, 2250 Highway 50, Delta, CO 81416, 303/874-7691. Includes forestland on north slopes of the San Juan Mountains and Grand Mesa (farther north).

Rio Grande National Forest, 1803 W. Hwy. 160, Monte Vista, CO 81144, 303/852-5941. Includes Wheeler Geologic Area and parts of the Weminuche Wilderness and South San Juan.

San Juan National Forest, Federal Bldgs., 701 Camino del Rio, Durango, CO 81301, 303/247-4874. Includes Lizard Head and parts of the Weminuche Wilderness and South San Juan.

C. Intermountain Region, Region IV, Federal Building, 324 25th Street, Ogden, UT, 84401, 801/625-5352—information for Utah.

Dixie National Forest, 82 North 100 East, PO Box 580, Cedar City, UT 84720, 801/586-2421. Includes forestland around Cedar City, St. George and Panguitch.

Fishlake National Forest, 115 East 900 North, Richfield, UT 84701, 801/896-4491. Includes forestland west and north of Capitol Reef.

Manti-LaSal National Forest, 599 West Price River Drive, Price, UT 84501, 801/637-2817. Includes forestland in southeast Utah.

IV. United States Geological Survey

For topographical maps and geological publications.

Western Regional Headquarters, 345 Middlefield Road, Menlo Park, CA 94025, 415/853-8300. Information for Arizona.

Central Regional Headquarters, Federal Center, Bldg. 810, PO Box 25046, MS 512, Denver, CO 80225, 303/236-7477. Information for Colorado, New Mexico and Utah.

For maps of Canyonlands, write Utah Geological Mineralogical Survey, University of Utah, Salt Lake City, UT 84112.

V. National Park Service

(see tour section for addresses of individual parks)

An annual Golden Eagle Passport allows your vehicle to enter national parks and monuments for free. If you are visiting several of these, it can be a good way to save money. Passports are available at the offices of the National Park Service, Forest Service, Bureau of Land Management, and at most ranger stations, or write to the National Park Service Headquarters, U.S. Department of the Interior, 18th and C Streets N.W., Washington, DC 20240. Cost is $25.

Western Regional Office, 450 Golden Gate Avenue, PO Box 36063, San Francisco, CA 94102, 415/556-4196. Information for most of Arizona.

Rocky Mountain Regional Office, 655 Parfet, Box 25287, Denver, CO 80225, telephone 303/969-2504. Information for Colorado and Utah.

Southwest Regional Office, Box 728, Santa Fe, NM 87504-0728, telephone 505/988-6375. Information for New Mexico and northeastern Arizona.

REGIONAL

I. State Parks and Outdoor Recreation

Arizona State Parks, 800 W. Washington, Suite 415, Phoenix, AZ 85007, 602/542-4174. An annual pass for free day-use at all Arizona state parks is $30 per vehicle. Camping in all state parks is on a first-come, first-served basis.

Colorado Division of Parks and Outdoor Recreation, 1313 Sherman, Room 918, Denver, CO 80203, 303/866-3437. An annual parks pass for day-use is available for $30 per vehicle. The charge for a daily pass is $3. For campground reservations, call 800/365-2267, in Denver 671-4500.

New Mexico State Parks and Recreation Division, Natural Resource Department, Villagra Building, PO Box 1147, Santa Fe, NM 87504-1147, 505/827-7465. An annual pass per vehicle is $30 for day-use, a daily pass is $2. No camping reservations are accepted.

Utah State Division of Parks and Recreation, 1636 W. North Temple, Room 116, Salt Lake City, UT 84116, 801/538-7221. For camping reservations, call 800/284-2267.

II. State Game and Fish

For fishing maps and information on fishing regulations and licenses.

Arizona Game and Fish Department, 2222 West Greenway Rd., Phoenix, AZ 85023, 602/942-3000

Colorado Division of Wildlife, 6060 Broadway, Denver, CO 80216, 303/297-1192. For recorded fishing information, 292-FISH.

New Mexico Dept. of Game and Fish, Villagra Building, Santa Fe, NM 87503, 505/827-7882

Utah Wildlife Resources Division, 1596 W. North Temple, Salt Lake City, UT 84116, 801/533-9333. For recorded fishing information, 530-1298; recorded fish and wildlife update 522-2473

APPENDIX B

TOURIST INFORMATION

STATE TOURISM BUREAUS

For a list of campgrounds, accommodations, maps, tour guides, calendar of events, and general information.

Arizona Office of Tourism, 1480 E. Bethany Home Road, Phoenix, AZ 85014, 602/255-3618

Colorado Tourism Board, 1625 Broadway, Suite 1700, Denver, CO 80202, 800/433-2656 or 303/592-5510.

New Mexico Tourism and Travel Division, New Mexico Commerce and Industry Department, Joseph Montoya Building, 1100 St. Francis Drive, Santa Fe, NM 87503, 505/827-0291 or 800/545-2040

Utah Travel Council, Council Hall-Capitol Hill, 300 N. State Street, Salt Lake City, UT 84114, 801/538-1030. Especially good maps of the state, including campgrounds, points of interest, National Parks, etc.

CHAMBERS OF COMMERCE AND VISITORS BUREAUS

ARIZONA

Camp Verde
P.O. Box 1665
Camp Verde, AZ 86322
602/567-9294

Flagstaff
101 West Santa Fe Avenue
Flagstaff, AZ 86001
602/774-4505

Fredonia
PO Box 537
Fredonia, AZ 86022

Grand Canyon
PO Box 3007
Grand Canyon, AZ 86023

Holbrook-Petrified Forest
100 E. Arizona
Holbrook, AZ 86025
602/524-6558

Jerome
PO Box 788
Jerome, AZ 86331
602/634-5716

Page-Lake Powell
PO Box 727
Page, AZ 86040
602/645-2741

Sedona-Oak Creek Canyon
PO Box 478
Sedona, AZ 86336
602/282-7722

Verde Valley
(Clarkdale and Cottonwood)
1010 S. Main Street
Cottonwood, AZ 86326
602/634-7593

Williams/Grand Canyon
PO Box 235
Williams, AZ 86046
602/635-2041

Winslow
PO Box 460
Winslow, AZ 86047
602/289-2434

COLORADO

Alamosa
Cole Park
Alamosa, CO 81101
719/589-6531

Pagosa Springs
PO Box 787
Pagosa Springs, CO 81147
303/264-2360

Cortez
343 E. Main
Cortez, CO 81321
303/565-3414

Silverton
PO Box 565L
Silverton, CO 81433
303/387-5654

Durango
PO Box 2587
Durango, CO 81301
303/247-0312

Telluride
PO Box 653
Telluride, CO 81435
303/728-3041
Central Reservations
800/525-3455 or 303/728-4431

Ouray
PO Box 145
Ouray, CO 81427
303/325-4746

NEW MEXICO

Albuquerque Chamber
of Commerce
401 2nd NW
Albuquerque, NM 87102
505/842-0220

Aztec
203 North Main
Aztec, NM 87410
505/334-9551

Bloomfield
PO Box 1570
Bloomfield, NM 87413
505/632-8013

Albuquerque Convention and
visitors Bureau
PO Box 26866
Albuquerque, NM 87215
505/243-3696 or 800/321-6979

Chama
Box 306-A
Chama, NM 87520
505/756-2306

Española
417 Big Rock Center
Española, NM 87532
505/753-2831

Los Alamos-White Rock
PO Box 460
Los Alamos, NM 87544
505/662-8105

Farmington Chamber
of Commerce
PO Box 267
Farmington, NM 878499
505/325-0279

Santa Fe Chamber of Commerce
PO Box 1928
Santa Fe, NM 87501
505/983-7317

Farmington Convention and
Visitors Bureau   401
203 W. Main, Suite 401
Farmington, NM 87401
505/326-7602 or 800/541-
1398-332832 on touch tone
phone only

Santa Fe Convention and
Visitors Bureau
PO Box 909
Santa Fe, NM 87501
505/984-6760 or 800/528-5369

Gallup
PO Box 1395
Gallup, NM 87301
505/772-2227 or 800/242-4282

Taos
PO Drawer I
Taos, NM 87571
505/758-3873 or 800/732-8267

Grants
PO Box 297
Grants, NM 878020
505/287-4802

UTAH

Cedar City
286 North Main
Cedar City, UT 84720
801/586-4484

Grand County Travel Council
PO Box 550
805 North Main Street
Moab, UT 84532
801/259-8825

Green River
240 Main Street
Green River, UT 84525
801/564-3526

Hanksville
Visitor Information
Hanksville, UT 84734

Kane County Visitor Center
(Kanab)
48 South 100 East
Kanab, UT 84741
801/644-5033

Moab
805 N. Main
Moab, UT 84532
801/259-8825 or 800/635-MOAB

Monticello
Box 217
Monticello, UT 84535
801/587-2231 ext. 29

St. George
97 East St. George Boulevard
St. George, UT 84770
801/628-1658

San Juan County Travel Council
PO Box 490
117 South Main Street
Monticello, UT 84535
801/587-2231

INDIAN

For information on visiting the Indian reservations, contact the tribal offices.

Havasupai Tribe, PO Box 10, Supai, AZ 86435, 602/448-2961

Hopi Tribe, PO Box 123, Kykotsmovi, AZ 86039, 602/734-2445

Jicarilla Apache Tribe, Tourism and Outdoor Recreation Department, Box 313, Dulce, NM 87528, 505/759-3442

Kaibab Tribal Council, Tribal Affairs Bldg., Pipe Springs, AZ 86022, 602/643-7245

Navajo Visitor Services, Box 308, Window Rock, AZ 86515, 602/871-4941

Paiute Tribe, 600 North 100 East, Cedar City, UT 84720, 801/586-1111

Southern Ute Tribal Council, PO Box 737, Ignacio, CO 81137, 303/563-4525

Ute Mountain Tribal Park, General Delivery, Towaoc, CO 81334, 303/565-3751

Nineteen Indian Pueblos of New Mexico

For information and a booklet on the Eight Northern Indian Pueblos, contact Eight Northern Indian Pueblos council, PO Box 969, San Juan Pueblo, NM 87566, 505/852-4265

Acoma, PO Box 309, Acomita, 87034, 505/552-6604

Cochiti, PO Box 70, Cochiti 87041, 505/465-2244

Isleta, PO Box 317, Isleta 87022, 505/869-3111

Jemez, PO Box 78, Jemez 87024, 505/834-7359

Laguna, PO Box 194, Laguna 87026, 505/243-7616

Nambe, Rt. 1, Box 117-BB, Santa Fe 87501, 505/455-7752

Picuris, PO Box 127, Penasco 87553, 505/587-2519

Pojoaque, Rt. 11, Box 71, Santa Fe 87501, 505/455-2278

San Felipe, PO Box A, San Felipe Pueblo 87001, 505/867-3381

San Ildefonso, Rt. 5, Box 315-A, Santa Fe 87501, 505/455-2273

San Juan, PO Box 1099, San Juan Pueblo 87566, 505/852-4400

Sandia, PO Box 6008, Bernalillo 87004, 505/867-2876

Santa Ana, PO Box 37, Bernalillo 87004, 505/867-3301

Santa Clara, PO Box 580, Espanola 87532, 505/753-7330

Santo Domingo, PO Box 99, Santo Domingo 87052, 505/465-2214

Taos, PO Box 1846, Taos 87571, 505/758-8626

Tesuque, Rt. 11, Box 1, Santa Fe 87501, 505/983-2667

Zia, General Delivery, San Ysidro 87053, 505/867-3304

Zuni, PO Box 737, Zuni 87327, 505/782-4481

For a list of Indian arts and crafts dealers, order the free Source Directory from the Indian Arts and Crafts Board, Room 4004-N, US Department of the Interior, Washington, DC 20240.

APPENDIX C

LODGING
INFORMATION

For complete information on lodging in the Southwest, invest in one of the many good guidebooks on the market.

BED AND BREAKFAST

Two guidebooks that include information for children are *Bed and Breakfast U.S.A.: Guide to Guest Houses and Tourist Homes*, by Betty Rundback and Nancy Kramer, published by E. P. Dutton, which includes information on whether or not children are welcome, and *Bed and Breakfast Colorado and Rocky Mountains West*, by Buddy Mays, published by Chronicle Press (most places mentioned in the book welcome children.)

CAMPING

National and State Parks

Reservations for campsites in Colorado State Parks can be made through Select-a-seat for a $3 reservation fee, 3915 E.

Exposition, Denver, CO 80209, 303/778-6691.

Reservations in Utah State Parks can be made by calling 800/284-2267. A $5.25 handling fee is charged.

No reservations are accepted in Arizona or New Mexico state parks.

Camping in the national parks is on a first come-first served basis except in the Grand Canyon (602/638-2401). For a complete listing of services and facilities available, order *National Parks Camping Guide* from the U.S. Consumer Information Center, BHG, Pueblo, CO 81009. Send $3.50 and ask for Item 152R.

Private Campgrounds

KOA (Kampgrounds of America), Box 30558, Dept. BHG, Billings, MT 59114. Send $2 for a list of their private campgrounds throughout the country.

National Campground Owners Association, 804 D St. NE, Washington, DC 20002. Send a self-addressed, stamped envelope for a list of state campground associations.

Rand McNally publishes a western edition of their *Campground and Trailer Park Guides*. It includes state maps with tent and trailer campgrounds marked. Woodall's also publishes a complete camping guide.

HOME EXCHANGE

The easiest way to swap or rent a home, condominium or apartment is through an exchange club. You can also try advertising, either in a professional journal or the local newspaper at your destination, or try asking friends and acquaintances if they know anyone where you plan to stay that would be interested in renting or swapping. Leave yourself plenty of time to search—9 or 10 months isn't too long.

There are numerous agencies that will help you with a home exchange for a fee. International Home Exchange Service/INTERVAC U.S., PO Box 3975, San Francisco, CA 94119, 415/382-0300 lists rentals, exchanges, hospitality exchanges (guests in a home), and Youth Exchanges. Vacation Exchange Club, 12006 Eleventh Avenue, Unit 12, Youngtown, Arizona 85363, 602/972-2186, is the world's largest home exchange agency.

For information about home exchange and a listing of agencies, read *Home Exchanging: A Complete Sourcebook for Travelers at Home or Abroad* by James Dearing, published by East Woods Press.

HOTEL/MOTEL CHAINS

For a listing of budget motels in each city, including nightly rates, check *National Directory of Budget Motels* edited by Raymond Carlson, published by Pilot Books, Babylon, N.Y.

If you call the central reservation numbers for the hotel/motel chains, they will send you a free directory.

Best Western, 800/528-1234
Cribs available for a small fee; children under 12 usually stay free

Budget Host Inns, 817/626-7064
Cribs available for $2 to $5 per night

Comfort Inns/Quality Inns, 800/228-5150 for Comfort Inns, 800/228-5151 for Quality Inns
Kids under 16 stay free; cribs available (at some places free, some charge a fee)

Days Inns of America, Inc., 800/325-2525
Children under 18 stay and eat free at many; free cribs available

Econo Lodges of America, 800/446-6900
Free cribs; children under 18 stay free

Friendship Inns International, 800/453-4511
Children's rates vary with each inn

Hampton Inns, 800-HAMPTON
Kids under 18 stay free; in-room movies and free continental
breakfast

Hilton Hotels, 800-HILTONS
Free cribs; children of any age stay free with parent; babysitting listings available

Holiday Inns, 800-HOLIDAY
Free cribs; children and teens stay free

Howard Johnson, 800/654-2000
Free cribs; under 18 stays free in many

LaQuinta Motor Inns, 800/531-5900
In most, kids under 18 stay free; free cribs

Marriott Hotels and Resorts, 800/228-9290
Free cribs; children under 17 stay free

Motel 6, 505/891-6161
Cribs free: 1 child per adult stays free

Ramada Inns, 800/2-RAMADA
Free cribs; under 18 stays free

Regal 8 Inns, 800/851-8888
Free cribs; Swimming pools in all

Sheraton Hotels & Inns, 800/325-3535
Children under 17 stay free

Super 8 Motels, 800/843-1991
Children's rates vary; cribs available for free or a small fee

TraveLodge/Viscount Hotels, 800/255-3050
Cribs $3; children's rates vary

Another option is a suite hotel. Most have one or two bedrooms, separate living room, dining area, and kitchen. Some offer complimentary breakfast, newspapers, stocked refrigerators, and baby-sitting services. Try Embassy Suites, 800/ EMBASSY or the Residence Inn Company, 800/331-3131.

YOUTH HOSTELS

American Youth Hostels, Box 37613, Dept. BHG, Washington, DC 20013-7613, telephone 202/783-6161. Membership ($30) includes nationwide directory and monthly newsletter. You can purchase the directory separately for $5 plus $2 postage and handling.

APPENDIX D

GLOSSARY OF SPANISH WORDS

Part of the richness of the Southwest is in the various languages spoken there. Here are a few words that mean about the same thing in English, Spanish and Navajo.

ENGLISH	SPANISH	NAVAJO
one	*uno*	*i-sly*
two	*dos*	*nockee*
three	*tres*	*taw*
four	*cuatro*	*ting*
five	*cinco*	*ishklaw*
six	*seis*	*hawstaw*
seven	*siete*	*sosit*
eight	*ocho*	*saypee*
nine	*nueve*	*nystie*
ten	*diez*	*neznaw*
water	*agua*	*toe*
hello	*hola*	*ya-ta-hey*
beautiful	*hermoso*	*neezhoni*
baby	*bebe*	*ahway*
horse	*caballo*	*kleent*

house	*casa*	*bahogan*
sheep	*oveja*	*debay*
little boy	*niño*	*ishkee yazzie*
little girl	*niña*	*a-tay yazzie*
mother	*madre*	*a-muh*
father	*padre*	*a-zay*
goat	*cabra*	*clizzie*
yes	*si*	*ooh*
no	*no*	*do-taw*
corn	*maiz*	*naw-taw*
hot	*caliente*	*dez-too-ee*
cold	*frio*	*suh-kuzz*

These are common Spanish words you might see.

SPANISH	ENGLISH
acequia	irrigation ditch
adios	goodbye
ahora	now
algodon	cottonwood
amiga(o)	female friend (male)
amor	love
aqui	here
arroyo	gulley
banco	bank, or the bench
bueno	good
bultos	carved images often of saints
caballeros	gentlemen
camino	road
cañon	canyon
carne	meat
conquistador	conqueror
corazon	heart
Cristo	Christ
cruz	cross
damas	ladies
dia	day

Don	title meaning Sir
Doña	title meaning Madam
fiesta	party
frijoles	beans
gracias	thank you
grande	large
hacienda	property, the farm, the ranch
hermana(o)	sister (brother)
hija(o)	daughter (son)
hombre	man
horno	oven
hoy	today
huevos	eggs
leche	milk
mañana	tomorrow
mariposa	butterfly
me gusta	I like
noche	night
norte	north
patio	courtyard
patron	master, boss
pequeño	small
perdon	I beg your pardon
picante	spicy hot
plaza	park
por favor	please
por que?	why
posada	lodging
pronto	soon
pueblo	village
puerta	door
queso	cheese
rancho	ranch
rio	river
salsa	sauce
San	saint (male)
sandia	watermelon

Santa	saint (female)
santuario	shrine
señora	married woman
señor	gentleman
señorita	young lady
sierra	mountain
siesta	afternoon nap
tarde	afternoon
tortillas	flat bread
trucha	trout

Reading List

The Southwest has inspired many excellent books. This list is by no means comprehensive. Here are a few we've discovered.

CHILDREN'S AUTHORS
Several children's authors have written more than one book pertaining to the Southwest. Look for these and other titles by them.

Byrd Baylor—These longer picture books also work well with older elementary schoolchildren. They are poetically written to give a feel for the Southwest.

Before You Came This Way, Dutton, 1969. Southwestern rock art inspired this text about the ancient dwellers of the desert.

The Desert Is Theirs, MacMillan, 1975. Describes life in the desert.

When Clay Sings, MacMillan, 1987. Inspires children to think about the ancient potters and what they produced.

Joe Hayes has storytelling tapes and picture books about the

Southwest. These are written in English and Spanish.

Coyote and: Native American Folk Tales, Mariposa Books, 1983. Collection of tales from many tribes about the antics of Coyote.

The Day It Snowed Tortillas: Tales from Spanish New Mexico, Mariposa Books, 1985.

Scott O'Dell writes children's novels on many subjects. These pertain to the Southwest.

The King's Fifth, Houghton Mifflin, 1966. This story of the conquistadores is told through the eyes of a Spanish boy who goes with them.

Sing Down the Moon, Houghton Mifflin, 1970. A Navajo girl named Bright Morning is captured by Spanish slavers. Later the United States government forces her and her people to leave their homes and go into exile.

CHILDREN/FICTION

And Now Miguel . . . , Joseph Krumgold, Harper and Row, 1987. An award-winning novel recounts the life of a New Mexican boy who goes to the Sangre de Cristo Mountains with the men in his family to herd their sheep.

Annie and the Old One, Miska Miles, Little, Brown, 1971. A Navajo girl learns about the circle of life when her grandmother announces she will die when the rug she is weaving is taken from the loom. Short novel.

Arrow to the Sun, Gerald McDermott, Viking, 1974. This well done picture book from an award-winning illustrator recounts a Pueblo Indian legend about a boy whose father is the Sun.

The Boy Who Made Dragonfly, Tony Hillerman, University of New Mexico Press, 1988. Retells a Zuni myth about a little boy who saves his people from a disastrous drought. For older children.

Clementina's Cactus, Ezra Jack Keats, Viking, 1982. A wordless picture book about a little girl, her father and a cactus.

Grandmother's Adobe Dollhouse, Mary Lou Smith, New Mexico Magazine, 1984. In this picture book a young boy describes his grandmother's dollhouse and gives information about the art and culture of New Mexico.

In My Mother's House, Ann Nolan Clark, Viking, 1941. The life of his people is described by a Pueblo Indian boy. Look in the library for this one.

Knots on a Counting Rope, Bill Martin Jr. and John Archambault, Henry Holt, 1987. A blind Indian boy's grandfather tells him the story of his life to show how each act of courage has helped him learn to overcome his handicap. Excellent picture book.

The Mouse Couple, Ekkehart Malotki, Northland, 1988. This Hopi folktale is retold in a longer picture book.

One Green Mesquite Tree, Gisela Jernigan, Harbinger House, 1988. Things found in the desert are used to teach numbers.

Trails, Tales and Tommyknockers: Stories from Colorado's Past, Myriam Friggens, Johnson Publishing Co., 1979.

Walk the World's Rim, Betty Baker, Harper Jr., 1965. After a Spanish shipwreck, de Vaca and the men with him were forced to walk across the desert Southwest.

Why the North Star Stands Still and Other Indian Legends, William R. Palmer, Zion, 1978. This is a collection of Paiute Indian tales.

CHILDREN'S NONFICTION
Agave Blooms Just Once, Gisela and Wesley Jernigan, Har-

binger House, 1989. Alphabet book of desert dwellers with letters based on Hobokam designs.

Arizona in Words and Pictures, Dennis Fradin, Regensteiner Publishing, 1980.

Beaver at Long Pond, William T. George and Lindsay Barrett George, Greenwillow, 1988. Excellent picture book about the life of a beaver.

Digging Up Dinosaurs, Aliki, Crowell, 1981. Wonderful drawings show children how scientists find, study and display dinosaur bones.

Evolution, Joanna Cole, Crowell, 1987. Aliki's drawings accompany a text which clearly explains evolution to children.

Glow in the Dark Night Sky Book, Chris Hatchett and Stephen Marchesi, Random House, 1988. The star map in this book can be used indoors or out.

Golden Nature Guides are written for children and illustrated with line drawings. They cover a variety of topics.

The Kachina Doll Book, Donna Greenlee, Fun Publishing Co., 1972. Line drawings and text tell about some of the Hopi kachinas.

Magic School Bus Inside the Earth, Joanna Cole, Scholastic, 1987. Lively drawings illustrate this story of a school class of children who learn about geology by taking a field trip to the inside of the earth.

Native Americans: The Pueblos, Richard Erdoes, Sterling, 1983. Text and photographs describe the history, land and culture of the Pueblo Indians.

New Mexico in Words and Pictures, Dennis Fradin, Children's Press, 1981. A picture tour of New Mexico is presented along with facts and information about the state.

The Old Ones, Jeff Brian and Jodi Lynn Freeman, The Think Shop, 1986. Line drawings and photographs illustrate this book about the everyday life of the Anasazi. (Coloring books to go with it are "Anasazi Coloring Book" which includes a narrative and "My Coloring Book About the Old Ones" for preschool. They are available from the Zion Natural History Association, Springdale, Utah 84767.)

The Pueblo, Charlotte Yue, Houghton Mifflin, 1986. The daily life, history and beliefs of the Pueblo Indians are described in this excellent book.

Signs Along the River, Kayo Robertson, R. Rinehart Inc., 1986. Young children are shown clues animals leave behind.

Spanish Pioneers of the Southwest. Joan Anderson, Lodestar Books, 1989. Photographs taken at La Cienege recreate the life of Spanish colonists.

Wild Babies, A Canyon Sketchbook, Irene Brady, Houghton Mifflin, 1979. Wild animal babies are the subject of this picture book.

Wildlife of Cactus and Canyon Country, Marj Dunmire, Pegasus Graphics, 1988. Well illustrated picture book.

Young Naturalist, Hobby Guide Series, A. Mitchell, EDC, 1984. A practical guide to becoming a naturalist.

ADULT/TEENAGER

Authors who have written a number of fiction and nonfiction books about the area are Zane Grey and Louis L'Amour. Also look for books by the following authors. We've listed a few of their works.

Edward Abbey
Desert Solitaire, Ballantine Books, 1968. The beauty of life in the seemingly stark Southwest is revealed in this classic.
The Monkey Wrench Gang, Avon, 1983. A fictionalized account of a radical group of environmentalists who try to blow up Glen Canyon Dam.
Slickrock: The Canyon Country of Southeast Utah, Gibbs & Smith, 1987.

Tom Bahti
Southwest Indian Tribes, KC Publications, 1968. Numerous photos illustrate this book about the life and history of southwestern tribes.
Southwest Indian Ceremonials, KC Publications, 1982. Excellent introduction to the southwestern Indian ceremonials.

C. Gregory Crampton
Land of Living Rock, G. M. Smith, 1985. Covers the geology and geography of the high plateau area of Arizona, Utah and Nevada.
Standing Up Country: The Canyon Lands of Utah and Arizona, Peregrine Smith Books, 1983.

Richard Erdoes
American Indian Myths and Legends, Pantheon Books, 1984.
The Rain Dance People, Random House, 1976. Presents information about the beliefs and lifestyle of the Pueblo Indians who live in the dry Southwest.

Tony Hillerman
The Great Taos Bank Robbery, and Other Indian Country Affairs, University of New Mexico Press, 1980. Humorous collection of stories told in New Mexico.
Dance Hall of the Dead, Avon, 1975. One of several myste-

ries centered around the Navajo Reservation.

David Lavender
Colorado River Country, Dutton, 1982. Factual account of
the people who explored and settled the Colorado River Country.
The Southwest, University of New Mexico Press, 1984. An
historian explores the land, people and history of the Southwest.

John Nichols
Milagro Beanfield War, Holt, Rineholt and Winston, 1974.
This excellent book about the effect of the modern world on
one New Mexico town was recently made into a movie.
The Last Beautiful Days of Autumn, Holt, Rinehart &
Winston, 1982. The author uses personal anecdotes to bring
to life the people and places around Taos.
On the Mesa, Gibbs & Smith, 1986. Words and pictures
capture the splendor of the Taos Mesa.

Marc Simmons
New Mexico, a Bicentennial History, W. W. Norton and
Company, 1977. Factual account by a respected southwestern
author.
*Ranchers, Ramblers and Renegades: True Tales of Territorial
New Mexico*, Ancient City Press, 1984.

Wallace Stegner
The Gathering of Zion, McGraw Hill, 1964. Your library
might have this well-detailed account of the Mormon trek to
Salt Lake City.
The Sound of Mountain Water, University of Nebraska
Press, 1985. Covers the natural beauty of the Southwest, man's
destructive actions there and the contributions of the West to
American civilization.

Stephen Trimble
Blessed by Light, Peregrine Smith Books, 1986. Outstanding collection of writings and photographs about the Southwest.
The Bright Edge: A Guide to the National Parks of the Colorado Plateau, Museum of Arizona Press, 1979.

Frank Waters
Book of the Hopi, Penguin, 1977 ed. A noted expert on the Southwest gathered this classic collection of the beliefs of the Hopi.
People of the Valley, Ohio University Press, 1941. A New Mexico town must face the modern world when a new dam is proposed. Fiction.

Ann Zwinger
Beyond the Aspen Grove, University of Arizona Press, 1988. Explores the aesthetics and relationships of life on 40 acres in the Colorado Rockies.
Wind in the Rock: The Canyonlands of Southeast Utah, Harper & Row, 1978, reprinted by the University of Arizona Press, 1986. The author explores, mostly on foot, 5 canyons in southeastern Utah.

GENERAL SOUTHWEST
American Indian Food and Lore, Carolyn Neithammer, Mac-Millan, 1974. Recipes, rituals and descriptions of plants used by the Native Americans.

Anasazi, Ancient People of the Rock, photographs by David Muench with text by Donald G. Pike, Harmony Books, 1974. This popular collection of photos gives background information on the Anasazi.

Arizona the Beautiful, Herb and Dorothy McLaughlin photographs, Don Dedera text, Doubleday, 1974. Wealth of interesting information from a former editor of the magazine "Arizona Highways."

Between Sacred Mountains: Navajo Stories and Lessons from the Land, ed. by Sam Bingham and Janet Bingham, University of Arizona Press, 1984. Excellent book written to give Navajo schoolchildren an understanding of their heritage and modern issues facing the tribe.

Colorado, Magnificent Wilderness, John Ward, Westcliffe Publishers, 1986. Beautiful color photographs celebrate Colorado's wilderness.

Coronado's Children: Tales of Lost Mines and Buried Treasures of the Southwest, J. Frank Dobie, University of Texas Press, 1978. Legends and stories of the Southwest are retold.

Death Comes for the Archbishop, Willa Cather, Alfred A. Knopf, 1927. This classic is based on the life of the first Catholic Bishop of Santa Fe.

Delight Makers, Adolph Bandelier, Harcourt Brace Jr., 1971. This novel of life among the Anasazi was based on the knowledge available at the time.

Explorations of the Colorado River and Its Canyon, John Wesley Powell, Penguin, 1987. This is a reprint of Major Powell's journal.

Grand Canyon: Today and All Its Yesterdays, Joseph Wood Krutch, Sloane, 1958. Respected geological and historical account of the Grand Canyon.

Handbook of American Indian Games, Allan and Paulette Macfarlan, Dover, 1958. Collection of various games played by the North American Indians.

The Hidden Canyon, A River Journey, John Blaustein and Edward Abbey, Penguin Books, 1978. Words and photographs show the majesty of the Grand Canyon.

The Hidden West, Rob Schultheis, North Point Press, 1983. Well written book describes the author's experiences in the American "outback."

Land of Journey's Ending, Mary Austin, University of Arizona Press, 1983. First published in 1924, this poetic book still captures the spirit of the Southwest.

Lost Treasures on the Old Spanish Trail, George Thompson, Publishers Press, 1986. Legends and history are woven into an interesting account of the Spanish Southwest.

The Man Who Walked Through Time, Colin Fletcher, Alfred A. Knopf, 1968. This well-respected author recounts his experiences and adventures on a two month hike through the Grand Canyon.

Maria, the Potter of San Ildefonso, Alice Marriot, University of Oklahoma Press, 1979. This is the story of the Pueblo Indian woman who revived the ancient art of pottery making.

New Mexico, David Muench, text by Tony Hillerman, Graphic Arts Center Publishing, 1974. Collection of photographs about the land and people of New Mexico.

No Life for a Lady, Agnes Morley Cleaveland, University of Nebraska Press, 1979. First-person account of a woman living on a New Mexico cattle ranch in the last part of the 19th century.

The Old West Quiz and Fact Book, Rod Gragg, Harper and Row, 1986. Interesting information about the Southwest is presented in a question and answer format.

One-Eyed Dream, Terry Johnston, Green Hill, 1988. Part of a fiction trilogy about the mountain men.

The Place No One Knew: Glen Canyon on the Colorado, Eliot Porter photos, edited by David Brown, Sierra Club Books, 1963. The lost Glen Canyon is remembered in this striking book by a noted photographer.

Southwest Indian Arts and Crafts, Mark Bahti, KC Publications, 1983. Good place to start for learning about authentic southwestern arts and crafts.

Stampede to Timberline: The Ghost Towns and Mining Camps of Colorado, Muriel Sibell Wolle, Ohio University Press, 1974. Historical account of the Colorado mining boom.

The Taos Trappers: The Fur Trade in the Southwest 1540-1846, David J. Weber, University of Oklahoma Press, 1980. An historical account.

Those Who Came Before: Southwestern Archaeology in the National Park System, Robert Lister, SW Parks and Monuments Association, University of Arizona Press, 1983. Photographs and information about the prehistory of the southwestern parks and monuments by a noted archaeologist.

To the Inland Empire: Coronado and Our Spanish Legacy, Stewart L. Udall, Doubleday, 1987. Account of Coronado's journey.

Utah, Magnificient Wilderness, Tom Till, Westcliffe Publishers, 1989. Stunning full color photographs give a feel for the diverse Utah wilderness.

Voices in the Canyon, Catherine Viele, Southwest Parks and Monuments, 1980. Photographs and information about Navajo National Monument are presented in this book.

The West, An Illustrated History, Henry Steele Commager ed., Exeter Books, 1976. The elements which created the West of legend and reality are examined.

SCIENCE AND NATURE

The Amateur Naturalist, Gerald Durrell, Knopf, 1982. This excellent guide to becoming an amateur naturalist contains a wealth of information on the natural world.

Field Guides by Audubon and Peterson give desriptions and pictures which identify various plants and animals in the Southwest.

Peterson Field Guides Coloring Books (Birds, Butterflies, Reptiles, Mammals and Wildflowers). Written for older youths.

Poisonous Dwellers of the Desert, Natt N. Dodge, . Southwest Parks and Monuments, 1976. Venomous wildlife of the Southwest is described in pictures and words.

Sharing Nature with Children, J. B. Cornell, Ananda Publications, 1979. This guide presents a series of fun, easy activities to foster nature awareness and appreciation in children.

Starting Small in the Wilderness: The Sierra Club Outdoors Guide for Families. Marlyn Doan, Sierra Club Books, 1979. Information is given on how to have safe outdoor adventures with children as young as infants.

TRAVEL GUIDES

Backpacking One Step at a Time, Harvey Manning, Random House, 1980. Practical tips are given to have a safe, enjoyable backpacking experience.

Canyon Country Guidebook series, F. A. Barnes, Wasatch Publishers, Inc. Trail guides and topographic maps for the area around Moab.

The Complete Family Guides to Navajo-Hopi Land, Bonnie Brown and Carol Bracken, co-published by the Navajo tribe, 1986. Send $9.95 to Navajo Tribal Museum, Box 308, Window Rock AZ 86515. Most comprehensive guide to the reservations currently available.

Enjoying the Southwest, Catryna Ten Eyck Seymour, J. B. Lippincott, 1973. Practical information and interpretative comments are included.

Journey to the High Southwest, Robert Casey, Pacific Search Press, 1985. This excellent guide includes places to stay and eat, as well as a wealth of information about the Southwest.

National Directory of Budget Motels, Raymond Carlson and Maria Maiorino, Pilot Books. Revised annually. Look for it in your public library.

New Mexico, A New Guide to the Colorful State, Lance Chilton, University of New Mexico Press, 1985. A wealth of interesting information on what to see and do in New Mexico.

Sierra Club Guides will give you complete information on natural areas in the public domain. Some examples are listed below:
  Adventuring in the Rockies, Jeremy Schmidt, 1986.
  Guide to the Natural Areas of Colorado and Utah, John Perry and Jane Givens Perry, 1985.
  Guide to the Natural Areas of New Mexico, Arizona and Nevada, John Perry and Jane Givens Perry, 1986.

Utah, A Family Travel Guide, Tom Wharton, Wasatch Publishers, Inc., 1987. This useful book describes places in Utah that are enjoyable for children.

TRAVEL WITH CHILDREN

Family Travel Times, published by TWYCH, 80 Eighth Ave., N.Y., NY 10011. $24 for 12 monthly issues with a wealth of travel tips for families.

Traveling Games for Babies, Julie Hagstrom, A & W Visual Library, 1981. This book presents general activities for children from infants to 5 years old.

HANDICAPPED

National Park Guide for the Handicapped, U.S. Department of the Interior, U.S. Government Printing Office, Washington, DC 20402 stock #2405-0286. This lists each park and monument and gives information to help handicapped visitors plan their visit.

Travel Tips for the Handicapped, Consumer Information Center, Pueblo, CO 81009. Free brochure.

Index